The Single Market Review

IMPACT ON TRADE AND INVESTMENT

EXTERNAL ACCESS TO EUROPEAN MARKETS

The Single Market Review series

EUROPEAN COMMISSION

The Single Market Review

IMPACT ON TRADE AND INVESTMENT

EXTERNAL ACCESS TO EUROPEAN MARKETS

The Single Market Review

SUBSERIES IV: VOLUME 4

OFFICE FOR OFFICIAL PUBLICATIONS
OF THE EUROPEAN COMMUNITIES

KOGAN PAGE . EARTHSCAN

This report is part of a series of 39 studies commissioned from independent consultants in the context of a major review of the Single Market. The 1996 Single Market Review responds to a 1992 Council of Ministers Resolution calling on the European Commission to present an overall analysis of the effectiveness of measures taken in creating the Single Market. This review, which assesses the progress made in implementing the Single Market Programme, was coordinated by the Directorate-General 'Internal Market and Financial Services' (DG XV) and the Directorate-General 'Economic and Financial Affairs' (DG II) of the European Commission.

This document was prepared for the European Commission

by

University of Sussex & South Bank University

It does not, however, express the Commission's official views. Whilst every reasonable effort has been made to provide accurate information in regard to the subject matter covered, the Consultants are not responsible for any remaining errors. All recommendations are made by the Consultants for the purpose of discussion. Neither the Commission nor the Consultants accept liability for the consequences of actions taken on the basis of the information contained herein.

The European Commission would like to express thanks to the external experts and representatives of firms and industry bodies for their contribution to the 1996 Single Market Review, and to this report in particular.

Office for Official Publications of the European Communities
2 rue Mercier, L-2985 Luxembourg
ISBN 92-827-8799-0   Catalogue number: C1-70-96-004-EN-C

Kogan Page . Earthscan
120 Pentonville Road, London N1 9JN
ISBN 0 7494 2333 1

Table of contents

List of tables

List of figures

List of abbreviations

ACP	African, Caribbean and Pacific countries parties to the Lomé Convention
ASEAN	Association of South-East Asian Nations (Brunei Darussalam, Indonesia, Malaysia, Philippines, Singapore, Thailand)
ATC	Agreement on Textiles and Clothing
CBE	Cocoa butter equivalent
CEECs	Central and Eastern European Countries
CENELEC	European Committee for Electrotechnical Standardization
CET	Common External Tariff
CN	Combined Nomenclature
CRS	Computerized Reservation System
CSFR	Czech and Slovak Federal Republic
CT	Community Transit
EAC	European Coordination for Accreditation of Certification
EAL	European Coordination for Accreditation of Laboratories
EAs	Europe Agreements
EC	European Community
ECJ	European Court of Justice
ECU	European currency unit
EEA	European Economic Area
EFTA	European Free Trade Association
EU	European Union
FDI	Foreign direct investment
FSU	Former Soviet Union
GATS	General Agreement on Trade in Services
GATT	General Agreement on Tariffs and Trade (UN)
GPA	Agreement on Government Procurement
GSP	Generalized System of Preferences
HS	Harmonized System
IAs	Interim Europe Agreements
ISO	International Organization for Standardization
MFA	Multifibre Arrangement
MFN	Most-favoured Nation
MRA	Mutual Recognition Agreement
MTE	Import Tariff Equivalent
NACE	General Industrial Classification of Economic Activities within the European Communities
NAFTA	North American Free Trade Agreement
NIC	Newly industrialized country
NTB	Non-tariff barrier
OECD	Organization for Economic Co-operation and Development
OETH	Observatoire européen du textile et de l'habillement
OPT	Outward-processing traffic
QR	Quantitative restriction
QU	Quota utilization
SAD	Single administrative document
SM	Single market
SMP	Single market programme
US(A)	United States (of America)
VAT	Value-added tax
VER	Voluntary export restraint
WTO	World Trade Organization

Acknowledgements

Part I: Legal and descriptive analysis

Part I of the project was directed by Christopher Stevens (Institute of Development Studies – IDS) in collaboration with Alasdair Young (Sussex European Institute – SEI).

Other project members were: Arianna Calza Bini, Ulrike Hotopp, Jane Kennan, Paul Marsden and Costanza de Toma.

The project members received research guidance from an independent academic study advisory board comprising: Professor Helen Wallace (SEI), Professor Iain Begg (South Bank University), Dr Stephany Griffith-Jones (IDS), Dr Nigel Grimwade (South Bank University) and Professor Alasdair Smith (SEI). Dr Peter Holmes (SEI) attended meetings of the board in his capacity as a consultant to the Commission in the overall programme of studies on the effects of the single market programme.

Part II: Quantitative analysis

Part II of the project was carried out by Professor Iain Begg, Nigel Grimwade and Tannis Seccombe-Hett (European Institute, South Bank University). The authors are grateful to Professor Ian Wooton of the University of Glasgow for overall guidance and help in constructing the simulation model presented in Chapter 16; to Volker Stabernak of World Systems for supply of trade and production data and to Dr Peter Holmes for scientific advice.

PART I: Legal and descriptive analysis

1. Summary

1.1. Aims and methodology

The aim of Part I of this study is to identify and prioritize the effects of the changes stemming directly from the single market programme (SMP) on the conditions under which third-country products (defined to include goods and internationally traded services) can gain access to the European market. This is achieved through a qualitative and targeted assessment, supported by quantifiable indicators where possible, of the changes in market access regime. This analysis identifies clearly the balance of probabilities concerning the way in which third-country products have been affected.

The study strikes a balance between a very narrow definition of SMP measures and the broader policy environment in which they have been implemented. To a degree, the SMP changes, narrowly defined, are neutral *vis-à-vis* third parties: their actual impact has been conditioned by the environment in which they have been implemented.

The methodology used to assess and prioritize change is based upon an eclectic use of empirical observation and literature on perceptions of gain and loss (Chapter 3). This reflects the methodological and practical problems of measuring some effects in a wholly objective fashion and the differing stages of implementation. In cases where the SMP measures are not yet fully implemented, the analysis seeks to identify the type and scale of effect that will accrue once implementation is complete.

1.2. Findings

1.2.1. National barriers to trade

In terms of the immediacy and directness of impact, the dismantling of national barriers to trade has had the most effect on conditions of access for those third-party suppliers that were adversely affected by them. Before the SMP there existed a bewildering array of formal and informal national-level trade restrictions, given practical effect through national control of internal frontiers and the use of Article 115 of the Treaty of Rome (Chapter 4). The number of these restrictions was well into five figures, most but by no means all on textiles and clothing. Although a precise measurement of their effect in practice is prevented by methodological and data problems, there are good reasons to suppose that they did restrict imports of some products from some suppliers.

The SMP has swept away most of these formal restrictions, other than those relating to textiles and clothing and to China. Although some formal barriers may have been replaced by informal controls, it seems clear that the scale of sub-Community restrictions on market access has been much reduced by the SMP (Chapter 5). Change in market access as a result of the SMP is very much a product-market-specific affair. However, the countries that will have gained most from communitization are the East Asian and South Asian states that were the most frequent targets of national quantitative restrictions (QRs).

1.2.2. Technical barriers to trade

Of more widespread and, in the longer term, greater importance for the conditions of access of third-country products are the SMP changes in relation to technical barriers to trade (Chapter 6). Before the SMP, differing technical standards were one of the most serious impediments to the free movement of goods within the Community.

The process of technical harmonization and standardization has largely improved market access for products from outside the Community: transparency and legal certainty have increased, and design and production costs have probably been reduced. Where mutual recognition applies, barriers between Member States are removed without being replaced by barriers at the Community level. Under new approach Directives, EC measures are relatively flexible and, therefore, tend not to affect trade very adversely.

To the extent that the SMP might have made market access more difficult, it is most likely to have done so with regard to technical harmonization. These measures are detailed and inflexible and thus harder to comply with than new approach Directives. In addition, there is reason to believe that, at least in some cases, in the pursuit of legitimate public policy objectives EC harmonization may have raised the stringency of some Member States' regulations, thus potentially impeding access for EC and third-country products to their markets.

The impact of such market access changes cannot be assessed precisely because it will vary according to the nature of the firms that are affected. Technical barriers are the most important barriers to intra-EC imports and, therefore, relatively more important than for extra-EC imports. Also EC firms may be better able to take advantage of opportunities to exploit economies of scale. Although access to some Member State markets for some products may have been made more difficult by the SMP, the strong balance of probabilities is that trade in products for which gains will be unambiguous is much larger than in products which may be subject to new restrictions.

1.2.3. Barriers to establishment and the provision of services

A range of SMP measures tend to reduce barriers to the provision of services and to rights of establishment (Chapter 7). These may affect third parties but, for the most part, they do so by making it easier for foreign firms to establish operations in the EC. Hence, they fall within the ambit of this study only to the extent that such establishment facilitates the access to the EC market of third-country products. Since intra-firm trade represents a significant part of the total, there are likely to be such spill-overs. The gains will accrue mainly to countries with firms able to consider establishing themselves in the EC market, such as the USA.

1.2.4. Changes to the business environment

To the extent that changes to company law, taxation, intellectual and industrial property rights, and the free movement of persons make it easier for foreign-owned firms to operate within the Community, and to the extent that this facilitates intra-firm trade utilizing extra-EC products, then the changes may be relevant to this study (Chapter 8). In most cases, the changes to the business environment do represent an improvement for third-country producers, even though progress in some areas has been slow. High profile contrary cases, such as the 'Television without Frontiers' Directive, are relatively limited in extent.

1.2.5. Public procurement

Public procurement is one area in which trade even within the EC has been heavily restricted in the past, and the removal of barriers represents an important element of the SMP (Chapter 9). Even though the SMP regulatory regime permits a degree of discrimination against third countries, it provides some restriction on the scope of that discrimination. As a result, the EC's public procurement regime should provide better access for foreign companies than did the pre-SMP national preference regimes. Extra-EC supplies, however, form a tiny proportion of total public procurement, and so any gains are likely to be relatively modest in absolute terms, at least in the short to medium term.

1.2.6. The liberalization of regulated industries

The liberalization of the telecommunications and energy markets is unlikely to have major effects on the conditions of access for third-country products in the short term, but might have substantial effects in the future. When complete it could provide opportunities for third-party suppliers to enter the telecommunications and energy markets. By and large, foreign firms will have to establish themselves in the EC in order to take advantage of these opportunities. Thus, these changes are not the focal point of our study.

1.3. Conclusions

On balance, the SMP has improved rather than worsened the conditions under which third-country products may be placed on the European market. In several ways the SMP has made it easier for third-country firms to participate in the EC market. Examples include eliminating national quantitative restraints, harmonizing customs procedures, increasing transparency and legal certainty, and decreasing market fragmentation.

But since these changes will have affected firms in different ways, it is not feasible to produce a single, firm judgement on gains and losses. Even where no discrimination exists between European and third-country firms in the formal SMP measures, there could have been a practical difference in the effect of these changes.

In a few limited cases, including financial services and public procurement, the SMP explicitly provides for discrimination against non-EC firms. This largely reflects the absence of comparable market access conditions in the EC's main trading partners. In spite of these provisions, market access conditions for third-country firms are probably better, and almost certainly not worse, than before the SMP.

Because of the diversity of SMP measures, and of the pre-SMP situation as it affected particular suppliers, the actual impact of change will vary widely, depending upon the precise characteristics and circumstances of the product and supplier in question. Hence, it is perfectly possible that the overall conclusion of third-party gain is compatible with the existence of some cases in which particular third parties have suffered a clear deterioration in access for some products.

2. Introduction

2.1. Aim of the study

The purpose of Part I of this study is to contribute to the understanding of the external consequences of the SMP. It is not the only element in the programme of studies launched by the European Commission[1] on the SMP that deals with external consequences, and its scope is influenced strongly by its relationship with these other studies and the need not to duplicate work. In particular, its parameters have been established in relation to the quantitative evaluation of the SMP in a number of sectoral case studies (Part II of this report) and by the other studies in Subseries IV (Impact on trade and investment).

The essential characteristic of this study is summed up in the study proposal issued by the European Commission:

> The purpose of this study is not to provide a quantitative analysis of changes in trade or investment flows occasioned by these adjustments in market access. Rather the objective is to identify and prioritize any changes and conditions under which third-country products can be placed on the markets of the EU Member States which stem directly from completion of the Internal Market.

Among the key words in this quotation are that the study should be concerned with:

(a)   identification and prioritization;
(b)   products;
(c)   changes stemming directly from the SMP.

The aim of the report is to establish a clear picture of the ways in which the various elements of the SMP could have had external impacts, how the direction of these and their scale might be judged, and what such judgements would imply for countries and sectors. Where (as will often be the case) there exists scope for reasonable differences of opinion to exist over the judgement that should be made, the report aims to make it possible to identify the consequences of such changes for the conclusions reached.

2.2. Boundaries of the study

2.2.1. The approach adopted

These directional beacons are important because the SMP is an enormously complex exercise of a nature and in a context that make the identification, let alone prioritization, of external effects a matter of considerable judgement. A strong emphasis has been put, therefore, on a mode of analysis that identifies clearly:

(a)   the approach adopted;
(b)   the choices made and the reasons for them;
(c)   the assumptions underlying the analysis and any qualitative or quantitative prioritization.

---

[1]   Known as the 'Commission of the European Communities' in legal matters, its usual title now is 'European Commission'.

The report presents a qualitative and targeted assessment of the changes in the market access regime for third-country products (defined to include goods and internationally traded services). This has involved varying levels of detail in the description of what has happened, why, and to what effect. In each case, the level of analysis has been selected in the light of the potential scale of effect on market access and of the amount of detail required to understand what has happened or might happen.

This approach has involved choices in defining the boundaries of the study. These have been made in a measured way taking account, on the one hand, of the need established in the terms of reference to disregard changes 'not strictly related to the completion of the Internal Market' and, on the other, the requirement to explain sufficiently the contextual changes that have given the SMP measures their flavour. Many of these detailed choices are described in the relevant chapters of the report. The fundamental choices affecting the overall boundaries of the study are described in this introductory chapter and the next.

2.2.2. The complexity of the SMP

The complexity of the SMP is well known, but can perhaps be illustrated by the fact that this report reflects only one study out of a total of 39. The bulk of the research programme is concerned with identifying the nature of the changes and their impact on sectors, regions and policies within the European Community (EC).[2]

The nature of the SMP exercise also adds complications since it was oriented primarily towards conditions on the European market, with little direct relation to the rest of the world. It is highly likely, therefore, that most of the external effects will be indirect in the sense of being consequences of SMP activities rather than their principal, or even secondary, objective. The absence of strong, tangible and direct external effects is evident in many of the sectoral, thematic and regional studies undertaken in this programme.

2.2.3. The context of the SMP

The most important complicating factor is the fact that the SMP did not occur in isolation. On the contrary, it occurred at a period of very substantial and particularly rapid change in other areas. This is likely to have had analogous and complementary effects on third parties. To a significant degree the SMP changes, narrowly defined, are neutral *vis-à-vis* third parties. Their actual and potential impact has been conditioned by the environment in which they have been implemented. A different environment would (and possibly could still) produce very different effects.

These contextual changes include not only such obvious parallel activities as the negotiation of the General Agreement on Tariffs and Trade (GATT) Uruguay Round, the creation of the European Economic Area (EEA), the enlargement of the EC, the collapse of Communism in Eastern Europe and the negotiation of the Europe Agreements. They also include the substantial changes in conventional attitudes in recent years towards the role of the public and

---

2   The events analysed in this report straddle a period in which European nomenclature has changed. Although the terms 'European Communities' or 'EC' remain valid when referring to legislation implementing the Treaty of Rome, the term 'European Union' has obtained widespread use following ratification of the Treaty on European Union. To avoid confusion, this report uses the terms 'EC' and 'Community' throughout when referring collectively to the Member States.

private sectors in economic affairs which contributed to, and were affected by, the SMP process.

Some examples may illustrate the situation. The change in access conditions for third-country products resulting from the phase-out of national restrictions was the result both of the replacement of national with Community-level trade instruments (an SMP effect) and the nature of those successor instruments (which in some cases were shaped by the GATT and regional trade negotiations). Similarly, the effect of provisions on the abolition of bilateral restrictions on air transport between Member States (an SMP measure) on third-party access will be strongly influenced by the (non-SMP) trend towards liberalization of air service provision in many Member States.

An illustration of the potential scope of the changes associated with the SMP is to be found in the following quotation drawn from a well regarded text on the EC (Wallace and Young, 1996:127):

'Several themes ... run through the story of the single market:

- the impact of new ideas, as views about the European 'Welfare State' altered and Keynesianism was forced to compete with neo-liberalism as an alternative and potentially predominant paradigm in economic policy;
- the mobilization of industrial opinion and pressure in novel ways as a transnational phenomenon and a stimulus to policy change;
- the critical conjunction of changes to EC decision-rules with alterations in the relationships between the business community and policy-makers and in business responses to global markets;
- evidence of policy 'entrepreneurship', especially by the Commission, backed by a new coalition of supporters of change and the recasting of the old argument about 'Community preference';
- the impact of 'statecraft' by and 'collusion' between top policy-makers from key Member States;
- the pervasive impact of European law and rulings from the European Court of Justice ... on the ways in which policy options were defined;
- the external dynamic of third-country competition and technological innovation; and
- the external projection of EC policy.'

2.3. Guiding principles

Two conclusions drawn from this review of the nature of the SMP have formed guiding principles for the study:

(a) In many cases, access conditions have been shaped not by the SMP changes in isolation, but by the context within which they have been implemented. A judgement is required at many points to determine what are, and what are not, justifiably described as effects of the SMP on conditions of access for third-country products to the EC market.

(b) In this grey area of the study, one of the most important objectives is to identify clearly the balance of probabilities in terms of the implications of the SMP, not least so that appropriate adjustments to the conclusions can be made by those who would form a different judgement on the appropriate range of factors that have been taken into account.

Another complicating aspect of the SMP that has added two more guiding principles concerns implementation. Despite its earlier association with '1992', the SMP is a process and not a date, and its extent varies between sectors. Some aspects with potentially major implications for the conditions of access of third-country products to the EC market have not yet been adopted, others are not fully implemented in practice, and others are in operation but have not been in position for long enough for their effects (if any) to be measurable in publicly available statistics.

Given the task of the study, it would be inappropriate to concentrate only on those measures for which adequate, quantifiable data are available. The study's aim is to set out the ways in which all changes that might affect the conditions of access of third-country products to the EC market would produce these effects if implemented fully. To the extent that the rigorous analysis of data within tightly drawn parameters is an important part of the process of assessing the external effects of the SMP, it is more appropriately performed by Part II as well as by the other studies in the group on the impact on trade and investment.

Because the study must cover the effects of instruments at different stages of implementation, for which different levels of data are available, it is not feasible to adopt a single methodology. Rather, the broad methodological approach described in Chapter 3 is applied in different ways in relation to the characteristics of each element of the SMP. Hence, the third and fourth guiding principles for the report are that:

(c)   an eclectic approach is required that gives highest importance to describing the ways in which a measure might affect third-party access to the EC market when it is fully implemented and if this is done in a particular way;

(d)   the methods used to assess the direction and scale of any such effects will vary considerably between measures according to the nature of the case.

2.4. The research team and sources

The principal authors of Part I of this report are Christopher Stevens and Alasdair Young. They have been supported by a research team at the Institute of Development Studies comprising: Arianna Calza Bini, Ulrike Hotopp, Jane Kennan, Paul Marsden and Costanza de Toma. An independent academic Study Advisory Board has provided research guidance. The Board's members are: Professor Helen Wallace (chair), Professor Iain Begg, Dr Stephany Griffith-Jones, Dr Nigel Grimwade, Professor Alasdair Smith. Dr Peter Holmes has attended the meetings of the Board in his capacity as a consultant to the Commission on the overall programme of studies on the effects of the SMP.

A wide range of published and unpublished data and analyses have been consulted in this study. Some of it, but by no means all, has been supplied by the Commission. A number of international organizations have kindly made available information and documents that are not in the public domain; for obvious reasons neither these nor the views expressed by the officials concerned are referenced. The study has attempted to move substantially beyond what is already available in the many reports, articles and books dealing with the SMP and has succeeded in this aim at least in terms of the detail and breadth of coverage as well as in the precision of some of the quantification made. Nonetheless, the conclusions drawn represent no more than the authors' interpretation of limited information.

2.5. Organization of Part I of the report

Chapter 3 sets out the main methodological parameters of the study and identifies, *inter alia*, the principal groups of SMP activity that are considered important for analytical purposes. Each of these is then subjected to review and analysis in the remaining chapters of Part I.

Because of their complexity, as well as their direct and substantial implications for the conditions of access of third-party products, national trade barriers are reviewed in two chapters. Chapter 4 assesses the pre-SMP situation and shows the range of national trade barriers that were in force, the countries that most frequently imposed them, the products that were covered, and the extra-EC states most directly affected. Chapter 5 assesses the implications of the SMP changes, and the contextual measures that have coloured their effect. Because the implementation of national trade barriers (and their removal) has been closely associated with national control over cross-border traffic, the SMP changes to customs veterinary and phytosanitary procedures are dealt with alongside the other elements of Chapters 4 and 5.

The important changes affecting technical barriers to trade are dealt with in Chapter 6. This analyses the changes in terms of their potential implications for the access of third-country products, and supplies a broad basis for prioritizing favourable and potentially unfavourable changes.

Many of the other SMP changes have limited implications for conditions of access of third-country products when viewed in isolation although, when taken together and fully implemented, their effect may be more substantial. For this reason, they are grouped in the last three chapters of Part I. Chapter 7 deals with barriers to the provision of services, rights of establishment and free movement of capital. Chapter 8 clusters changes that can be described as the removal of barriers in the business environment. These include elements such as intellectual and industrial property, company law, taxation and the media. Chapter 9 deals with the SMP changes in relation to public procurement and Chapter 10 to barriers in regulated industries such as energy and telecommunications.

Finally, Chapter 11 draws the threads of the analysis together and presents them in different ways in order to identify and prioritize the effects of the SMP on the conditions of access to the European market for third-country products.

3. Methodology

3.1. A typology

3.1.1. The extent of the SMP

Adopting systematically a wide-ranging approach to the SMP such as described by Wallace and Young (Section 2.2.3) is clearly beyond the terms of reference for this study. But it is often difficult to distinguish clearly between effects on third parties that result solely from the SMP narrowly defined and are not influenced, at least in part, by these broader aspects. The methodology adopted must accommodate such problems and provide guidance on how they are to be resolved.

The problem of definition is made more difficult because direct external provisions are spread widely through many documents and because there is ground for reasonable disagreement even on the scope of a narrow definition of the SMP.[3] The problem of scope is exemplified by the arrangements made since 1992 for the European banana market. These changes have often been described as a consequence of the SMP and, indeed, are listed in European Commission reports on the single market (see, for example, CEC, 1994a:57-60). Yet, although the new common market organization for bananas might have been an indirect consequence of the SMP, it is not part of the legislation in the SMP, and its legal basis is a 1968 Regulation (Council Regulation (EEC) No 827/68). Hence, it could be argued that it falls outside the terms of reference of this study since its relationship is too tenuous and it is not an effect that 'stems directly from' the SMP.

In order to produce a convincing analysis of the potential effects of the SMP on third parties it is necessary to step a little beyond the narrowest confines of the Directives and to consider modes of implementation and ancillary effects. An OECD Working Paper which provided an early 'post-1992' review of the SMP, for example, concluded that the 'single market initiative should have had a strong impact on trade flows' that would benefit third parties, but it continued that 'whether trade diversion occurs will partly depend on external trade policy changes' (Hoeller and Louppe, 1994:26, 33). Such changes will not all fall within the confines of the SMP, even broadly interpreted. But, once the path towards broader study boundaries is embarked upon, it is difficult to find clear, objective milestones that can be used to halt the slide into wide analysis of the kind indicated by Wallace and Young.

3.1.2. Different modes of effect

What may be learned from existing classification systems of the SMP measures to help deal with the particular needs of this study? Several different approaches have been adopted for classifying the various SMP measures into broad categories. The Commission in its progress reports has begun, for example, to distinguish between White Paper Directives and Single Market Legislation, as well as between elements within each group.

---

3   The first problem is illustrated by a detailed review undertaken by the Commission of those elements of EC documents related to the SMP that contain explicit references to third parties (CEC, 1992a). It identifies some 172 EC documents (Council Regulations, Directives, opinions of the European Parliament and of the Economic and Social Committee, etc.) that contain references to the treatment of third parties. But the great majority of these references are in the form of one or two (usually brief) articles in documents, the bulk of which do not refer to third parties.

One categorization of the SMP measures employs the widely used fourfold classification of measures in the White Paper (CEC, 1985) concerned with: market access, competitive conditions, market functioning and sectoral policy, as defined in Pelkmans and Winters (1988:12). In all four categories, there are effects on goods and services (the primary focus of this study), persons and labour, and capital. Although the origins of the classification pre-date much of the SMP and, hence, the examples used are not always still apposite, it is helpful to use these examples to illustrate the main characteristics of the four categories of effect.

(a)   **Market access** measures for products, as identified by Pelkmans and Winters, include the abolition of intra-EC frontier controls, and the approximation of technical regulations. For services, they include mutual recognition and 'home-country control', the removal of licensing restrictions for banking and insurance, dismantling of quotas and freedom of cabotage for road haulage, access to inter-regional air travel markets. For capital, market access involves the abolition of exchange controls, the admission of securities listed in one Member State to another, and measures to facilitate industrial cooperation and migration of firms. In the case of persons and labour, the measures include the right of establishment for various highly educated workers.

(b)   Market measures in the White Paper on **competitive conditions** with respect to products are said to include, for example, liberalization of public procurement. For services, they include the introduction of competition policy in service industries such as air transport.

(c)   **Market functioning** measures include those on voluntary standards, trade marks and corporate law. In services they include the approximation of requirements in service industries, for consumer protection in relation to insurance, together with EC-wide permits for road haulage. In the case of capital they include harmonization of industrial and commercial property laws and the European company statute. In the case of persons and labour, the measures include various training provisions and mutual recognition of diplomas.

(d)   **Sectoral policy** measures include the approximation and mutual recognition in agriculture of veterinary and phytosanitary policies. Services examples are proposals for common air transport policy on access, capacity and prices, together with common rules on mass-risks insurance.

Although this classification system is helpful for examining the overall effects of the SMP, it is not necessarily best suited to classifying external effects. One problem is that the elements affecting market access for third countries are spread across several categories which also contain elements with no direct impact on access conditions for products.

3.1.3. An economic framework for analysing trade effects

Evidently, none of the existing systems is ideal for the present study. The SMP was designed to remove internal barriers to trade and to reduce discrepancies in regulations within Europe; possible external effects were not a prominent feature of the measures adopted. This section and the next review some classification systems and major methodological considerations, as a prelude to a description, in Section 3.2, of the approach adopted for this study.

Economic analyses that focus on the central core of the SMP, i.e. its promotion of intra-EC trade, tend to identify four welfare-enhancing effects. These are: an initial reduction of costs as a result of the dismantling of customs and administrative barriers to trade; lower costs due to economies of scale and learning; the efficiency-inducing effects of stronger competition; and non-price effects such as enhanced innovation and organizational change (Hoeller and Louppe, 1994:16).

When the analysis extends to consider the external dimension, economists have introduced an additional set of factors which often emphasize the importance of policy changes as a determinant of the scale and direction of change (see, for example, Koekkoek *et al.*, 1990). These include the effects of income growth on demand for extra-EC imports of products, enhanced European competitiveness, changes to trade policy and also, when examining effects outside the EC market, changes to the terms of trade.

The SMP is anticipated to result in faster European economic growth than would occur otherwise. This could be expected, other things remaining equal, to result in increased European demand for products, both those produced within the EC and those that are imported. This 'trade creation' effect forms an important element in exercises that undertake a formal quantification of the external impact of the SMP. But an equally important focus for attention, that is given relatively more weight in Part I (which complements Part II), is the validity of the 'other things remaining equal' assumption.

Another anticipated consequence of the SMP is that European producers will become more competitive. This will enhance European welfare but could result in the replacement of products previously imported by the, now, more competitive European supplies. Although frequently, and confusingly, referred to as 'trade diversion' in the SMP context, such a change would result in a reduction of welfare only if it were accompanied by new market distortions, such as might be produced by trade-related policy. Again, this emphasizes the importance of checking the 'other things remaining equal' assumption.

The critical element that may be overlooked is whether trade-related policies have changed. If they have, this could be in a direction that extends the welfare-enhancing effects of the SMP. This would be the case if, for example, national governments became unable to support ailing domestic industries from intra-EC competition and as a consequence lost the need to protect them also against extra-EC imports; European trade policy might become more liberal as a result of this realignment of political forces. This is certainly the case made in favour of the abolition of national trade barriers, as analysed in Chapters 4 and 5 (see, for example, WTO, 1995: 57). But the opposite could have happened: through a combination of new policies, governments might have attempted, at a national or Community level, to offset for ailing firms the consequences of the increased SMP competition by raising new barriers to the access of extra-EC imports. Because such action need not have been in the form of transparent, conventional 'trade policies', any analysis that aims to establish a balance of probabilities must spread its net widely.

The typology of barriers to market access developed by Emerson *et al.* (1988) identified:

(a)   tariffs;
(b)   quantitative restrictions;
(c)   cost-increasing barriers (border formalities, technical regulations, certification);
(d)   market-entry restrictions (public procurement, restrictions on establishment, provision of
        services and ownership);
(e)   market distorting subsidies and practices (subsidies, collusion, abuse of dominant
        position).

Not all of these barriers have been affected by the SMP, which related only to categories (b) to (d). The differing ways in which the SMP's set of internally oriented measures could affect external trade relations was well summarized in the GATT *Trade Policy Review* of the EC in 1993 (GATT, 1993:64). The internal market reforms, it argues, fell into two groups:

> (i) measures which have an immediate impact on access, such as the abolition or 'communitization' of residual national import quotas, or the treatment of external deliveries under the new EC procurement rules; and (ii) measures which, while not directed at imports, can nevertheless be expected generally to change access conditions for external suppliers as well for EC producers, such as the recognition or harmonization of technical regulations among the Member States or the abolition of internal border controls.

In order to rank the effects of the different SMP changes on third countries' market access it is necessary to know the relative importance of each of these barriers in restricting market access. Unfortunately it is very difficult to quantify the effects of many of these barriers. This is particularly the case for non-tariff barriers (NTBs). Three principal difficulties are that there is no precise definition of NTBs, many NTBs are not transparent, and NTBs can vary greatly in their restrictiveness (see OECD, 1985). The problems are such that even in the context of the 'Cost of non-Europe' evaluation the quantification of the costs associated with technical barriers was possible in only a few cases, and could not be aggregated (Emerson *et al.,* 1988).

Given the variety of SMP effects and the well-known problems of measuring some of them, the most appropriate methodology for assessing the scale and direction of changes and an appropriate counterfactual will differ between broad categories of change. Some elements of the SMP fall clearly into one or other category, while others may straddle boundaries or their influence may be strongly affected by interplay with measures in the other category (as with the removal of internal border checks which undermined national QRs permitted under Article 115).

3.1.4. Differential effects on third parties

There is the possibility of SMP measures having differential effects with respect to third parties in both absolute and relative terms. If, for example, access to the European market for products from third parties were to be subject to an absolute restriction, as some had feared with their evocation of a 'Fortress Europe', then there would have been a clear differential change as between foreign and domestic suppliers.

Hence, an important distinction is between changes that apply equally to external and to non-national EC suppliers and those that apply specifically to foreign suppliers.

(a)   An example to illustrate the first type of measure is that the removal of physical barriers to trade within the EC has similar effects for Netherlands-based companies exporting to Germany and for external imports cleared through Rotterdam for onward shipment to Germany.

(b)   By contrast, the requirement in the Excluded Sectors Directive (see Chapter 9) clearly establishes a differential treatment between EC and external suppliers in its rule that third-country offers that are less than 3% more advantageous on price (and no more advantageous on other grounds) must be rejected.

But even in cases where there is apparently equal treatment of EC and foreign suppliers, there may still be differential effects in practice which the methodology adopted should seek to identify. This is because market access is not just an absolute, but is also a relative affair. Identifying such relative differential access is much more difficult and contentious than simply looking for absolute changes.

A relative deterioration could have occurred if, for example, the improvement resulting from the removal of the barriers to trade between one Member State and another were less marked for external suppliers than for European producers. This could happen if, say, the removal of internal borders and the accompanying strengthening of external borders increased the difference between the formalities faced by European and foreign suppliers. To continue with the illustrative example cited above, the combination of abolishing the customs posts between the Netherlands and Germany and strengthening customs control in the Rotterdam Europort could make market access absolutely easier for both Dutch and non-EC suppliers, but relatively more difficult for the latter as compared with the former.

The scope for disagreement is widened when account is taken of a second type of differential impact. This is between one third party and another. Not all of the pre-SMP restrictions on imports had the effect only of protecting domestic industries in the Member State imposing the restriction. To the extent that the controls did not apply to all third-party suppliers, they will have tended to restrict competition between the most constrained suppliers and all non-constrained (or less constrained) suppliers, including those outside the Community. Hence, the removal of the partial restrictions will have improved market access for those suppliers that formerly bore the brunt of the restrictions but, by the same token, increased competition for those suppliers (external as well as domestic) that had not previously been affected (or not to the same extent).

3.2.   The analytical framework adopted

Almost all the changes of the SMP are likely to have some impact on third parties, if only through their effect on the rate of European growth. But since the demand effects of the SMP are the subject of other studies in the research programme, they are not the direct concern of this report. Only some aspects of the SMP will affect 'conditions of access of third countries' products'.

3.2.1.   Types of external effect

Taking into account the different bases for classification and the range of potential effects on third parties, an analytical framework has been developed for this study. This is summarized in Table 3.1, which uses the broad classification system employed by the Commission in its 1994 progress report (for rows) and in the columns classifies each of the sets of SMP change according to:

(a)   the nature of the pre-SMP barrier and its external effects;
(b)   the nature of the change; and
(c)   the potential external effects of these changes.

Table 3.1.   Analytical typology of SMP change and third parties

Pre-IMP barrier	External effect	Nature of change	Potential external effect of change
QRs in Member States	Discrimination between internal and external	Removal of QRs	Better access for externals
		Substitution of EC QRs	Complex change
	Discrimination among third parties	Removal of QRs	Better access for some; more competition for others
		Substitution of EC QRs	Complex change
Physical barriers between Member States (e.g. controls on borders)	No differential effects vis-à-vis domestic supplies	Removal of barriers	Increased ease of supply
Technical barriers (e.g. regulations and standards)	No differential effects	Mutual recognition	Access to new markets, more competition in old
		Harmonization	Complex change
	Discrimination among third parties (e.g. MRAs)	Mutual recognition	Access to new markets, more competition in old
		Harmonization	Complex change
Barriers to provision of services, right of establishment and free movement of capital (e.g. financial services, transport)	No differential effect	Primarily liberalization	Greater ease of establishment
Barriers in the business environment (e.g. intellectual and industrial property, company law, taxation and media)	No differential effect	Primarily approximation	Simpler operating conditions
Public procurement	No differential effect	Some liberalization	Mix of opening plus continued discrimination
Barriers in regulated industries (e.g. energy and telecommunications)	No differential effect	Primarily liberalization	Improved access

The justification for some of the judgements made in the table is provided in the following chapters.

In the case of the pre-SMP QRs in Member States, there were two types of external effect: discrimination between internal and external suppliers, and discrimination among third parties between the relatively favoured and the relatively disfavoured. In both cases, the QRs have either been removed or replaced by EC QRs.

In the former case, the nature of the change is related to the type of external effect of the pre-SMP barrier. The removal of national QRs will result in better access for external suppliers, but this improvement will be stronger for those suppliers that bore the brunt of the former restrictions. Those states that were not so affected may even face increased competition as a result of the change.

In the latter, the nature of the change for third parties as a result of the SMP will depend very much on the nature and the implementation of the new restrictions as compared with the old. This will differ case by case.

In the case of physical barriers between Member States, it is not clear that there is any major direct differential effect on third parties compared with domestic suppliers other than nationals of a particular Member State market. The removal of these barriers as part of the SMP will increase demand in the EC, and this is likely to affect external as well as domestic suppliers. The main aim of this study is to identify any special aspects of the removal that might have a direct bearing on the access conditions for third countries' products. Since these are likely to be small in relation to the overall effect on demand for imports resulting from market enlargement, quantification is more appropriately captured by formal dynamic models of the impact of the SMP.

In the case of technical barriers to trade between Member States (such as differing regulations and standards), the SMP change can be summarized as a mixture of mutual recognition of national measures and approximation of national measures (although this has taken different forms). It is not always straightforward to distinguish between 'direct SMP effects' and the consequences of changes in the policy environment within which the SMP occurred. As explained above, the consequences of the changing regulatory environment are, in most cases, beyond the terms of reference of this study.

The old regime had effects on third parties that were equivalent to those of the QRs in Member States. To an extent the restrictions discriminated between domestic and foreign (including other EC) suppliers, and in some cases may have also discriminated among foreign parties (such as in the case of bilateral agreements on the mutual recognition of certifications between individual Member States and certain third countries). The harmonization of Member State measures simplifies access to the EC market as a whole by reducing the number of regulations with which importers must comply, but might, depending on the specifics of the harmonized measure, make access more difficult, even to traditional markets, by raising the standard that must be attained. As in the case of Member State QRs, there are differential improvements between third parties depending on the extent to which they were more or less favoured by the old regime.

A rather similar picture applies with regard to the other SMP measures. Most pre-SMP measures governing the provision of services, rights of establishment, the business environment or tendering in public procurement largely discriminated against non-national EC firms and non-EC firms alike, although firms from some foreign countries might have received preferential treatment. In most cases the changes have been a mixture of harmonization and liberalization, in which non-EC suppliers have benefited to a certain degree. Where establishment is required to reap the gains of the removal of barriers, it is EC firms that would benefit, together with those third-country firms able to establish a presence in the EC. Consequently, it is more likely that gains will accrue to firms from the United States of America (USA) than to those from, for example, Bangladesh. Similarly, where reciprocity is required it is more likely to be firms from countries that are of reciprocal interest to the EC that will gain.

3.2.2. Relative external impacts of SMP measures

An assessment of how the different SMP changes have affected market access conditions for third countries' products requires the relative importance of each of these barriers in restricting market access to be established. Unfortunately, as is explained in Section 3.1.3, it is very difficult to quantify the effects of many of these barriers, particularly NTBs. Work currently being undertaken under the auspices of the OECD bears out these methodological and data problems. It tends to support the approach to dealing with them that is adopted in Chapter 5.

Although a definitive assessment of the relative importance of market access restrictions is not possible, it is feasible to identify in general terms the sectors in which SMP changes are likely to have the most significant impact on third countries' products. The same SMP change will have a more significant impact on market access in a sector in which tariffs or other trade barriers are low than in a sector in which they are high. Likewise SMP changes will have less impact in sectors where competition is restricted than in ones where it is open. As tariff levels decline as a result of the Uruguay Round, remaining NTBs will become relatively more significant as restrictions on market access.

EC producers will experience relatively larger cost reductions as a result of the SMP than third-country producers because of the persistence of some trade barriers, such as tariffs and customs formalities. Consequently, it is possible that although barriers to market access decline for third-country producers, they may lose market share to EC producers that have experienced greater cost reductions (Koekkoek *et al.*, 1990:115; Hoeller and Louppe, 1994: 19).

3.2.3. Subjective views

The emphasis given to SMP measures in this study is broadly in line with views expressed by some observers of the SMP process. Given the problems of identifying unambiguous quantitative conclusions on some aspects of the SMP, the qualitative assessments of third parties could form an important input. They are used at appropriate places in the following chapters.

In order to obtain as wide a range of such views as feasible, several sources were consulted.[4] Three of these are sufficiently detailed and general enough to be synthesized in this section (in addition to the issue-specific references elsewhere in the report). They are: US government reports on the SMP (USITC, 1993; 1996), a survey of European trade associations commissioned as part of the overall programme of studies (DRI, 1995), and a business opinion survey (Eurostat, 1997).

The USA had initially feared the formation of a 'Fortress Europe' as the 1992 programme led to increasing competition among the 12 Member States, causing EC industry to seek more protection against imports from third countries (USITC, 1993:xix). Later USITC reports

---

[4] These included the European Free Trade Association (EFTA) states, which are among the third parties most likely to find the market access of their producers affected by the SMP. But the EFTA Secretariat's analyses consulted did not address the issues in such a way as to be a direct input into this study (for example EFTA, 1992; Gardener and Teppett, 1992). They attempted to predict rather than evaluate the effects and to include modifications of EFTA's relations with the EC in the analysis. Moreover, since the EFTA states were engaged in bilateral free trade agreements for manufactures prior to the SMP most of the external trade measures did not apply to them. Hence, their analyses are of limited validity for other third parties.

indicate that these fears have been largely dissipated. However, certain issues like standards, broadcasting, public procurement and intellectual property remain a source of concern and will continue to be monitored by the US government and the private sector (USITC, 1993:72–5, 79–90).

Table 3.2 tabulates the areas of interest identified in the syntheses of US and trade association reports. A brief indication of the reason for the area being the focus of attention is provided in the two columns labelled 'Hopes' and 'Fears'. The table is not intended as a definitive list, but simply a very broad-brush review of expectations. It must be understood, as well, that it does not offer any commentary on the validity or otherwise of either the hopes or the fears that are recorded.

Table 3.2.   SMP effects: subjective priorities

Area	Hopes	Fears
1. By third parties – USA		
Standardization	Uniformity will facilitate exports	
Testing		May inhibit exports
Intellectual property	Support for trade-related intellectual property rights	
Public procurement	Potential US exports	Fear of exclusion (Utilities Directive)
Financial services	Potential US exports	
Free movement of goods	Will facilitate US exports	
Residual QRs		May inhibit exports (e.g. US-Japanese cars)
Taxation	Will facilitate US exports	
2. EC trade associations		
Residual QRs		Removal will increase import competition Non-removal will reduce SMP boost for EC firms
Regulations		Extravagant social and environmental controls will increase costs
Free movement of capital		Will attract hostile FDI

3.3.   Methodological options for analysis

3.3.1.   The research tasks and data availability

Different methodological options are required for this variety of measures. Most are constrained because of the wide range of potential effects and the limited availability of evidence (qualitative or quantitative) on their impact. The aim has been to use explicit empirically supported criteria for prioritizing SMP effects on market access wherever these are available. However, in many cases they are not available, either because of technical problems with the data that limit their use (at least within the time scale of this study) or because of the nature of the SMP changes. The methodological options are illustrated in Table 3.3.

In the case of both the removal of the Member State QRs and the harmonization of regulations and standards, the most appropriate methodology would be to compare data on trade patterns before and after the change, either in a formal analysis or in a less structured fashion as necessary. For example, when evaluating pre-SMP restrictions to judge the potential impact of the SMP-induced abolition of national QRs (Chapter 4) it would have been very helpful to be able to compare, for the products concerned, the pattern of EU trade in, say, 1985 and 1995. But this is not possible for reasons of structure and availability of trade data. The problem of structure derives from changes in the nomenclature used to classify products.[5] The problem of availability arises because the latest year for which full annual EC trade data are in the public domain (1994) is too early to capture many post-SMP effects. Unfortunately, EC measures formally communitizing all remaining national QRs were only adopted in March 1994, and although a number of technical harmonization measures have been in effect for some time, some have only come into force recently and significant work remains to be done in developing the European standards to give effect to some of the new approach Directives (CEC, 1996a:30). Therefore in both cases the change has been too recent for any effects to be observable in published trade statistics.

In the case of the removal of Member State QRs, therefore, what has been adopted is an eclectic identification of the main pre-SMP distortions and of the changes that have been introduced. This uses a combination of quantitative and qualitative data, with attention focused on a sufficiently small sub-set of the whole to allow them to be collated, absorbed and assessed within the time constraints of this study. This provides a level of quantification that goes significantly beyond any previous work in this area known to the authors, but even so the empirical analysis does not resolve beyond reasonable doubt many of the more important questions that arise concerning the SMP. When combined with qualitative data and broader considerations it is possible to obtain a view that establishes a reasonable 'balance of probabilities'.

---

5   The QRs were mainly established at the most disaggregated item level. The Nimexe system of product nomenclature (in use in 1985) and the Combined Nomenclature (CN, used since 1988) are not fully compatible at the most disaggregated level. Even within the period since 1988, when the CN has been operative, there have been many changes in the 8-digit details between years that bedevil attempts to make systematic comparisons at the required level of disaggregation over time.

Table 3.3.   Methodological options for prioritizing SMP change

SMP change	Research task	Methodology	Data required	Data availability
Removal of Member State QRs	Identify suppliers and scale of change	Analysis of trade flows before and after	Import time series before and after	Not available (change too recent)
	Identify items covered by QR and regime details	Eclectic and incomplete identification of pre-SMP distortions	Data on direction and value of imports into QR-imposing Member State	Available
Harmonization of regulations and standards	Identify indicators of scale	Analysis of trade flows before and after	Import time series before and after	Not available (change too recent)
	Describe changes	Qualitative identification of issues and, where possible, quantitative indicators of broad scale	Literature on perceptions of gain or loss; relevant trade statistics	Moderate availability
Removal of barriers to the provision of services and right of establishment	Describe changes	Broad-brush, qualitative identification of type of effect and of states more or less likely to take advantage	Literature on perceptions of gain or loss	Moderate availability
	Identify effects on suppliers and indicators for scale of change			
The business environment	Describe changes with potential effects for market access	Broad-brush, qualitative identification of type of effect and of states more or less likely to take advantage	Literature on perceptions of gain or loss	Moderate availability
Public procurement	Describe changes	Use existing study on SMP and public procurement	Procurement study	Available
	Identify indicators for scale of change			
Regulated industries	Describe changes with potential effects for market access	Broad-brush, qualitative identification of type of effect and of states more or less likely to take advantage	Literature on perceptions of gain or loss	Moderate availability

In the case of harmonization of regulations and standards, the methodology focuses more heavily on qualitative than quantitative measures. This involves an assessment of the EC's different approaches to removing technical barriers to trade, to identify the areas in which third countries are most likely to be directly adversely affected. This broad assessment is supplemented by the perceptions of EC and external suppliers.

In the case of the removal of barriers to the provision of services and improvement to the business environment, a much more broad-brush, qualitative analysis is all that is feasible. Our first step is to analyse the market opening potential of the SMP, paying particular attention to measures that have at least the potential to discriminate against firms from third countries. The literature on third parties' perceptions of gain and loss is used to round out this assessment. This is also an important source of information on procurement, but is supplemented by another study in this Programme which focused on the SMP changes to procurement practice.

3.3.2. Evidence of change in practice

Part of the problem of weighing the relative importance of the various SMP measures concerns the extent to which they have altered the practical conditions within which businesses operate. This is a separate issue from that concerning the degree of implementation, although the two are linked. A flavour of the problem may be obtained from a survey of business associations undertaken as part of the overall programme of studies.

The 431-page report entitled 'Survey of the Trade Associations' Perception of the Effects of the Single Market' is the result of 200 face-to-face interviews with European trade associations conducted between February and June 1995 (DRI, 1995).

The overall message of the report is that whilst the single market programme may have had an overall positive effect on the economy, and therefore indirectly on business in general, few of the measures contained in the White Paper were perceived to have directly impacted on the different business sectors represented by the trade associations. The list of perceived obstacles to the establishment of the SMP is summarized in Appendix A to Part I.

There is no explicit evaluation in the report of the external impact of the single market programme. Neither the interview guide nor the respondents (European trade associations) particularly lent themselves to such an analysis. However, several questions and issues tackled in the report were of indirect relevance to the external impact of the single European market. The responses need to be interpreted in the knowledge of the respondents' role. They are, essentially, comments from European lobbying groups, with their own interests.

One external impact of the SMP, according to the business survey, has been the increase in external interest in Europe as an entity and investment opportunity. This has been manifested by an increase in merger and acquisition activity as well as joint ventures and alliances. The single market programme is perceived by Europe's trade associations as a successful exercise in attracting external investment.

There is a concern that high production and infrastructure costs in Europe together with environmental and social policies may encourage both EC and non-EC companies to relocate, often to Eastern Europe or the Mediterranean Rim. This perceived high burden of costs is held to have allowed non-EC companies to compete successfully on price. In order to exploit this strategy, non-EC companies have created alliances, or established European 'shop windows' by merging with or taking over EC companies.

A similar set of conclusions is to be drawn from another Business Opinion Survey undertaken as part of the overall programme of studies (Eurostat, 1997). The results were first published in an internal EC document in April 1996. No indication was made in the report as to when the actual fieldwork took place. The study was conducted using self-completion closed questionnaires that were sent to EUR-12 businesses by mail. The sample size was 20,000 and the response rate was 65%, yielding 13,000 completed questionnaires.

Among the questions were three of some relevance to this study. They were:

Question 2.4 (i)   Change in the number of non-EC competitors
Answer   Increased, but less than increase from EC competitors.

Question 2.4 (ii)   Change in competition based on price from non-EC companies
Answer   Increased, but less than increase from EC and domestic competitors.

Question 2.4 (iii)   Change in level of competition on quality from non-EC firms
Answer   Increased, but less than increase from EC and domestic companies.

4. National trade barriers: identification

A whole host of import restrictions maintained at a national level have been swept aside and either replaced by Community-wide restrictions or abolished altogether. The removal of these national barriers to trade, which were maintained on at least some products by all Member States prior to the SMP, is an extremely important aspect of the SMP for this study. This is because it has had clear effects on the conditions of access of third-country products and because it is a direct effect of the SMP. This view is shared by the World Trade Organization (WTO), which has argued that 'quantitative restrictions are possibly the area where the single market has most directly improved access conditions across a wide variety of "sensitive" product categories' (WTO, 1995:57).

A first step in evaluating the impact of the SMP in this area is to establish the extent and effect of the national barriers to trade. Although their existence was well known and their extent has been commented upon by many analysts, there does not exist in the secondary literature a definitive list and estimates of their extent have varied widely. An OECD Working Paper, for example, stated that there were 6,417 country-specific restrictions at the start of 1993, but the exercise undertaken in the present study and reported in this chapter found the total to be one-third greater (Hoeller and Louppe, 1994:34) The identification of the pre-SMP national QRs presented in this chapter is believed to go well beyond anything previously available from secondary sources in the public domain and, as far as is known, from restricted sources.

The pre-SMP national barriers fell into one of three main groups:

(a)   residual QRs that were in force before the countries entered the Community or before the agreement of the common commercial policy and which were allowed to continue after joining;

(b)   national quotas on textiles and clothing established as part of the Community's overall trade policy in this area; and

(c)   a disparate collection of barriers of varying opaqueness introduced to affect trade flows into particular Member States.

The first two of these are treated together in the next sub-section because their extent is reasonably well documented in official Community publications. The third group is treated as a separate sub-section because accurate documentation is sparse.

Which countries imposed restrictions on which products from which suppliers? Have these restrictions been abolished, or replaced by Community-wide measures? And, in the case of the latter, how do these differ from the national restrictions that they have replaced? Neither the *status quo ante* nor the *status quo* are clear-cut with respect to these questions.

4.1. Residual quantitative restrictions

An analysis of the 'last-before-1992' Council Regulations in the *Official Journal of the European Communities* has established the nature of the *status quo ante* immediately before the SMP as it related to national trade barriers in the form of authorized residual QRs.

The same methodology was employed for assessing the pre-SMP extent of national QRs for products from both state and from non-state trading countries, although due to differences in the data available and to changes in EC policy following the collapse of Communism some of the analyses were not conducted for the state trading countries. Because of these differences in implementation of the common methodology, the procedures for these two types of trading partner are set out in separate sub-sections.

4.1.1. Non-state trading countries

Official listings of QRs

Council Regulation (EEC) No 288/82 built upon earlier Regulations and, as subsequently amended, established common rules for imports up to the SMP from non-state trading countries. It provided a framework for EC monitoring of the QRs that were maintained by the member governments. Over the following decade the number of national QRs was periodically changed in the light of economic and commercial circumstances. Council Regulation (EEC) No 196/91 represented the last major amendment before the completion of the single market, replacing entirely previous lists of exceptions. It was further amended twice, but only in relation to the QRs imposed by Spain, France and Italy.

In 1991, some 7,269 national QRs were authorized in respect of products imported from non-state trading countries (Council Regulations (EEC) Nos 196/91 of 21 January 1991, 2978/91 of 7 October 1991 and 2875/92 of 21 September 1992). In most cases, each QR referred to a specific (8-digit) item of the Combined Nomenclature (CN) that was restricted in whole or in part in relation to imports from a specified source. Two-thirds of the QRs were with respect to textiles and clothing.

This total includes QRs covered by the derogations granted to Spain and Portugal upon their accession. Since their elimination was not a single market effect, it is appropriate to disregard them. This brings the total down to 6,421 (three-quarters for textiles and clothing). The vast majority of these restrictions were total, in the sense that they covered the whole of a CN item.

The products and countries involved

The 10 Harmonized System (HS) chapters with the most restrictions were (in descending order of the number of items within the chapter subject to QRs):

(a)   52 (cotton);
(b)   62 (articles of apparel and clothing accessories, not knitted or crocheted);
(c)   55 (man-made staple fibres);
(d)   61 (articles of apparel and clothing accessories, knitted or crocheted);
(e)   85 (electrical machinery and equipment and parts thereof);
(f)   54 (man-made filaments);
(g)   63 (other made up textile articles);
(h)   87 (vehicles other than railway or tramway rolling-stock, and parts and accessories thereof);
(i)   60 (knitted or crocheted fabrics);
(j)   51 (wool, fine or coarse animal hair).

Only two chapters were subject to QRs by all of the Member States. They were Chapter 9 (coffee, tea, maté and spices) and Chapter 21 (miscellaneous edible preparations, including processed coffee). Both were, presumably, in support of the International Coffee Agreement quotas. But in most other chapters there was a broad spread of quota-imposing states: more than half of the then Member States maintained national QRs in all chapters except 60 (four imposing states) and 87 (three imposing states).

Even after the expiration of its derogations, Spain maintained the most national QRs overall, followed by the UK (mostly on textile and clothing imports from Laos and Cambodia), Italy, Greece, France and Portugal. Excluding textiles and clothing, Spain imposed the most QRs, followed by Portugal, Italy, France and the UK. The Benelux customs union had the fewest QRs, followed closely by Denmark.

Japan was far and away the country most specifically targeted by national QRs. QRs directed only at Japan accounted for more than 60% of non-general national QRs. After Japan came Laos and Cambodia (all UK QRs), Taiwan, Zone II countries,[6] and non-members of the International Coffee Agreement.

Adding to and interpreting the lists

The list of products provided in these Regulations is extensive, but there are reasons to suppose that it is not complete. It would appear that there were errors and omissions in the published text of Council Regulation (EEC) No 196/91. In some cases, these dealt with residual QRs that had, in the view of the national government concerned, been omitted erroneously from the list, and in others it dealt with changes to CN codes that had not been fully reflected in the Regulation. In at least one case, and probably in others, these errors and omissions were notified to the Commission and taken into account in the implementation of import policy. However, they appear not to have been put into the public domain as a formal combined list.

The analysis in this report is based on a complete record of one Member State's (the UK's) national residual QRs, but does not take account of any similar errors and omissions in Council Regulation (EEC) No 196/91 identified by other Member States.

A more substantial limitation of the information derived from Council Regulation (EEC) No 196/91 and its subsequent amendments for the purposes of this study is that, although it lists the products on which Member States had QRs, it does not provide any detailed information on the nature of the restrictions. There is every reason to suppose that there may have been substantial differences in some cases, but it is not possible to discern from the Regulations which products are most likely to have been affected.

There is no way of determining, for example, whether a Member State actually enforced any of these QRs. There may well have been reasons to keep redundant authorizations 'on the books' so that they would be available should demands arise for import limitation. But, if this occurred, it is not easy to discern. One observer writing in 1989, for example, recorded that 'the United Kingdom government claims to have revoked all [non-textile and clothing] QRs

---

[6]   Zone II refers to QRs imposed by France, and includes: Libya, Republic of South Africa, Namibia, Mexico, Guatemala, Honduras, El Salvador, Nicaragua, Costa Rica, Panama, Haiti, Dominican Republic, Colombia, Venezuela, Ecuador, Peru, Brazil, Chile, Bolivia, Paraguay, Uruguay, Argentina, Iraq, Iran, Saudi Arabia, North Yemen, Afghanistan, Pakistan, India, Bangladesh, Maldives, Sri Lanka, Nepal, Bhutan, Burma, Thailand, Indonesia, Philippines, South Korea, Japan, Taiwan, Australia, Australian Oceania, New Zealand, New Zealand Oceania.

other than on footwear, leather gloves, ceramics, hats, television sets and matches imported from various Eastern European countries and China and, as a curiosum, ceramics from Vietnam' (Davenport, 1990:190). Yet, the 1991 Regulation lists the UK as imposing on non-state trading countries QRs in no fewer than 10 chapters outside the textile and clothing sectors. Were these enforced?

Even where national QRs are known to have been enforced, neither their nature nor their coverage is clear from the lists in the Council Regulations. The nature of this problem may be illustrated in relation to controls on the import of bananas (CN 08030010). This is a product for which actions taken in relation to (but not necessarily as part of) the SMP are known to have had consequences for third parties, and in which the national regimes in operation prior to 1992 were complex. No hint of this complexity is provided by Council Regulation (EEC) No 196/91. The Regulation implies that Spain, France, Greece and Portugal all imposed complete restrictions, that the UK imposed a complete restriction with regard to the dollar area except for Liberia, and that Italy did so with regard to Mediterranean states, EFTA and Zone A3.[7] Yet the facts belie this implication. The UK imported bananas from dollar zone countries (but under licence), while the apparent complete restriction of France did not prevent that country importing bananas from Côte d'Ivoire, Cameroon, Colombia, Egypt, Chile and other Latin American countries in 1992.

4.1.2.   State trading countries

Official listings of QRs

As with the non-state trading countries, the move towards a common approach with regard to QRs on products from state trading countries began in the early 1980s and over the ensuing decade the number of national QRs was gradually changed. The 'last-before-1992' regulations dealing with the issue were Council Regulation (EEC) No 3420/83, as amended, together with Council Regulation (EEC) No 3419/83 which treated Romania separately.

In addition to changes in economic conditions, the liberalization of QRs on state trading countries had a great deal to do with the internal politics of the countries in question. For example, for years Romania received more favourable treatment than the other state trading countries and following the collapse of Communism a spate of new agreements with countries in Central and Eastern Europe radically changed the trading regimes between those countries and the EC. Council Regulation (EEC) No 3049/91 of 29 July 1991 was the last substantive amendment prior to the '1992' target date and set out a definitive list of national QRs exempted from the common approach.

---

[7]   Afghanistan, United Arab Emirates, Andorra, Angola and Cabinda, Saudi Arabia, Argentina, Australia (and territories under Australian administration), Azores, Bahrain, Bangladesh, Bermuda, Bhutan, Burma, Bolivia, Brazil, Busingen (German territory of), Cambodia, Canada, Canary Islands, Ceuta and Melilla, Chile, Colombia, South Korea, Costa Rica, Cuba, Dominican Republic, Ecuador, El Salvador, Philippines, Gibraltar, Greenland, Guatemala, Haiti, Honduras, Hong Kong, India, Indonesia, Iraq, Iran, Kuwait, Laos, Libya, Macao, Malaysia, Maldives, Mexico, Mozambique, Nauru, Nepal, Nicaragua, New Zealand (and territories under New Zealand administration), Oman, Pakistan, Panama, Paraguay, Peru, Qatar, Singapore, Sri Lanka, United States of America (and territories under United States administration), South Africa, Taiwan, Thailand, Uruguay, Venezuela, North Yemen, South Yemen (People's Republic).

In 1991 there were 4,800 authorized national QRs in respect of products other than textiles and clothing imported from state trading countries (Council Regulation (EEC) No 3049/91 of 29 July 1991). In addition, there were a large number of restrictions on textile and clothing products which have not been totalled for technical reasons.[8] When the Spanish and Portuguese transitional QRs are taken into account, this figure falls to 4,138. The principal target of these national QRs was China. According to Commission sources, over 4,000 quotas were in respect of China.

The products and countries involved

Even excluding textiles and clothing, under the *status quo ante* more products from state trading countries faced Member State QRs than did products from non-state trading countries. Of those products, the following faced the most restrictions (in descending order of the number of items within the chapter subject to QRs):

(a)   85 (electrical machinery and equipment and parts thereof);
(b)   72 (iron and steel);
(c)   73 (articles of iron and steel);
(d)   63 (footwear, gaiters and the like, parts of such articles);
(e)   87 (vehicles other than railway or tramway rolling-stock, and parts and accessories thereof);
(f)   48 (paper and paperboard; articles of paper pulp, of paper or of paperboard);
(g)   29 (organic chemicals);
(h)   84 (nuclear reactors, boilers, machinery and mechanical appliances; parts thereof);
(i)   70 (glass and glassware);
(j)   39 (plastics and articles thereof).

In no chapter did all Member States impose QRs, and in only four did over half of the Member States maintain national QRs – Chapters 85, 73, 64 and 70.

The fact that these figures do not include QRs on textiles and clothing needs to be borne in mind when assessing their incidence among Member States. Spain maintained by far the most national QRs, accounting for 40% of the total. Only Italy came close to imposing as many national QRs. Together they accounted for 66% of national QRs. Ireland imposed the fewest QRs, followed by Germany and France.

4.2. Other national barriers

The lists in the *Official Journal* did not cover all the measures that tended to restrict imports in relation to particular EC Member States. As stated in GATT 1991 (p. 97):

> The absence of quotas in an individual Member State does not necessarily mean that access is unlimited. For example, imports of passenger cars from Japan (subject to quotas in Italy) are under administrative import barriers in France and industry-to-industry restraint arrangements in the

---

8   The data do not include information on textiles and clothing for two reasons:
     (a) They are provided in terms of MFA codes, and so are not directly comparable with the other data for state trading countries or with those for the non-state trading countries;
     (b) The Regulation supplements the bilateral agreements with many state trading countries. Since there has not yet been time to analyse all of these agreements, the information derived from Council Regulation (EEC) No 3049/91 alone would not be representative.

United Kingdom. Japan moderates its exports of colour TV sets to the EC as a whole and, specifically, to Germany; other Member States (France and Italy) have implemented quotas.

By their nature, these less transparent restrictions are difficult to catalogue and, if they depend upon industry-to-industry collaboration, the effective change brought about following the SMP may also be very difficult to discern. As the GATT argued, in a subsequent *Trade Policy Review*:

> The individual measures may differ widely with regard to trade coverage, restrictiveness and potential implications on third countries. Retrospective Community surveillance, as an example, may be considered a merely statistical exercise without any impact on trade flows. However, as a possible precursor to trade restraints, it may also serve as a warning signal to the suppliers concerned. In other cases, it may be used to monitor compliance with price or quantitative undertakings given (GATT, 1993:71).

This ambiguity is underlined in a 1990 study by Winters. This concluded that:

> ... more often than not the imposition of import surveillance, which ostensibly entails *only* collecting detailed trade information, curtails imports ... [S]ince surveillance barely affects the actual costs of trading, its effects must stem from its influence on exporters' perceptions of their environment (Winters, 1990).

Moreover, some voluntary export restraints (VERs) may not even be known to the Member State governments. One observer has claimed, for example, that in the late 1980s Taiwan continued to restrict its footwear exports to UK by agreement with the British Footwear Manufacturers' Association, even though the government believed the VER to have expired in 1986 (Davenport, 1990:191).

Given the uncertainty in this area, it is important to limit unnecessary controversy by focusing attention on those trade restrictions for which there is some quasi-official acceptance. For this reason, a list has been compiled of known voluntary restraints, surveillance and similar measures affecting imports identified by the GATT in the early 1990s which were enforced at a sub-Community level (Table 4.1). No other more detailed and equally authoritative source is available, at least in the public domain. Since the table combines information relating to more than one time period, not all of the restrictions will necessarily have been in force at the same time. The purpose of the table is to illustrate the range of measures in place, the products affected, and the external suppliers that were constrained.

Table 4.1. Other national trade barriers[1]

Product	Imposing state	Target state	Type of measure
Frozen squid	Italy	Rep. of Korea	Reference prices
Slippers and sandals	France	China	Autolimitation
Footwear	Ireland	Rep. of Korea	Industry-to-industry arrangement
	UK	Czech Rep., Slovakia, Romania, Poland	Industry-to-industry arrangement
Machine tools	France	Japan	Restraint arrangement
Colour TVs	Germany	Japan	Export moderation
	UK	Singapore	Export restraints
TV tubes	France	Japan	Industry-to-industry arrangement
Video recorders	France	Japan	Industry-to-industry arrangement
Passenger cars	UK	Japan	Industry-to-industry arrangement
Automobiles	Belgium	Japan	Price fixing subject to administrative authorization
Metal flatware	Benelux	Rep. of Korea	Industry-to-industry arrangement
Umbrellas	France	Singapore, Taiwan, Thailand	Industry-to-industry arrangement
Pottery and chinaware	UK	Japan	Export restraints
Clothing	UK	Japan	Export approval
Travel goods	Belgium, Germany, France, Italy, Netherlands, UK	Rep. of Korea	Export recommendation

[1] Explanatory notes in original tables excluded.
Source: GATT, 1991:Table IV.5; GATT, 1993:Table IV.2.

The products covered range from frozen squid to passenger cars, via, among others, consumer electronics, machine tools and spoons. Eight Member States are identified as having imposed restrictions. The restrictions themselves are of a kind that is not easy to monitor (such as industry-to-industry arrangements).

4.3. Use of Article 115

4.3.1. Scope and application of Article 115

The practical application of national QRs is closely associated with the use of Article 115 of the Treaty of Rome which may be used if the import of a product is restricted at a level lower than that of the EC, usually the Member State level. The Article provided a safety valve for national governments facing internal economic difficulties to seek protection by preventing goods, the import of which was restricted at Community level, from crossing their borders via other Member States. The scope and application of Article 115 has changed, but the situation over the time period covered by this report is best reflected in terms of the Commission's Decision 87/433/EEC in 1987. This stated that:

> ... at the present stage of establishment of the Common Market the measures under Article 115 of the Treaty should be authorized only where deflections of trade lead to economic difficulties or jeopardize the effectiveness of commercial policy measures taken by Member States pursuant to the Community's international obligations (OJ L 238/26, 21.8.1987).

Under the pre-SMP procedures for the implementation of Article 115, a procedure was established through which requests for protection were channelled upwards from the affected industries via national governments to the Commission (Velia, 1996:86). The first stage of the procedure was for the industry, mostly through national associations, to provide their national authorities with the necessary information. Supported cases were then passed on to the Commission for examination. The Commission based its judgement on indicators of change in the levels of employment, production and use of capacity, bankruptcy rates, total and direct imports, price and profit levels, and turnover plus consumption in the current and two preceding years. Under this procedure, discretion on whether or not to put forward an application lay with the Member State, while responsibility for taking a final authorization either to restrict licences or to grant intra-Community surveillance rested with the Commission.

Without the opportunity afforded by Article 115 to restrict imports from other Member States of goods originating outside the Community, the enforcement of national QRs would have been much more difficult or, depending upon the nature of the product and market, impossible. The Article has not been removed as a result of the SMP, but it appears to be no longer enforceable given the disappearance of internal border controls. Under the rewording of the Article in the Treaty on European Union, national measures require *ex ante* approval. Hence, Article 115 is not a separate feature of the SMP with implications for the access of third-country products, but it forms part of the context within which changes have been made to conditions of access.

4.3.2. National customs control

The application of Article 115 was facilitated by the physical barriers to trade at national frontiers. Until 1988, each Member State retained its own form of customs declaration required for all cross-border trade. In 1988, a single document, the Single Administrative Document (SAD), was developed to bring some consistency to the paperwork and data collected. This remained in force for all trade until the end of 1992.

Until the SAD was introduced Member States used many different individual forms for the purposes of customs export and import declarations and Community transit (CT). The total number of different 'boxes' on customs forms before the SAD was over 150. This was reduced to 54 in the SAD, and a good degree of consistency in the individual Member States' requirements for data was achieved.[9]

---

9   This section draws on the study on Customs and fiscal formalities at frontiers undertaken as part of the broader programme of research on the SMP, in *The Single Market Review*, Subseries III, Vol. 3, Luxembourg: Office for Official Publications of the EC and London: Kogan Page/Earthscan publishers, 1997.

Until 1 January 1992, customs warehousing was governed by a fairly generally worded Directive and implemented in quite different ways in different Member States. New basic and implementing Regulations were applied from this date and brought a much more standard approach to this important procedure.

An important feature to note is that controls for customs warehousing have also progressed. In the 1980s there was an emphasis on physical control over the security of the premises and checking of the goods themselves. This has tended to change to a control based on records, especially computerized records.

In the past, customs usually required a bond or guarantee to cover the duty and taxes suspended in warehouse (hence the old expression 'bonded warehouse'). Customs today often will not require such a bond for the warehousing procedure.

Before 1993 CT documents were used to cover free circulation goods which moved through another country *en route* from the Member State of export to that of destination. They also covered goods moving directly from one Member State to another, but the goods were to be customs-cleared inland and not at the frontier.

4.4. The scale and incidence of national QRs

Bearing in mind the methodological pitfalls and the greyness of the situation before and after the SMP, it is not the task of Part I of this study to attempt a formal modelling of the effects of removing national QRs. As explained in Section 3.3, data are not available to make a systematic comparison of a 'before and after' kind, and as indicated in Section 4.1 the codified information on formal national QRs (let alone informal ones) is insufficiently detailed to permit wide-ranging, empirically supported conclusions to be drawn without substantial qualification. In this difficult situation the study has undertaken a range of quantitative exercises designed to contribute to a set of indicators of the probable scale and incidence of the pre-SMP restrictions. Because each of these exercises looks at only a part of the overall picture, the process of undertaking them could continue for a very long time without exhausting all useful approaches. The time constraint has been the principal limiting factor in the extent of the exercises reported in this chapter. Nonetheless, the data presented in this section do represent the fruits of a significant level of research and a considerably more detailed and wide-ranging quantification of national QRs than, as far as is known, is available elsewhere.

4.4.1. Ranking HS chapters by quota ratios

In Section 4.1 the CN chapters most affected by residual QRs were identified, but any analysis conducted at a chapter level of restrictions that are, in most cases, established in relation to particular items, cannot be very rigorous. One simple refinement is to adjust for the number of items in any chapter. A chapter with a large number of items may have a higher number of national QRs than one with only a few items, but what does this imply? It is not possible to establish without closer scrutiny whether a chapter in which 50 out of 100 items are subject to quotas is more or less substantially affected than a chapter in which nine out of ten items are covered. But at least an attempt should be made to distinguish between these different cases.

All 54 chapters in which national quotas on imports from non-state trading countries were recorded in the Regulation have been analysed to indicate the proportion of the number of

8-digit items that were subject to quotas. A similar exercise has been undertaken for all 61 chapters in which imports from state trading countries were subject to national restrictions in the Council Regulation. This exercise, when combined with others (see below), directs attention towards those product groups that appear to have faced more, and those that have faced fewer, restrictions.

Summary information on all those chapters in which more than 20% of the items were subject to national quotas is provided in Table 4.2 (for non-state traders) and Table 4.3 (for state traders). These supply information on the number of quotas imposed, the number of EC Member States imposing them, and a column headed 'ratio'. The ratio is produced by dividing the number of quotas by the number of countries imposing them, and expressing the result as a percentage of the total number of 8-digit items within that chapter. The chapters are then presented in declining order of ratio.

Table 4.2.   Top HS chapters subjected to national QRs on imports from non-state trading countries (all HS chapters with quota/item ratio > 20%)

HS chapter	Description	No of quotas	No of countries	Ratio (%)
65	Headgear and parts thereof	15	1	83
60	Knitted or crocheted fabrics	183	4	83
61	Articles of apparel and clothing accessories, knitted or crocheted	751	6	74
62	Articles of apparel and clothing accessories, not knitted or crocheted	924	7	69
52	Cotton, including yarns and woven fabrics thereof	985	8	69
55	Manmade staple fibres, including yarns and woven fabrics thereof	780	8	58
87	Vehicles, and parts and accessories thereof	274	3	51
66	Umbrellas, walking sticks, whips, etc., and parts thereof	4	1	50
54	Manmade filaments, including yarns and woven fabrics thereof	347	7	47
50	Silk	33	3	44
64	Footwear, gaiters and the like; parts of such articles	141	4	43
58	Special woven fabrics; tufted textile fabrics; lace; etc.	164	7	41
63	Other made-up textile articles; worn clothing; etc.	279	8	40
51	Wool, fine and coarse animal hair; yarn and fabrics of horsehair	170	7	35
31	Fertilizers	42	3	35
95	Toys, games and sports equipment; parts and accessories thereof	47	2	31
89	Ships, boats and floating structures	11	1	28
57	Carpets and other textile floor coverings	35	3	25
27	Mineral fuels, mineral oils and products of their distillation	47	2	25
53	Other vegetable textile fibres	21	2	21

Sources: Eurostat, 1995; Council Regulations (EEC) Nos 196/91 and 197/91 of 21 January 1991.

Hence, for example, in Table 4.2 it is indicated that 15 quotas were imposed by one Member State on Chapter 65 which, because it contained only 18 items, represents a ratio of 83%. In the case of Chapter 60 there were 183 quotas, but they were imposed by four Member States. The ratio will vary depending on whether the four imposed QRs on different items (i.e. 183 items were affected) or all targeted the same items. Given the objective of providing a focusing device rather than a precise ranking (an infeasible objective given the uncertainty over implementation), an arbitrary assumption was made. This was that each imposing state targeted the same items, i.e. in this example there were 45 or 46 quotas per Member State, which is equivalent to some 83% of the total number of items in the chapter.

Table 4.3.   Top HS chapters subjected to national QRs on imports from state trading countries (all HS chapters with quota/item ratio > 20%)

HS chapter	Description	No of quotas	No of countries	Ratio (%)
65	Headgear and parts thereof	15	1	83
18	Cocoa and cocoa preparations	40	2	77
64	Footwear, gaiters and the like; parts of such articles	357	8	54
66	Umbrellas, walking sticks, whips, etc., and parts thereof	8	2	50
87	Vehicles, and parts and accessories thereof	324	4	45
36	Explosives; pyrotechnic products; matches; etc.	17	4	43
31	Fertilizers	80	5	40
93	Arms and ammunition; parts and accessories thereof	27	2	39
45	Cork and articles of cork	3	1	38
48	Paper and paperboard; articles of paper pulp, paper or paperboard	191	3	33
39	Plastics and articles thereof	144	2	32
79	Zinc and articles thereof	13	3	29
78	Lead and articles thereof	4	1	29
27	Mineral fuels, mineral oils and products of their distillation	78	3	27
38	Miscellaneous chemical products	75	3	26
42	Articles of leather	2	4	25
72	Iron and steel	437	4	23
89	Ships, boats and floating structures	27	3	23
41	Raw hides and skins (other than furskins) and leather	12	1	21
29	Organic chemicals	187	2	21
73	Articles of iron or steel	388	7	21
32	Tanning or dyeing extracts; tannins and derivatives; etc.	27	2	20

Sources: Eurostat, 1995; Council Regulation (EEC) No 3049/91 of 29 July 1991.

A number of salient features appear from Table 4.2:

(a)   Only a relatively small number of chapters were affected by a broad range of national quotas. Out of the 54 chapters considered, only 20 have a quota/item ratio of more than 20%. Clearly, a ratio below this threshold does not necessarily mean that the quotas were not important in one sense or another; a quota on just one item could have a very strong effect if that item were either of considerable importance to a particular country or group of countries, or covered the most important traded good within a chapter. Nonetheless, the finding, when combined with other focus criteria, provides a basis for identifying the sectors in which national QRs were most wide-ranging.

(b)   There exists a fairly strong polarization between those chapters in which most Member States imposed quotas and those in which very few did so. Because the Benelux is treated as one unit, the maximum number of countries imposing quotas is 10. Of the 20 chapters in Table 4.2, eight were subject to quotas by six or more Member States, while 10 were targeted by three states or fewer.

(c)   This polarization is closely associated with the type of product. Thirteen were textiles or clothing of some kind, and this group included all the chapters in which six or more Member States imposed quotas. In five of the remaining seven cases, the number of imposing states was three or fewer.

The salient features of Table 4.3 are similar to those of Table 4.2, although this is partly because textile items were excluded from the analysis:

(a)   Once again, only a relatively small number of chapters were affected by a broad range of national quotas. Out of the 61 chapters considered, only 22 have a quota/item ratio of more than 20%.

(b)   With textiles absent, most chapters faced restrictions in only a few national markets (as was the case for non-textile items in Table 4.2). Of the 22 chapters in Table 4.3, only two were subject to quotas by six or more Member States, while 15 were targeted by three states or fewer.

4.4.2.   Ranking HS chapters by value of trade

Evidently, the quota/item ratio is only one of several approaches to prioritizing the national QRs in order to identify those with the most wide-ranging potential impact on third parties. The value of trade in the products subject to national QRs is also a very relevant consideration (but not an unambiguous one, which is why it must be assessed alongside other measures).

Data have been collected on the value of EC imports in 1992 of HS chapters subject to national QRs on imports from non-state trading countries, and on the value of imports of the items within these chapters covered by national QRs.[10] In order to cover the possibility that the value of extra-EC imports of items subject to national QRs was restricted because of them, data were collected on both extra-EC and intra-EC imports.

This information has been processed in two ways, and the most important features are presented in Tables 4.4 and 4.5. The first approach lists the chapters in declining order of

---

10   It was agreed between the authors and the Commission to focus attention on non-state trading countries.

value of imports (intra + extra) of items within the chapter subject to national QRs. Table 4.4 indicates, in declining order of intra + extra import value, all of those chapters:

(a) in which the value of imports (intra + extra) of the items subject to national QRs exceeded ECU 500 million in 1992; and

(b) which were not included in Table 4.2.

Table 4.4. **HS chapters subject to national QRs, by value of imports (chapters not included in Table 4.2)**

(million ECU)

HS chapter	Description	Total EUR-12 imports of QR items, 1992, from:	
		intra- + extra-EC	extra-EC
85	Electrical machinery and equipment and parts thereof	65,991	31,280
84	Nuclear reactors, boilers, machinery and mechanical appliances; parts thereof	14,396	5,685
90	Optical, photographic, medical etc. instruments and parts	10,698	5,487
04	Dairy produce; birds' eggs; natural honey; edible animal products n.e.s.	8,258	495
40	Rubber and articles thereof	6,568	1,657
22	Beverages, spirits and vinegar	4,670	620
12	Oil seeds and oleaginous fruits; misc. grains, seeds and fruit	4,444	3,291
72	Iron and steel	4,192	1,724
08	Edible fruit and nuts; peel of citrus fruit or melons	3,475	2,291
82	Tools, implements, cutlery, spoons and forks, of base metal	3,467	1,493
09	Coffee, tea, maté and spices	2,698	2,209
42	Articles of leather	2,572	1,710
07	Edible vegetables and certain roots and tubers	2,568	491
91	Clocks and watches and parts thereof	2,474	2,251
15	Animal or vegetable fats and oils and their cleavage products	2,220	971
20	Preparations of vegetables, fruit, nuts, or other parts of plants	2,181	752
59	Impregnated, coated, covered or laminated textile fabrics	2,048	518
56	Wadding, felt and non-wovens; special yarns; ropes, etc.	2,042	504
69	Ceramic products	2,020	736
16	Edible preparations of meat, fish, crustaceans, molluscs, etc.	1,830	513
94	Furniture; stuffed furnishings; lamps n.e.s.; prefab buildings	1,674	458
71	Precious/semi-precious stones; precious metals; imitation jewellery; coin	690	491
11	Products of the milling industry	552	18

Sources: Eurostat, 1995; Council Regulations (EEC) Nos 196/91 and 197/91 of 21 January 1991.

The second approach presents the data in proportionate rather than absolute value terms. The chapters are listed in relation to the proportion of the value of imports of the items subject to national QRs in total imports of the whole chapter within which they fall. Again, it is intra- + extra-EC imports that are used for this ranking exercise. Table 4.5 identifies from this list those chapters:

(a)   in which the proportion of imports of the items subject to national QRs exceeds one-third of the total value of imports in the chapter; and

(b)   which were not included in Table 4.2.

Table 4.5.   HS chapters subject to national QRs, in declining order of proportionate value of quota-restricted items (chapters not included in Table 4.2)

HS chapter	Description	Total EUR-12 imports, 1992, from:		Proportion of value of QR imports to total:	
		intra+extra-EC (million ECU)	extra-EC (million ECU)	intra+extra-EC (%)	extra-EC (%)
59	Impregnated, coated, covered or laminated textile fabrics	2,077	521	99	99
56	Wadding, felt and non-wovens; special yarns; ropes, etc.	2,115	532	97	95
12	Oil seeds and oleaginous fruits; misc. grains, seeds and fruit	5,788	3,871	77	85
09	Coffee, tea, maté and spices	3,521	2,821	77	78
91	Clocks and watches and parts thereof	3,415	2,784	72	81
85	Electrical machinery and equipment and parts thereof	96,862	44,302	68	71
04	Dairy produce; birds' eggs; natural honey; edible animal products n.e.s.	12,528	772	66	64
93	Arms and ammunition; parts and accessories thereof	520	194	62	57
82	Tools, implements, cutlery, spoons and forks, of base metal	5,734	2,441	60	61
42	Articles of leather	4,772	3,278	54	52
22	Beverages, spirits and vinegar	9,646	962	48	64
40	Rubber and articles thereof	13,608	4,168	48	40
15	Animal or vegetable fats and oils and their cleavage products	4,851	1,781	46	55
11	Products of the milling industry	1,285	55	43	33
16	Edible preparations of meat, fish, crustaceans, molluscs etc.	4,733	1,946	39	26
69	Ceramic products	5,616	1,233	36	60
36	Explosives; pyrotechnic products; matches, etc.	365	173	35	44

Sources: Eurostat, 1995; Council Regulations (EEC) Nos 196/91 and 197/91 of 21 January 1991.

Combining the data in Tables 4.4 and 4.5 indicates the additional chapters, not already covered in Table 4.2, that combine both relatively high import value (implying that they are of wide potential interest to third parties) and were characterized by a relatively high proportion of the value of the chapter in items subject to national QRs (implying that external suppliers may have been strongly affected). The chapters concerned, and the number of QR-imposing states for each, are listed in Table 4.6.

Table 4.6.   Most important HS chapters, ranked by value

HS chapter	Description	No of countries
85	Electrical machinery and equipment and parts thereof	6
04	Dairy produce; birds' eggs; natural honey; edible animal products n.e.s.	2
40	Rubber and articles thereof	4
22	Beverages, spirits and vinegar	3
12	Oil seeds and oleaginous fruits; misc. grains, seeds and fruit	2
82	Tools, implements, cutlery, spoons and forks, of base metal	1
09	Coffee, tea, maté and spices	10
42	Articles of leather	1
91	Clocks and watches and parts thereof	3
15	Animal or vegetable fats and oils and their cleavage products	2
59	Impregnated, coated, covered or laminated textile fabrics	7
56	Wadding, felt and non-wovens; special yarns; ropes, etc.	5
69	Ceramic products	6
16	Edible preparations of meat, fish, crustaceans, molluscs, etc.	2
11	Products of the milling industry	3

Sources: Tables 4.4 and 4.5.

One-third of the 15 additional 'most affected' chapters added to the list in Table 4.6 are agricultural products. Five cover products that fall under the common agricultural policy (CAP), while a sixth (coffee) reflects the EC's adherence to the International Coffee Agreement. Of the remainder, two are textiles, and beverages, leather goods, cutlery, ceramics, electrical machinery and watches make up the picture.

The polarization between widely and narrowly imposed QRs is more marked than was the case for the top 20 chapters selected in relation to the quota/item ratio (Table 4.2), especially if coffee is disregarded. Nine of the chapters in Table 4.6 were subject to national QRs in three or fewer states. Apart from the case of coffee, only three chapters were subject to QRs in six or more states. In the case of quota/item ranking, half of the top 20 chapters were subject to QRs in three or fewer states; with the value ranking in Table 4.6, the proportion is almost two-thirds. Similarly, just under one-third of the chapters in Table 4.2 were subject to national QRs in six or more Member States; in Table 4.6 the share is just over one-fifth.

4.5. The countries affected

This sorting process provides some guidance on:

(a)   the Member States that made the most use of national QRs (identified in Sections 4.1 and 4.2 above and also in Section 5.3 below);

(b)   the products most subjected to national QRs and, hence, most likely to experience a change in market access as a result of the SMP (identified in Section 4.4);

(c)   the third parties most frequently targeted by national QRs and, hence, most likely to be affected directly by the SMP (identified in Section 5.3 below).

However, these exercises do not indicate in any precise way either the impact of the national QRs on the direct imports even of the imposing states (leaving aside the methodological debate on trade deflection summarized in Section 5.2 below), or the extent to which they may have altered the geographical pattern of trade (by disfavouring, for example, targeted states relative to other third parties).

A full quantification of such effects is well beyond the scope of this study (not least because of the manifold problems of complexity and lack of data noted above), but a number of illustrative exercises have been completed to facilitate the prioritization process. These are designed to identify whether or not the existence of national QRs was associated with a complete absence of imports into the imposing state, and whether the geographical pattern of imports from the QR-imposing state was different from that of the EC as a whole.

4.5.1. Cases of zero imports

Data have been collected on an item-by-item basis to show the level of imports into QR-imposing states and into the Community as a whole. These cover the HS chapters listed in Tables 4.2 and 4.6.[11]

There are a significant number of occasions on which the existence of a national QR is associated with a complete absence of imports into the imposing Member State. In over one-third of the cases covered in Table 4.7, the imposing state recorded zero imports in 1992 for 25% or more of the items on which it imposed national QRs. In one-quarter of 1,068 national QRs covered by the table, the imposing state recorded zero imports.

Whilst there exists reasonable room for doubt over whether a given positive level of imports has been influenced by a national QR (with the counterfactual having to take account of consumption patterns, etc.), there must be some strong suspicion that the absence of imports is a QR effect. If market and consumption characteristics were such that imports were not demanded (or were prohibited by other measures) there would be no need, after all, for the national QR.

---

11   For technical reasons, Chapter 85 is excluded.

Table 4.7.   Authorized national QRs: An indicator of the frequency of discrimination against external suppliers

HS chapter		QR-imposing state	No of items:		
			with QR	with zero imports:	
				No	%
04	Dairy produce, eggs, etc.	Spain	66	41	66
		France	1	1	100
09	Coffee	Benelux	4	0	0
		Denmark	4	1	25
		Germany	4	0	0
		Greece	4	1	25
		Spain	4	0	0
		France	4	0	0
		Ireland	4	1	25
		Italy	4	0	0
		Portugal	4	0	0
		UK	4	0	0
11	Products of the milling industry	Spain	43	37	88
		Germany	2	0	0
		UK	1	0	0
12	Oilseeds	Portugal	22	8	36
		Spain	1	0	0
		France	1	0	0
15	Animal fats and oils	Portugal	48	32	67
		Spain	4	3	75
		France	1	1	100
16	Edible meat and fish preparations	Spain	20	9	45
		France	5	1	20
22	Beverages, spirits, vinegar	Spain	41	16	39
		France	19	2	11
		Portugal	18	13	72
		Denmark	3	3	100
27	Mineral fuels	France	33	6	18
		Spain	13	5	39
31	Fertilizers	Benelux	14	6	43
		Spain	14	8	57
		Greece	14	6	43
40	Rubber	Spain	15	0	0
		Portugal	15	0	0
		Greece	5	0	0
		Ireland	2	0	0
42	Articles of leather	Spain	24	0	0
		UK	4	0	0

Table 4.7.   (continued)

HS chapter	QR-imposing state	No of items:		
		with QR	with zero imports:	
			No	%
56 Wadding, felt and non-wovens	France	11	0	0
	UK	9	0	0
	Italy	9	0	0
	Spain	3	0	0
	Greece	1	1	100
59 Impregnated, coated, etc. textiles	UK	12	2	17
	Spain	6	3	50
	Greece	5	4	80
	France	4	0	0
	Portugal	4	2	50
	Germany	1	0	0
	Italy	1	0	0
66 Umbrellas	Spain	3	0	0
69 Ceramic products	UK	11	0	0
	Spain	9	0	0
	Portugal	6	1	17
	Denmark	5	0	0
	France	2	0	0
	Greece	2	0	0
82 Base metal tools, cutlery, etc.	Spain	70	0	0
87 Vehicles	Spain	138	20	15
	Italy	102	14	14
	Portugal	66	23	35
89 Ships, boats, etc.	Spain	12	5	42
	France	11	3	27
91 Clocks and watches	Portugal	16	0	0
	Spain	8	0	0
	UK	1	0	0
95 Toys and games	Spain	28	0	0
	Greece	23	1	4

Sources: Eurostat, 1995; Council Regulations (EEC) Nos 196/91 and 197/91 of 21 January 1991.

The exercise has added a further illustration of the ambiguous effect of national QRs and the fact that their role must be considered alongside data on national consumption and production patterns, as well as on the extent to which the QRs were actually enforced. In a significant number of cases the actual imports into the QR-imposing state were not less than might have been expected (based on that state's 'normal' share of EC imports and of total extra-EC imports of the item in question). On the contrary, they were more – sometimes considerably more. This suggests that on some products the QR-imposing state is one of the major markets in the EC. Whether this is because QRs may have been designed primarily to restrain but not necessarily to stifle imports that would otherwise have been even larger, or whether it reflects their non-enforcement, or whether it simply reflects different consumption patterns within the EC, is impossible to judge in the context of this study.

4.5.2. Differential effects on third parties

The national QRs did not simply restrict extra-EC imports into the Community. In the case of QRs affecting only some supplying countries, they may also have distorted the geographical composition of imports. Countries facing restrictions were disadvantaged but, by the same token, external suppliers not covered by the restrictions were relatively favoured.

Two sets of data were collected in relation to the products listed in Table 4.2, in the expectation that they might provide a broad indication of the extent to which such differential treatment may have occurred. The first concerns the main source of extra-EC imports into the QR-imposing state and into the EUR-12 as a whole. The second concerns the share of the most important supplying state in the extra-EC imports of the QR-imposing state and in the EUR-12. This information is summarized in Table 4.8.

Table 4.8. **Authorized national QRs: an indicator of the frequency of discrimination between external suppliers**

Chapter	QR-imposing state	No of items facing QR in which:			
		Main supplier is different from main EUR-12 supplier		Share of QR-imposing state is higher than of EUR-12[1]	
		No	%	No	%
27 Mineral fuels	France	17	70	21	78
	Spain	5	63	7	88
31 Fertilizers	Benelux	7	88	7	88
	Spain	5	83	3	50
	Greece	6	75	5	63
66 Umbrellas	Spain	3	100	3	100
87 Vehicles	Spain	65	55	88	75
	Italy	62	71	71	83
	Portugal	20	47	37	86
89 Ships, etc.	Spain	5	71	6	86
	France	3	38	5	63
95 Toys and games	Spain	22	79	18	64
	Greece	21	96	18	82

[1] Items in which the main extra-EC supplying state to the QR-imposing state has a share of the QR-imposing state's extra-EC imports that is one-quarter or more greater than its share of EUR-12 extra-EC imports.
Sources: Eurostat, 1995; Council Regulations (EEC) Nos 196/91 and 197/91 of 21 January 1991.

In the great majority of cases, the most important source of extra-EC imports into the QR-imposing state is different from the most important supplier of that item to the EUR-12. Column 4 of Table 4.8 shows, for each QR-imposing state in relation to each chapter, the proportion of items subject to QRs in which the main source of imports into the QR-imposing state and the EUR-12 was different. In all but two of the 13 instances reported in the table, the proportion of items in which there was a difference of supplier is greater than one-half, and in nine it is greater than two-thirds.

The two right-hand columns report the comparison between the import share of the main supplier to the QR-imposing state and that country's share of EUR-12 imports. In most cases, the main supplier to the QR-imposing state has a higher share of that country's imports than it does of EUR-12 extra-EC imports.

It may be the case that these results indicate the existence of an inter-third-party bias which results not only in a reduction in the total value of imports into the QR-imposing state but also in a shift in the source of supply. However, it was agreed between the authors and the Commission that further work on the differential impact of national QRs as between one third-party supplier and another was not a high priority for the limited resources available for this study.

4.6. Summary of findings

Unlike most of the other chapters in this report, the present one has attempted only to identify the pre-SMP situation. This is because the situation is sufficiently complex to require detailed exposition.

There were an extremely large number of national QRs in existence on paper, plus an indeterminate number of unauthorized restrictions that tended to distort particular national product markets. It is far from clear how many of these restrictions were actually imposed, and those that were in force are likely to have been applied in differing ways so that their effect on market access will not have been identical.

Despite these caveats, the overall effect of the restrictions will have been to limit market access for some products from some third parties to some extent. A very wide range of products may have been affected in this way. Textiles and clothing were clearly the most targeted products, but a wide range of other items were covered too (over 1,000 in the case of non-state trading countries, and over 4,000 in the case of state traders).

The Member States most frequently imposing national QRs on imports from non-state trading countries were Spain, the UK, Italy, Greece, France and Portugal. The fewest QRs were imposed by the Benelux and Denmark. In the case of imports from state trading countries, Spain and Italy imposed overwhelmingly the largest number of national QRs, with Ireland imposing the fewest. At least nine Member States imposed unofficial restrictions on imports.

The countries most frequently targeted by these national QRs were state traders, Japan and other East Asian states. Unofficial national trade barriers were directed almost exclusively at the East Asian countries.

5. National trade barriers: the effects of their removal

5.1. Changes to the *status quo ante* as a result of the SMP

5.1.1. The new regulations

An important aspect of the SMP is that:

> ... Member States may no longer enforce national trade restrictions against third countries, control regional supply targets that may be pursued by exporters, or operate technical barriers as substitutes for border measures (WTO, 1995:14).

Although provision is made for national derogations from harmonized policies on the grounds of 'major needs', such exemptions are supposed to be exceptional in character.

In 1994 the import regime described in Chapter 4 was replaced by a regime compatible with the single market. Two Council Regulations of 7 March 1994 (No 518/94 for non-state trading and No 519/94 for state trading) repealed, respectively, Council Regulations (EEC) Nos 288/82 and 3420/83, thereby eliminating all national QRs and surveillance measures on products (apart from textiles under Section XI of the CN) from both groups of countries. From 15 March 1994 all surveillance measures and decisions regarding the imposition of quotas have been at the EC level.

Council Regulation (EEC) No 517/94 of 7 March 1994 replaced Council Regulations (EEC) Nos 288/82, 3420/83, 1765/82 and 1766/82 as far as their application to clothing and textile products from countries without a bilateral agreement is concerned. (Countries covered by a bilateral agreement under the Multifibre Arrangement (MFA) are covered by Council Regulation (EEC) No 3030/93, see Table 5.2.)

Residual national QRs on products from non-state trading countries were suspended pending the entry into force of the Agreement on textiles and clothing resulting from the Uruguay Round of GATT negotiations at which point they were due to be abolished, although it is understood that this has not yet happened. Although no new formal equivalents have since been imposed for non-state trading countries and, as explained below, use of safeguard actions to achieve similar objectives has been very limited, there are some curbs in place that have similar effects. These include, for example, the 1991 Elements of Consensus Agreement with Japan on cars.

Council Regulation (EC) No 519/94 of 7 March 1994 generally prohibits individual Member States from applying national QRs or surveillance measures on products from the countries formerly governed by Council Regulations (EEC) Nos 3420/83, 1765/82 and 1766/82, excluding many of the countries of Eastern Europe.[12] It placed 'justified' existing national quotas on an EC footing. In effect this meant that it replaced national QRs with a limited

---

[12] The countries currently covered are Albania, Armenia, Azerbaijan, Belarus, China, Georgia, Kyrgyzstan, Kazakhstan, Moldavia, Mongolia, North Korea, Russia, Tajikistan, Turkmenistan, Ukraine, Uzbekistan, Vietnam.

number of EC restrictions on imports from China.[13] It also established restrictions on outward processing traffic (OPT) and detailed surveillance measures.

From the beginning of 1993, the Commission has rejected all but one application of Article 115. This exception was its use for six months in relation to imports of bananas from certain Latin American countries.

The net effect is that sub-EC level restrictions with respect to non-state trading countries have been largely removed, except for clothing and textiles, but that the situation is not so clear-cut with respect to states that are, or were formerly, state trading. The collapse of Communism meant that many states were changing category before the SMP was completed. In important respects the change in the EC's trade policy stance, especially towards the countries of Central and Eastern Europe, has been influenced by factors other than the SMP. This is not to say that the SMP was without any influence on the evolution of EC policy towards Eastern Europe, only that it was one factor among others, was not necessarily the most important, and any unique effects are not sufficiently identifiable to satisfy the tight requirements of the terms of reference for this study. Moreover, the state trading country that was most heavily targeted before the SMP, China, is still subject to restrictions and, hence, is in a different position to the non-state trading countries with respect to the effects of the SMP.

The broad picture on QRs is illustrated in Table 5.1. This indicates the situation pre- and post-SMP for textile and non-textile products from state trading and non-state trading states. It makes the point specifically that the removal of non-textile QRs from formerly state trading states not covered by Council Regulation (EC) No 519/94 should not be considered an effect of the SMP. Rather, it is a consequence of action taken by the Community following the collapse of Communism.

Table 5.1.   Changes on national QRs

Products	Countries	Pre-SMP	Post-SMP	Regulation
Textiles	Non-state trading	National QRs	Community QRs	(EEC) No 958/93 (EC) No 517/94
	State trading	National QRs	Community QRs	(EEC) No 958/93 (EC) No 517/94
Non-textiles	Non-state trading	National QRs	Abolition of QRs or Community QRs	(EC) No 518/94
	Eastern Europe	National QRs	No SMP effect	Trade and Cooperation Agreements Association Agreements
	Former Soviet Union and China	National QRs	Abolition of QRs or replacement with Community QRs	(EC) No 519/94

---

[13]   The following are the 2-digit HS chapter numbers followed, in brackets, by the number of products at the 8-digit level affected: 42 (1); 64 (9); 69 (2); 70 (1); 85 (2); 95 (3); quotas under Chapter 85 were eliminated in 1996.

5.1.2. Changes to customs procedures

An important stimulus to these changes has been the parallel movement in cross-border customs formalities, which has made national restrictions much more difficult to enforce. The SMP has been associated with changes designed to improve the efficiency and simplicity of customs procedures relating to all cross-border trade, intra-Community and third-country alike.

Such procedures were increasingly being developed at Community level before the SMP, but the objective of creating a barrier-free Europe added impetus to the effort.[14] There have, of course, been many other changes to customs procedures during the period covered by this study, but they are in the main not a direct consequence of the SMP but of other factors. As the study on Customs and fiscal formalities at frontiers notes, for example, many of the procedures which customs will administer for third-country trade are governed by the provisions of the Uruguay Round, while procedures on the ground are covered by the Commission's 'Customs 2000' vision and programme, which is also outside the review.

One change that is most directly attributable to the SMP is that external imports and internal cross-border traffic are now treated differently. The SAD (see Section 4.3.2) was discontinued from 1 January 1993 for intra-Community cross-border trade, and was replaced by the EC VAT and Intrastat reporting systems. The SAD is now used only for third-country trade.

On 1 January 1994 a Community Customs Code came into force, with Member States progressively introducing simplified customs procedures for approved traders and forwarders, together with computerization. These two changes, simplification and computerization, can lead to immense improvements in the efficiency of customs procedures, but it is reported that much remains to be done in terms of implementation and establishing commonality between the computerized applications adopted by different Member States.

To the extent that the new procedures apply to intra- and extra-EC trade alike, any improvement would have the potential to improve the conditions of access of third-country products into the European market. And, to the extent that the improvements have not yet been realized, there is no strong evidence that, apart from the difference in use of the SAD, it is because of rules or procedures that are differentially onerous for third parties; it is just that the changes have not yet been fully implemented and, hence, the gains not obtained.

An example provided in the report on Customs and fiscal formalities at frontiers refers to footwear. Certain types of footwear specially designed for a sporting activity, or involving special technology, are covered by special import regulations that do not apply to other forms of footwear. However, the interpretation in the Member States differs on the definition of the given rules. One result is that companies importing these goods choose the most favourable Member State for import clearance in order to avoid problems and additional administrative work.

---

[14] This section draws on the study on Customs and fiscal formalities at frontiers undertaken as part of the broader programme of research on the SMP in *The Single Market Review*, Subseries III, Vol. 3, Luxembourg: Office for Official Publications of the EC and London: Kogan Page\Earthscan, 1997.

Alongside the simplification and harmonization of customs procedures has been a harmonization of veterinary and health checks. These have had a similar effect in opening the European market (to external and non-national EC suppliers alike) and reducing the practical scope for implementing sub-Community import restrictions.

The changes in this area have overlapped with those analysed in Chapter 6. There has been activity to ensure adequate veterinary and phytosanitary standards in extra-EC imports. This has included fact-finding field visits to third countries and the granting of 'a large number of derogation decisions' (CEC, 1994b:70). For the most part, these were adaptations of previous derogations 'made necessary by the requirements of the new legislation and the concept of the internal market' (CEC, 1994b:70).

5.1.3. The implications for national restrictions

Does this mean that there can no longer be sub-Community restrictions on access to third-country products? The answer is no. In all three Regulations, the decision to impose QRs may be taken only at the EC level, but the possibility is raised that QRs will apply only to certain parts of the EC. The proviso is made that this will occur only if deemed necessary and most appropriate, and on an exceptional and temporary basis.

Clearly, without the enforcement mechanism of Article 115 or intra-EC border controls, the application of this provision will vary according to the characteristics of the product and its market, so that not all third-country products can be restricted successfully at a sub-Community level. As is clear from the review of non-authorized national QRs, it is possible to segment the European market for some products (depending upon the characteristics of suppliers, consumers and the goods in question) by a range of other, often informal, means.

There have been no formal safeguard actions to replace the pre-SMP restrictions. And, in any case, change in the use of safeguards by the EC is now more properly considered as a Uruguay Round and WTO effect than as a direct consequence of the SMP. Council Regulation (EC) No 518/94 was superseded by Regulation (EC) No 3285/94 to reflect the EC's WTO obligations.

Since 1988, the Commission has adopted only two safeguard measures (a third, on footwear from China in 1992, was proposed by the Commission but not accepted by the Council). The two were:

(a)   in 1992, in relation to certain steel products from the Czech Republic and Slovakia imported into Germany, Italy and France;
(b)   in 1993, in relation to unwrought aluminium imported from the former Soviet Union (FSU) into the Community as a whole.

But there may have been less formal, and visible, controls. In the period since the SMP, negotiations with third countries have occurred and there is some evidence that the 'cooperation' of third countries has been requested in order to keep their exports at a certain level and to avoid concentration in specific markets (Velia, 1996:85). A recent WTO *Trade Policy Review* on Japan lists various cases of export monitoring or restraints *vis-à-vis* the EC in addition to the 1991 'consensus' on cars. Some of these have sub-Community application. The products covered were: video tape recorders, forklift trucks (until December 1994), ball-bearings (until July 1993), cotton fabrics (export approval for one item since December 1994), pottery and chinaware (exports to the UK), and clothing (exports to the UK until December

1994) (WTO, 1995:67). WTO *Trade Policy Reviews* have also indicated that several Mediterranean countries have for years moderated their exports of 'sensitive' textiles and clothing in order to avoid EC safeguard actions under their bilateral agreements.

In addition to sub-Community and informal controls, national QRs have been replaced in some cases by formal Community-level restrictions. These are almost exclusively in relation to textiles and clothing or, in the case of non-textile products, those originating in China.

An overview of the provisions regarding textiles is presented in Table 5.2. Protocols exist on textile and clothing products under the EC's association agreements with Bulgaria, Hungary, Poland, Romania, the Czech Republic, and Slovakia; these provide for full liberalization by 1 January 1998. During 1993 the EC substituted bilateral quotas for previously unilateral restrictions on imports from Mongolia, Vietnam, Belarus, the Russian Federation, Ukraine and Uzbekistan, and the textile agreements with the Baltic states and other FSU states have surveillance provisions (WTO, 1995:58).

Table 5.2. Suppliers of textiles and clothing products with bilateral agreements or arrangements with the EC, 1 January 1995

I. MFA Agreements		II. MFA-type Agreements		III. Preferential Arrangements (Mediterranean countries)
ASEAN		Albania		
Indonesia		Armenia	(no restrictions)	Egypt
Malaysia		Azerbaijan	(no restrictions)	Turkey
Philippines		Belarus		Morocco
Singapore		Georgia	(no restrictions)	Tunisia
Thailand		Kazakhstan	(no restrictions)	Malta
		Kyrgyzstan	(no restrictions)	
South Asia		Moldova	(no restrictions)	**IV. Preferential Arrangements**
India		Russian Federation		**(Europe Agreement countries)**
Pakistan		Tajikistan	(no restrictions)	
Sri Lanka		Turkmenistan	(no restrictions)	Czech Republic
Bangladesh	(no restrictions)	Uzbekistan		Slovakia
		Ukraine		Hungary
Far East		Mongolia		Poland
Hong Kong		Vietnam		Romania
Republic of Korea		Estonia	(no restrictions)	Bulgaria
Macau		Latvia	(no restrictions)	
China		Lithuania	(no restrictions)	**V. Autonomous Arrangements**
		Slovenia	(no restrictions)	
Latin America				Chinese Taipei
Argentina				Bosnia-Herzegovina
Peru				Croatia
Brazil				Form. Yugoslav Rep. of Macedonia
Uruguay	(no restrictions)			People's Democratic Rep. of Korea
Colombia	(no restrictions)			
Guatemala	(no restrictions)			
Mexico	(no restrictions)			

Source: European Commission, cited in WTO, 1995:Table V.2.

In the case of non-textile products, Council Regulation (EC) No 519/94 (7 March 1994) introduced Community-wide quotas on imports from China of: working gloves, six types of footwear, tableware of porcelain or ceramics, glassware, car radios, and three types of toys. Council Regulation (EC) No 538/95 (6 March 1995) enlarged and amended the quotas and, according to Commission estimates, non-restricted items account for more than 65% of EC imports of footwear from China (WTO, 1995:58).

5.2.   Methodology for assessing the impact of change

Despite the caveats identified above, the assumed counterfactual must be that, in the absence of the SMP, national restrictions would have remained in force. Hence, the effect of the SMP on market access for non-state trading third countries is to be identified by comparing the *status quo ante* with the *status quo*.[15]

Assessing the effect of the SMP changes on third-country access to the EC market is complicated by:

(a)   the complexity and opacity of the *status quo ante*;

(b)   uncertainty concerning the *status quo* (given the continuation of some Community-wide quotas and some less formal means of restriction);

(c)   and methodological uncertainty concerning the impact of both pre- and post-SMP measures.

The first two of these have been described in Chapter 4 and Sections 3.3 and 5.1. The methodological uncertainty derives from theoretical and empirical arguments over the impact of national quotas on trade and prices (see, for example, Hamilton, 1991; Faini *et al.*, 1992). There are at least three relevant strands of argument.

Since national QRs restricted the entry into a Member State market only of goods produced outside the Community, it is possible that the intended protective effect on producers in the quota-imposing state were partly offset. If prices in the notionally restricted market were raised by the reduction of supply, they may have attracted increased intra-EC imports. In such a case, the extra-EC product may have been deflected into the national market of the exporting Member State. To the extent that this occurred, the anticipated restriction on third-party access to the EC market will have been dissipated. Hence, the SMP changes will have had less effect than would have been expected.

In addition, there is debate over the practical effect of switching from country sub-quotas to EC-wide quotas. The effect of identically sized quotas could be different for two (not mutually exclusive) reasons:

(a)   in one case, a Community-wide quota could be less restrictive than a set of national quotas with the same total volume. This is because the national system might result in a situation in which exports to one country reach constraining levels even though demand is unsatisfied, while quotas in other countries are underutilized because of inadequate demand;

(b)   in the other case, Community-wide quotas may be more rigorously administered than were some national quotas. If true, this would tend to affect third parties in the opposite direction.

---

15   As explained above, this counterfactual does not necessarily hold with respect to the formerly state trading countries with which the EC has agreed trade and cooperation and association agreements.

If the underutilization of quotas in some sub-markets reflects differential price levels between the sub-markets, and if the relatively high prices in the sub-markets with fully utilized quotas include a certain element of economic rent, then the gains to suppliers from a globalization of quotas may be less than might have been expected. This is because globalization of sub-quotas would tend to level out prices across the sub-markets, resulting in an increase in supply to the market in which, previously, the quota was underutilized, but a loss of revenue on exports to the markets with fully utilized quotas. Hence, the gains to suppliers from increased sales at higher prices to some markets will be offset to a degree by lower prices on their sales to other markets.

5.3.   Article 115 as a barometer

The use of Article 115 provides a helpful barometer to the extent to which the national QRs that existed on paper were actually enforced. As noted in Chapter 4, one of the problems of quantifying the effect of the SMP in terms of access to Member State markets is that there are no comprehensive and reliable data on the extent to which Member States made use of their authorizations to restrict imports, let alone of the use made of the more informal, unauthorized policies that had a restrictive effect. One broad indicator, however, of the use made of national QRs is provided by the applications made to the Commission by Member States to implement the provisions of Article 115.

Monitoring of the rate of applications for, and approvals of, Article 115 action can provide one indicator of:

(a)   the scale of national QRs;
(b)   the distribution of national QRs between product groups;
(c)   the frequency with which different Member States make use of national QRs;
(d)   and the supplying countries against which national QRs were most often enforced.

It is important to understand, however, that Article 115 usage is only one, very imperfect, such indicator. Its failings relate to the wide variety of restrictions covered by the regulations described in Section 4.1 for which systematic details are lacking, the absence of a complete overlap between the classification of authorized residual national restrictions, of trade flows and of Article 155 restrictions, and the methodological problems referred to in Section 5.2. Moreover, as indicated below, usage of Article 115 fell dramatically well before the SMP-associated changes in Council Regulations described in Section 5.1, complicating attempts to use it as an unambiguous, objective empirical element in establishing the relative and absolute importance of the SMP changes relating to national trade barriers.

5.3.1.   The incidence and product profile of Article 115 usage

Data have been collected by various analysts from the Commission's records on recourse to Article 115 (see, for example, Pelkmans, 1987; Davenport, 1990 and 1991; Langhammer, 1990; Schuknecht, 1992). The most up-to-date, extensive analysis is provided in Velia, 1996. These exercises normally distinguish only between textiles and clothing, on the one hand, and other products, on the other.

The use of Article 115 increased sharply at the end of the 1970s, reaching a peak in 1980, and then generally subsided so that by 1992 applications were already at a very low level (Figure 5.1). The decline in the usage of Article 115 is even more marked since the decline in applications at the end of the 1980s and start of the 1990s was mirrored by a drop in the rate of acceptance (Velia, 1996:95).

Figure 5.1.   Article 115 applications, 1971–92

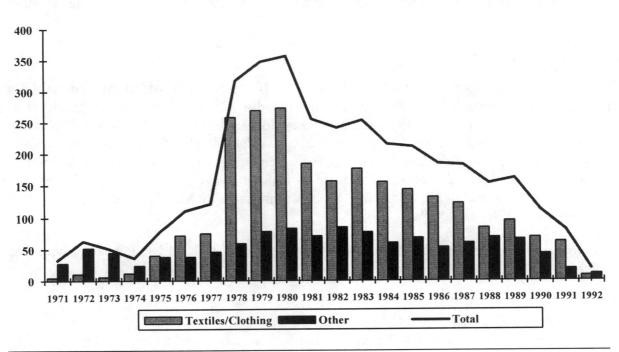

Source: Velia, 1996.

This pattern is influenced substantially by changes in practice with respect to textiles and clothing. A large part of the increased use of Article 115 in the late 1970s/early 1980s is the result of applications made with respect to textiles and clothing and, by the same token, the decline during the second half of the 1980s is similarly linked to this sector. The use of Article 115 in relation to textiles and clothing can be shown to have varied in a quite close relationship with the negotiations on the MFA over this period (Velia, 1996:94). Applications for products other than textiles and clothing were made at a broadly similar rate for much of the period covered in Figure 5.1, with a sharp decline in usage occurring only at the very end of the period.

5.3.2. Imposing states

There have been marked differences in the pattern of Article 115 use by different Member States (Table 5.3). Over the period 1984–92, France made the most frequent recourse to Article 115 for both textiles and clothing and other products. Ireland received the second highest number of acceptances for Article 115 applications in relation to textiles and clothing, but made very few applications in relation to other goods. Italy, by contrast, which was the second-most-frequent recipient of approvals for Article 115 action on goods other than textiles and clothing, made a much smaller number of applications for restrictions to textiles and clothing (even though it was the third-most-frequent recipient of acceptances for these products). Spain and the UK received a moderate number of acceptances for both types of product, acceptances for Benelux were restricted largely to textile and clothing products, and Denmark made only two applications (both accepted) for any Article 115 use over the whole period.

Table 5.3.   **Percentage of acceptances of applications by applying Member State, 1984–92[1]**

Member State	Textile and clothing applications		Applications for goods other than textiles and clothing	
	Acceptances	% accepted	Acceptances	% accepted
Benelux	17	100.0	4	66.7
Denmark	2	100.0	0	n.a.
Spain[2]	29	42.6	64	60.4
France	276	83.6	135	80.4
Ireland	255	80.4	9	90.0
Italy	67	82.7	111	85.4
United Kingdom	34	82.9	20	76.9

Note: Member States not mentioned in the table have not made applications in the period considered.
[1] Excludes 16 applications withdrawn by the Member States over the period.
[2] 1986-92.
Source: Velia, 1996.

5.3.3.   Target states

The great majority of Article 115 actions have been with respect to the East Asian newly industrialized countries (NICs) plus China (Table 5.4). Almost all of the applications which were not directed at these four countries were aimed at other developing countries or the USSR and Eastern European states (especially Romania and Czechoslovakia).

Within the NIC group, just over half of all applications applied to Hong Kong. But, this country's share of the total fell to a little over one-third in 1991. During the last five years of operation of the Article, applications against Korea rose.

Different Member States have tended to target specific trade partners. It is reported in Velia (1996:111) that France and Italy were by far the dominant applicants against Chinese and Pakistani textile and clothing imports, while the majority of applications against Hong Kong originated from Ireland, those against Taiwan from France, and those against South Korea from Spain. Importantly, a comparison of this pattern of applications with the relative share of different suppliers in the imports of applying countries suggests that in most cases there is no systematic relationship. In other words, the sensitivity of Member States against specific trade partners appears not to have been connected to import levels (Velia, 1996:112).

Table 5.4.   Applications by the Member States against third countries, 1985–92: number of cases[1]

Applications by ... against	Belgium	Denmark	France	Ireland	Spain	Italy	UK	Total
Poland			1					1
Czechoslovakia			4			9	1	14
Hungary	1		4			1	1	7
USSR					2[2]			2[2]
Romania	1		24	4		1	8	38
Hong Kong	1		45	106	16			168
Taiwan	1		29	38	9		1	78
South Korea		2	38	21	17	10	1	89
China	1		74	11	16	11	4	117
Thailand			18	5				23
Philippines			1	5	2			8
Indonesia			4	1				5
Malaysia			2					2
Macao			1	7				8
India			4	29	6	12		51
Pakistan			23	9		20	1	53
Sri Lanka			3					3
Yugoslavia			11	8			3	22
Peru			3					3
Brazil			6				1	7
Egypt						1		1
Turkey			7	7			2	16

[1] This table includes all withdrawn cases. The number of applications when added up do not match with the reported total number of applications made over the period. This is due to the fact that two applications withdrawn by France were omitted in the Commission Summary Statistics Tables.

[2] There were in fact three cases. One was withdrawn and was not reported in the Commission table either as a withdrawn or a rejected application.

Source: Velia, 1996.

Another important point for the methodology used in this study concerns the countries which are not listed in Table 5.4. As explained in Chapter 2, the trade policy changes associated with the SMP may have differential effects upon one third party *vis-à-vis* another. Article 115 could not be used against countries with which the EC had negotiated a trade agreement excluding the possibility of QRs. Hence, Article 115 could not be used against either EFTA or most of the EC's Mediterranean trade partners, or against imports from African, Caribbean and Pacific (ACP) states. Indeed, in the case of the most celebrated post-SMP dispute with a link to Article 115, bananas, the Article was used to protect producers not only in Member States but also in favoured third parties (i.e. the ACP).

5.4. Summary of findings

The SMP has affected national trade barriers substantially and, hence, has tended to improve the conditions of access for third-country products to the EC market. This effect has been reinforced by the considerably expanded legal powers given to the European Commission to enforce and protect the single market. And it is the case that the controls have not been reimposed.

However, on the evidence of the WTO, it has not completely removed sub-Community differences in the treatment of imports. Moreover, the continuation of such sub-Community differences is the result not of incomplete implementation of the SMP but of the continuation of policies that permit differentiation. Hence, the further implementation of the SMP will not substantially alter the conclusions to be drawn on its impact on external access.

The main vehicle for the reduction of sub-Community differences in access has been the removal of border controls. In consequence, while it is still possible to apply differential treatment for some products from some sources (depending upon the nature of the market), this now occurs on a much less substantial scale than before the SMP.

The most reasonable counterfactual against which the SMP changes are to be judged is that sub-EC barriers to trade with non-state trading countries would have continued, although the situation with respect to state trading countries is not so clear-cut. In the absence of the SMP, there might well have been problems in adapting the system of national restrictions to the tariffication requirements of the GATT Uruguay Round. However, it must be assumed that some way would have been found to permit the Community to continue to operate in the old way had the SMP not intervened. Given that conclusion, it is reasonable to conclude that the SMP has had a beneficial effect on the market access of some products from some third-party suppliers by removing national restrictions that, in most cases, have not been replaced by Community-level controls.

Despite the evidence provided by the empirical analysis reported in Chapter 4, the scale of this effect is unclear. This is because of uncertainty concerning the extent to which the pre-SMP national restrictions were actually enforced, and also because of methodological questions over the effect of such restrictions, and the uncertain empirical evidence on the extent to which the QRs restricted imports. Nonetheless, there is some reason to suppose that there will have been gains even though the true scale of these cannot be established with any precision.

These gains are likely to have accrued to a relatively small number of countries, and in only a few Member State markets. Only 11 states were subjected to more than 10 applications of Article 115 between 1985 and 1992. The great majority of these were Eastern European, East Asian or South Asian states, although Turkey and Yugoslavia were also represented. France, Ireland, Italy, Spain and the UK were the countries most often granted Article 115 rights.

Only a relatively small number of product chapters were affected by a broad range of national quotas. Textiles and clothing, footwear, vehicles, agricultural products, and a range of manufactured items figure prominently in the lists.

It is impossible within the scope of this study to provide any serious quantitative estimate of the scale of the restrictions. Too many other factors have to be taken into account when interpreting Member State import figures. However, the fact that a significant number of states which imposed national QRs recorded no external imports of the products in question in 1992 suggests that the national QRs had a real impact on trade, even though Article 115 usage had declined substantially since the late 1980s.

Because the application of national QRs was very restricted, the impact of their removal on external suppliers as a whole is likely to be different from that on the countries directly affected. It is likely that differential effects between third parties will be an important element of the overall picture. Hence, it is perfectly possible that a particular supplier in a non-EC state may believe that its relative access to the European market has deteriorated as a result of the SMP even though, absolutely, there has been an improvement in access. However, this was not a priority area for the study, which was intended to concentrate on absolute changes for all third parties – such as administrative simplification, the opportunities offered by a bigger market, and increased transparency in the replacement of 12 separate administrative processes with one.

6. Removal of technical barriers to trade

The free circulation of goods is one of the corner-stones for the creation of the single market. In the period after the formation of the customs union in 1968 differences between national technical regulations and standards – technical barriers to trade – became the principal impediment to the free movement of goods within the EC. Because of this, roughly half of secondary single market legislation is concerned with the production and marketing of goods. Removing national technical barriers to trade is also one of the aspects of the SMP that has been most successful in terms of implementation narrowly defined. Nonetheless, 258 complaints regarding obstacles to trade were recorded in 1995 and, according to the Commission, 'much remains to be done' in relation to standardization policy (CEC, 1996a:23 and 30). This is a view that is also reflected in the trade association survey (Appendix A to Part II). This chapter concentrates on identifying the changes that would accrue if and when the SMP is fully in operation.

The potential external impact of this process is not unambiguously unidirectional, and may vary according to the precise form that technical harmonization and standardization have taken. The next section outlines the bare bones of the process as a necessary basis for understanding this potentially differential effect.

6.1. The SMP changes

6.1.1. The *status quo ante*

Prior to the creation of the single market there was a profusion of national technical regulations and standards. In 1990 there were 20,000 standards on the books in Germany, 13,000 in France and 10,000 in the United Kingdom, compared to 1,250 European standards (CEC, 1990). Even considering that a significant proportion of the national standards were either identical or related to international or European standards, the number and diversity of national standards was extensive.

Thus the European market was fragmented and producers had to tailor their products to the respective national markets. This is likely to have had a negative impact on trade in relation both to goods originating outside the Community and to those produced in one Member State for sale in another.

This impediment to internal and external trade was compounded by the requirement that some products be certified by authorized independent bodies as conforming with the technical regulation or standard in question. In most cases the certification had to be carried out by an authorized body in the country of destination. This meant that multiple certifications were necessary.

6.1.2. The nature of the change

The creation of the single market in goods has five components (which, as explained in the next sub-section, may have had differential external effects):

(a)   notification of new national technical legislation or standards which could have implications for the free circulation of goods;

(b)   mutual recognition of national regulations and standards (requires equivalent levels of protection);
(c)   new approach Directives in which the EC adopts only the 'essential minimum requirements' for a measure and refers it to the appropriate European standardization body(ies) to develop the voluntary standards to achieve those requirements;
(d)   full harmonization in selected sectors where mandatory standards are necessary;
(e)   mutual recognition of national certification.

It is helpful to consider these components in three groups. The first two represent a decentralized approach; the second two a centralized approach; and the fifth is a necessary condition for mutual recognition and the new approach Directives to function properly.

Under the notification procedure the competent authorities in a Member State must notify the relevant European organization of a new law/standard. In the case of proposals for new technical regulations notification is to the Commission. For proposed standards, notification is to the appropriate European standards body. This procedure has two merits. It increases the transparency of national measures, and it provides an opportunity to revise the measures so that they do not impede trade.

Mutual recognition of national regulations and standards means that any good circulating legally in one Member State must also be free to circulate in any other part of the EC, except where a Member State can demonstrate that the rules of the Member State of origin do not afford equivalent protection of the essential public good.

Legislative harmonization at the EC level is necessary in the relatively few cases in which the national legislation of the Member States is not equivalent. It can take one of two forms: the 'new approach', where legislation is framed only in terms of essential requirements, or harmonization, where detailed specifications are provided.

Because new approach Directives lay down only essential minimum requirements, leaving the development of detailed specifications to the European standards bodies, each can cover an entire 'family' of products. Moreover, because they are based on reference to voluntary standards, manufacturers may choose to comply with a different standard, their own or that of another country. In order for goods produced to such standards to circulate freely in the EC, however, an authorized third party must certify that the standard used meets or exceeds the essential minimum requirements laid down in the Directive.

As of mid-1996 20 new approach Directives had been adopted (Atkins International Limited, 1996) regarding: toy safety, simple pressure vessels, construction products, electromagnetic compatibility, personal protective equipment, machinery, non-automatic weighing instruments, active implantable medical devices, electrical equipment for use in potentially explosive atmospheres, explosives for civil use, appliances burning gaseous fuels, new hot-water boilers fired with liquid or gaseous fuels, hydraulically and oil-electrically operated lifts, lifts, telecommunications terminal equipment, satellite earth station equipment, recreational crafts, and packaging and packaging waste.[16]

---

[16]   One new approach Directive (93/68/EEC) amended 12 previous new approach Directives to incorporate common rules for CE marking (Atkins (1996) forthcoming in *The Single Market Review*, Subseries III, Vol. 1: Technical Barriers to Trade, Luxembourg: Office for Official Publications of the EC and London: Kogan Page\Earthscan, 1997).

In some sectors the new approach is not considered adequate to ensure public policy objectives. In such areas detailed harmonized regulations are agreed at the European level. Technical harmonization is particularly important with respect to cars, foodstuffs, pharmaceutical products for human and veterinary use, and chemicals. Due to their special nature, the regulatory regimes governing the first three sectors deserve further description.

In the case of cars, 45 detailed specifications had been adopted by 1994 governing safety and emissions. These comprise the EC's type approval for cars. Cars that comply with all 45 measures can be sold anywhere in EC.

Foodstuffs are regulated using both horizontal and vertical measures. The former reflect the essential minimum requirement considerations of the new approach; the latter are detailed harmonized specifications. Horizontal measures include those that govern the additives that may or may not be used, how food products are labelled and how food hygiene is guaranteed. The vertical approach measures designate the composition of certain specific products, such as chocolate, honey, sugar and jams.

Because of their importance (direct and indirect) for human health, all pharmaceutical products for human and veterinary use must receive authorization from the competent authorities regarding quality, safety and efficacy as well as specifications concerning manufacturing and marketing. The safety criteria for veterinary products are particularly far reaching because of the need to protect consumers of animal-derived foods.

There are three procedures for obtaining market authorization for pharmaceutical products: centralized, decentralized and the national authorization of products for the domestic market. The centralized procedure applies to all biotechnology products and is available on request for other innovatory products and new chemical entities. It results in a single authorization by the European Medicines Evaluation Agency that is valid in all Member States. The decentralized procedure applies to the majority of products and allows the extension of an authorization granted by one Member State to another, which must decide swiftly whether to recognize the authorization. A procedure exists for resolving disputes. Member States remain responsible for authorizing products intended only for the domestic market.

There are two types of certification which can impede trade. The first is obligatory certification, which is required by public authorities to ensure that the product in question complies with certain, usually safety, requirements. This is the certification required in the full harmonization and new approach Directives discussed above. The second is voluntary certification, which may be required by consumers or producers in order to check quality, assess process control, or ensure compliance with customer specifications.

In the EC, as elsewhere, responsibility for obligatory certification may in some cases be assigned to competent and properly equipped manufacturers. In others it may have to be carried out by authorized, specialist third parties, such as testing laboratories and certification bodies, as in the case of pharmaceuticals above (see Table 6.1). The proportion of products which comes under mandatory certification systems in the Member States is small compared with the total quantity of products on the market (CEC, 1989). As noted above, however, private bodies may also require product certification.

Table 6.1. EC regulated products: certification options

Product type	Certification options
Toys	Manufacturer assurance
Construction products	At a minimum, manufacturer registration of production quality assurance system
Simple pressure vessels	EC type examination
Large pressure vessels	EC type examination and quality assurance
Electromagnetic compatibility	Manufacturer declaration
Machinery	Manufacturer declaration
Personal protective equipment	EC type examination with quality control system registration for higher risk equipment
Gas appliances	EC type examination and either quality assurance system registration or on-site checks
Non-automatic weighing instruments	EC type examination and quality assurance registration or EC verification
Active implantable medical devices	Declaration procedure requiring complete quality assurance system subject to surveillance or EC type examination and declaration of conformity or EC verification
Telecommunications terminal equipment	EC type examination or declaration of conformity with full quality assurance
Hot-water boilers	EC type approval and declaration of conformity
Hydraulically and oil-electrically operated lifts	EC type examination and inspection
Lifts	Declaration procedure requiring complete quality assurance system subject to surveillance or EC type examination
Medical devices	Declaration procedure requiring complete quality assurance system subject to surveillance or EC type examination and declaration of conformity or EC verification
Equipment intended for use in potentially explosive atmospheres	EC type approval
Explosives intended for civil uses	EC type examination and quality assurance or product verification or third-party unit verification
Satellite earth station equipment	Declaration procedure requiring complete quality assurance system subject to surveillance or EC type examination
Recreational craft	Various options depending on category and size of craft ranging up to EC type examination
Packaging and packaging waste	Procedures to be determined by the Member States

Sources: US Department of Commerce (cited in Kruger, 1992); Atkins International Limited, 1996; and relevant Directives.

6.2. External effects of change

Overall, technical harmonization and standardization are likely to benefit trade, to the advantage of foreign and EC firms alike. But some aspects of technical harmonization and standardization at the European level have specifically external implications.

The approximation of standards was the aspect of the SMP that most concerned the US business community (USITC, 1993:7–985), but US perceptions of the issue now are generally favourable. The elimination of technical barriers within the EC, it is believed, will greatly benefit trade, saving money and time, and creating the potential for more fully exploiting economies of scale.

The SMP has benefited third-country producers by providing greater transparency and legal certainty in many sectors (GATT, 1993). In addition, the elimination of technical barriers among potential markets reduces design, engineering, marketing and transport costs and, in some cases, might provide opportunities to exploit greater economies of scale.

6.2.1. Mutual recognition

Mutual recognition is a particularly beneficial way of eliminating technical barriers to trade from the point of view of third-country firms as it increases market sizes without replacing national barriers with European measures. Third-country producers may even enjoy an advantage over EC producers in that they can choose to export to the Member State with the most favourable regulatory regime, while EC producers must conform to the requirements of the Member State of production.

6.2.2. New approach Directives

The flexibility of new approach Directives also makes them quite favourable to third-country firms. Because their objectives are realized by only voluntary standards, a foreign firm may continue to use its national standard so long as a notified third party certifies that this standard conforms with the essential requirements of the relevant Directive. This helps to alleviate any European bias in the standards, which might occur for no reason other than that this is the expertise available in drawing up the standard.

Another attraction of this approach for foreign firms is that there is a high degree of congruence, particularly in the electrotechnical field, between European and international standards. According to the European Committee for Electrotechnical Standardization (CENELEC), in 1991 90% of the draft European standards in the electrotechnical sector were prepared at the international level (Nicolas and Repussard, 1995).

The relative transparency of the European standardization process means that third-country parties can gain access to, and comment on, draft standards, thereby facilitating adaptation to new European standards. It should be noted that the national standards institutes of the members of the EFTA are full members of the European standards bodies. As of early 1994, Bulgaria, Cyprus, the Czech Republic, Hungary, Lithuania, Poland, Romania, Slovenia, Slovakia and Turkey were affiliated members of the European Committee for Standardization, and all but Bulgaria, Cyprus and Lithuania were affiliate members of CENELEC. Thus they were able to attend as observers general assemblies, technical committees and sub-committees.

6.2.3. Full harmonization

If third-country firms face market access problems it is most likely to be with regard to products that are subject to technical harmonization (Woolcock, 1991). This is not to say that coping with one common regulation is not more straightforward than complying with multiple national ones nor that the new EC regulations are necessarily more restrictive than the national measures they replaced. Indeed, the benefits to third-country producers due to the creation of a single regulatory regime as well as to improved transparency and greater legal certainty mentioned above apply equally with respect to technical harmonization. However, because such regulations address risks that are considered to be too great to be entrusted to more decentralized approaches, harmonized measures are detailed and mandatory and therefore are harder to comply with than new approach Directives. It is possible that although they were adopted in order to realize public policy objectives – such as reducing pollution and ensuring consumer safety – and apply equally to domestically produced and imported goods, they may suit European firms better than foreign ones.[17]

The negative impact of detailed regulations on trade is illustrated by the high priority EC and US leaders have attached to reducing barriers to trade in cars caused by divergent safety and emissions regulations.[18] Similarly, the Japanese government has requested that the EC recognize the equivalence of its regulations on safety glazing materials for road vehicles (DG I, 1996).

Although it is easier in general for exporters to comply with one common standard than 12 different ones, because the harmonized regulations are detailed and mandatory it is possible that a product that had previously complied with one Member State's regulations would not conform with the European regulation. In such circumstances, in order to retain access to the Member State's market the third-country producer would have to adjust to the new measure, as would the domestic producer. It is possible, however, that the export market is not sufficiently important to the third-country firm for it to make that adjustment and thus it would lose market access. Such effects, while potentially significant for individual producers, are almost certainly negligible compared with the more general simplification of access.

Within the category of harmonized regulations, some types of measure may present greater problems for foreign firms than others. Some regulations not only govern product performance, they may also mandate the composition of the product or the way in which it is produced. Where there are requirements on product composition, this may affect suppliers of inputs (whether production is based inside or outside the EC). Where the regulations specify production processes, adaptation to fulfil the requirement may prove particularly difficult.

The sector in which compositional requirements are most common is foodstuffs, although they also occur in regulations on chemicals and cosmetics. The current attempts to amend the 1973 Chocolate Directive illustrate how such measures affect third countries. Currently Austria, Denmark, Finland, Ireland, Portugal, Sweden and the UK permit the use in chocolate of up to 5% cocoa butter equivalents (CBEs), while the other Member States require that only cocoa fats be used. Depending on the response of European producers and consumers, a measure that would permit the use of CBEs throughout Europe might benefit the producers of the components of CBEs, such as Burkino Faso and Mali, while potentially damaging cocoa

---

17   Divergent national regulations and standards exist because different countries and regions face different problems and different governments perceive and respond to risks differently (Héritier, 1996; Previdi, 1997). Further, it is standard practice to consult widely when developing regulations. Domestic firms, not surprisingly, tend to be more engaged than foreign firms and the resulting regulations are more likely to reflect their concerns. For these reasons European regulations are likely to be closer to the regulatory regimes under which European firms are used to operating than to those of third countries.

18   'Joint EU-US Action Plan', Madrid, 3 December 1995.

producers such as those in Ghana and Côte d'Ivoire. By contrast, a measure prohibiting the use of CBEs would tend to benefit the cocoa producers at the expense of the CBE exporters. Hence the actual external impact will depend on the precise form of the change. The current proposal will not prohibit the use of the term chocolate for confectionery containing some products other than cocoa, but it will impose stricter requirements on labelling and packaging. If the final decision is in line with this proposal then the ultimate effect will depend upon the behavioural patterns of consumers, and will therefore not be clear for some time.

Technical harmonization has been particularly contentious when it establishes requirements regarding how goods are produced. The EC's ban on imports of meat and meat products raised with the aid of growth promoting hormones, for example, is estimated by the USA to have cost it $97 million a year, and also affects Australia, Canada and New Zealand (USTR, 1996). The USA has complained that the Third-country Meat Directive requires strict compliance with EC standards and does not recognize equivalent protection offered by the exporting country's animal and public health regulations (USTR, 1996). If it were not for a derogation, EC regulations that require wine imports to be produced using only those oenological practices authorized for production of EC wines would prevent the importation of most US wines.

6.2.4. Certification

Another potential impediment to trade is the requirement of additional certification that a product conforms to specified standards or detailed regulations. How that requirement affects third parties varies according to the procedure adopted for particular types of product.

The obstacle is least significant when the manufacturer's declaration of conformity is sufficient, which is the case for a number of products covered by new approach Directives. For such a declaration by foreign firms to be considered adequate they may have to be certified as having a quality assurance programme in line with ISO 9000. Or they may be required to use another method of conformity assessment, such as a combination of a type test and a product check by an outside body (Nicolas and Repussard, 1995). For example, the EC does not accept the equivalence of Japan's certification of good medical practice and requires inspections of Japanese certified factories and manufacturing facilities which produce pharmaceuticals and medical equipment (DG I, 1996).

Multiple certifications are most problematic in sectors where it is logistically difficult and costly to transport the product to the notified testing body. Examples include heavy machinery, medical devices, pulp and paper and forest products. An Organization for Economic Cooperation and Development (OECD) survey of the telecommunications sector estimated that at least 2% of costs could be saved by mutual recognition of certifications (DG I, 1995b).

One indicator of the sectors in which multiple certification problems are considered most severe is provided by the list of sectors in which the EC is currently negotiating MRAs with various countries. This is provided in Table 6.2.

Table 6.2.   Sectors in which MRAs are being negotiated (as of December 1995)

Sector	Number of partners[1]
Telecommunications equipment	5 (1)
Electrical equipment (low voltage)	5 (1)
Electromagnetic compatibility	5 (1)
Medical devices	5 (1)
Pharmaceuticals	5 (1)
Machinery	3 (2)
Chemicals good laboratory practice	3 (1)
Recreational craft	3
Simple pressure vessels	2 (2)
Personal protective equipment	2 (1)
Vehicles	2

[1] Number in brackets denotes number of countries with which preliminary discussions are being held.

The need for additional certifications is likely also to impose a particularly heavy cost on small and medium-sized enterprises. These are likely to have smaller export volumes and are less likely to have the understanding and resources necessary to negotiate the European regulatory system (DG I, 1995b).

The EC has attempted to respond to the potential impediment to internal and external trade caused by the need for multiple certifications with its 'Global Approach to Certification and Testing'. This, among other things, established principles for negotiating MRAs with third countries. Although individual MRAs are not directly part of the SMP, they are only possible due to the creation of common standards and regulations and have, as acknowledged in the terms of reference (under 2b), the potential to enhance the initial impact of the SMP on conditions of access.

The Global Approach identified three requirements for the conclusion of an MRA:

(a)   the technical competence of the non-EC partner must be adequate;
(b)   the benefits flowing from the agreement must be equivalent; and
(c)   the agreement must be limited to designated bodies (CEC, 1989).

The Commission has also developed criteria for prioritizing negotiations with partner countries. These are:

(a)   the mutual interest in facilitating trade in regulated sectors;
(b)   interest expressed by EC economic operators;
(c)   subscription to the WTO Agreement on Technical Barriers to Trade;
(d)   and the volume of trade between the two parties (DG I, 1995a).

These two sets of criteria are likely to ensure that in the short and medium term MRAs will be negotiated only with the more developed countries. There may be, in consequence, differential effects of this aspect of the SMP between third parties. The first six countries with which discussions have commenced are Australia, Canada, Japan, New Zealand, Switzerland and the USA. It should be noted, however, that the negotiation of MRAs has proved difficult and slow. As of August 1996 only one MRA, with Switzerland, had been concluded. Thus any differential effects of MRAs on market access for different third countries are likely to be muted in the short to medium term. Provisions of the EEA Treaty, however, perform a role similar to MRAs for the participating countries.

In addition, under the 1985 Product Liability Directive the EC-based importer of a defective product is responsible under law for the defects. Because of this, it is possible that such importers may require third-party certification even when the Directives in question accept manufacturer assurance.

In the more general case of voluntary certification, third-country firms might have a more difficult time than their EC competitors, for instance, in furnishing their EC customers with third-party certification of the quality of the products. Even in Europe, the web of bilateral MRAs among laboratories and certification bodies in the voluntary sphere were melded into multilateral agreements covering all European members only relatively recently. The European Coordination for Accreditation of Certification (EAC) was only established in 1990, and European Coordination for Accreditation of Laboratories (EAL) was not formed until mid-1994, although precursors emerged during the 1980s. EAC/EAL have been engaged in negotiating MRAs with other countries and regions, notably the Asia Pacific Accreditation Council (Atkins International Limited, 1996).

6.3. Assessing the scale and direction of external effects

An indication of the product groups and characteristics for which technical barriers to imports are greatest is given by those that are the subject of MRA negotiations between the EC and third countries (see Table 6.3). It should be noted that almost all of these products appear to fall within the industrial sectors that Buigues *et al.* (1990) have identified as those likely to be most affected by the SMP.

It is not possible to indicate in anything other than the most broad-brush, illustrative terms the relative importance of the market enhancing and potentially market restricting effects of the SMP on external parties. The possible direction of effects will depend on a host of factors which are likely to vary between products, markets and suppliers. Although, according to one source, only 10% of goods sold in Europe are subject to EC legislation (US Chamber of Commerce, 1993), the US Department of Commerce estimates that EC legislation covering regulated products will eventually be applicable to 50% of US exports to Europe (USTR, 1996).

The precise impact of technical harmonization and standardization will depend on the specific relationship between the *status quo* and the *status quo ante*, which will differ between Member States, third countries and products. For example, the EC has been credited with raising the level of consumer safety and environmental protection in some, largely southern, Member States (CEC, 1991; Sbragia, 1993). To the extent that these measures govern product characteristics, they may have made access for third-country (along with EC) products to those previously less regulated markets more difficult, although access to the EC market as a whole would have been made more straightforward.

Table 6.3.   Sectors in which technical barriers to imports are greatest

Sector	Detailed harmonization	Subject of MRA negotiations
Vehicles	X	X
Chemicals	X	X
Cosmetics	X	
Foodstuffs	X[1]	X
Telecommunications terminal equipment		X
Electrical equipment (low voltage)		X
Electromagnetic compatibility		X
Medical devices		X
Pharmaceutical products		X
Machinery		X
Recreational craft		X
Simple pressure vessels		X
Personal protective equipment		X

[1] Applies to some products only.
Note: Harmonized measures are assumed to be more of an impediment to trade than certification. Rankings are based on extent of product group covered and number of countries with which MRAs are being negotiated.

The impact of the 'Global Approach to Certification and Testing' on conditions of access for third-country products likewise depends on the specifics of pre- and post-SMP conditions. To the extent that EC Member States required that products be certified by an authorized third party as conforming to standards, the creation of the single market has benefited foreign firms. Instead of having to get their products certified in each Member State, they need now do so only in one. The impact of the SMP, at least in the short to medium term, however, may not be unambiguously positive. There are some indications that prior to the SMP some Member States had MRAs with some third countries (Woolcock, 1991). Such agreements could not be extended automatically to all Member States as they had not been parties to the negotiations. Consequently, such agreements as there were had to lapse pending the conclusion of EC-wide MRAs. In addition, the 'Global Approach' meant that all the Member States had to employ the same certification procedures. Before the SMP some had accepted manufacturers' assurances. Others had required third-party certification: in some cases voluntary and in others mandatory (CEC, 1989). By requiring a common approach to certification, the SMP in some instances might have required some Member States to shift from voluntary to mandatory certification or from manufacturer assurance to third-party evaluation, thereby making access to the markets of particular Member States more difficult for foreign firms.

There are also differences concerning the extent to which SMP measures may affect all trade (internal and external alike) or may affect external suppliers differentially. All EC technical regulations and standards apply to EC and third-country firms equally. However, some standards and regulations, particularly those governing production processes, may favour EC firms. In addition, as noted earlier, complying with technical standards accounts for a larger share of the costs of imports from within the EC than those from outside because other price-raising barriers – notably tariffs and customs formalities – have been eliminated. Consequently, technical harmonization and standardization will benefit EC firms relatively more than third-country firms (Koekkoek *et al.,* 1990:115; Hoeller and Louppe, 1994:19). This is most likely to occur with respect to products governed by technical regulations and in which the costs of multiple certifications are particularly significant.

What is the relative importance of these differential effects? According to several US estimates, trade creation should significantly exceed trade diversion (Ahern, 1992). One broad indicator is to consider the relative importance in EC trade of the product groups identified as being subject to the greatest potential diversion. Accordingly, data have been collected on the level (and source) of EC imports of the product groups for which harmonized measures or third-party certification apply. This is an extremely broad-brush exercise, since the scope of the product groups covered is not specified in terms of the CN in the relevant Directives. Moreover, as noted above, there is only a potential for diversion.

With these caveats in mind, the total value of extra-EC imports in 1994 has been collected where possible for the HS or NACE codes that appear to relate to the products for which harmonized measures or third-party certification apply. When expressed as a proportion of total extra-EC imports in 1994, this exercise suggests that about two-thirds (by value) of imports should, if they are affected at all, benefit from unambiguous improvement in their terms of access, while one-third may be potentially subject to unfavourable changes.

6.4. Summary of findings

Before the SMP the European market was characterized by a proliferation of standards and technical regulations that had the effect of segmenting the market. This was a barrier to access into national markets of products both from outside the EC and from other Member States. Although the problems caused by differences in national standards have not yet been completely eradicated in practice, the most reasonable counterfactual is that without the SMP they would continue to be much more extensive than they are at the present time and will be when the process of removing technical barriers to trade is complete.

In many ways, the process of technical harmonization and standardization is unambiguously beneficial for market access for products from outside the Community: transparency and legal certainty are increased, while design and production costs are likely to be reduced. Where mutual recognition applies, barriers between Member States are removed without being replaced by barriers at the Community level. Under new approach Directives, the EC measures that are adopted are relatively flexible and, therefore, tend not to affect trade very adversely.

The greatest potential for the SMP to have adversely affected market access for third countries directly is with regard to technical harmonization. These measures are inflexible and thus harder to comply with than new approach Directives. In addition, there is reason to believe that, at least in some cases, in the pursuit of legitimate public policy objectives EC harmonization may have raised the stringency of some Member States' regulations, thus potentially impeding access for EC and third-country products to their markets. The product categories in which the potential for gain is likely to be most ambiguous are those listed in Table 6.3.

Market access for third countries' products may also suffer due to the impact of the SMP on EC firms' competitiveness. Not only are technical barriers the most important barriers to intra-

EC imports, and therefore relatively more important than for extra-EC imports, but EC firms may be better able to take advantage of opportunities to exploit economies of scale.

Given that countries with a strong supply capacity are most likely to be able to benefit from the market-enlarging effects of technical harmonization, it is probable that there will be differential effects between third parties. The OECD states and NICs will tend to gain most, and poor developing countries least.

It is not easy to identify plausible quantitative indicators of the likely scale of the effect separately from those that would be used in a modelling of the overall economic impact of the SMP. In qualitative terms, however, the effect of harmonization, while not as immediate and direct as the removal of national QRs, may turn out to be the more important in the longer term. Certainly, it has been welcomed by third parties such as the US Chamber of Commerce and the US International Trade Commission.

7. Removal of barriers to the provision of services and right of establishment

The freedom to provide services is one of the four freedoms at the core of the SMP, and is one of the issues of particular interest to third countries. The freedom to provide services has two components:

(a)   the freedom of establishment;
(b)   the free provision of services across borders.

It is the consequences of the second that are of most direct concern to this study, focusing as it does on access conditions for third-country products, although the former has relevance to the wider aims of the study and analysis must sometimes range over both to explain the nature of the change. While the objectives are the same in all service sectors, the measures necessary to achieve them differ significantly. Consequently they are addressed in separate categories below.

7.1.   Financial services

7.1.1.   The *status quo ante*

Even before the implementation of the SMP, there were few overt barriers to establishment by foreign (non-national EC and non-EC) banking and insurance firms, at least in most of the Member States (Price Waterhouse, 1988). National regulations, by and large, applied equally to domestic and foreign firms alike, although they may have imposed proportionally higher costs on foreign firms.

Most countries maintained controls on foreign acquisitions of domestic banks and often restricted the services that branches or subsidiaries of foreign banks could provide. In investment services the overt barriers were more pronounced, particularly regulations that prevented foreigners from being licensed as brokers.

In no financial service was there scope for providing services across borders, that is without establishment in the target market. Thus there were significant administrative obstacles to entering new markets.

7.1.2.   The nature of the change

Under the SMP a single authorization permits a financial service – be it a credit institution, an insurance undertaking, or an investment service – to operate throughout the EC.

This single licence system is predicated on the concept of home-country control. This means that the Member State issuing the authorization is responsible for regulating activities throughout the EC. Only mass risks in non-life assurance and the regulation of an investment service's conduct may be subject to some host-country control.

In order for home-country control to be practicable, a degree of harmonization of national regulatory regimes was required. Thus, for banks and other credit institutions EC measures were adopted to set minimum capital requirements, common rules on the supervision of internal management and accounting, and to regulate relations with customers in areas such as payment cards and cross-border transfers. In insurance there are common rules regarding annual accounts, insurance contracts, winding up firms, etc. Minimum capital adequacy requirements were established for investment services.

7.1.3. Implications for third countries

To a significant extent the single market measures will benefit third-country firms in the same way, and to the same extent, as they do non-national EC firms. They grant them access to a much larger market with relatively little increase in regulatory burden.

There are, however, some elements of the legislation that have the potential to deny third-country firms access to the single market (see Table 7.1). All the Financial Services Directives require that firms be established in a Member State.

Table 7.1.   Service sectors in which there are restrictions on third-country firms

Sector	Reciprocity	Additional restrictions
Air services	Regarding slot allocation and aviation-related services	EC national control
Maritime transport		EC national control
Inland waterway		EC national vessels
Road transport		Governed by Member State of establishment
Banking	Yes	Wholly incorporated subsidiary
Insurance	Yes	Wholly incorporated subsidiary
Investment services	Yes	

Although most of the Directives apply equally to EC and non-EC firms, all the Directives explicitly regarding the freedom to provide services contain reciprocity provisions in order to avoid unilaterally liberalizing third-country access to the EC's financial services market (CEC, 1994c). These provisions require Member States to deny authorization to subsidiaries or branches of third-country firms from countries that do not provide national treatment or effective market access to equivalent EC firms. As of November 1995, however, these reciprocity clauses had not been invoked (WTO, 1995:113).

These requirements do not apply to the members of the WTO by virtue of most-favoured-nation treatment. The entry into force of the new WTO Agreement on Financial Services on 1 September 1996 has not changed this.

There are other impediments to third-country participation in the SMP for services. In the banking and insurance sectors only wholly incorporated branches of non-EC-owned firms are allowed to open additional branches or provide services from one Member State to another (WTO, 1995:116). It is also possible that non-EC firms may face more obstacles than EC firms in listing securities on EC stock exchanges, as some restrictions on such activity are prohibited only with respect to companies or legal persons which are nationals of a Member State.

These potential problems are clearly not considered to be dominant by the most interested foreign parties. US financial services companies have indicated that they anticipate benefiting from the SMP through increased economies of scale and the creation of new business opportunities, particularly in insurance and investment services (US Chamber of Commerce, 1993:95). Easier movement across Member State borders, and the ability to establish and expand operations in the investment and insurance areas, would help US banks to diversify both geographically and in terms of product line. This would decrease their vulnerability to changes in a particular market.

7.2. Transport services

7.2.1. The *status quo ante*

Prior to the introduction of the SMP, road and air transport services between the Member States were governed by a patchwork of bilateral agreements that regulated access to the international transport market and the conditions under which such services could be provided. There were no QRs on the provision of international transport on the EC's inland waterways.

In no transport services were foreign operators (non-national EC or non-EC) permitted to provide transport services entirely within another Member State (cabotage). Due to the degree of public ownership and the importance of public service obligations, the liberalization of national railways, a prerequisite for the freedom to provide services, is only just beginning.

7.2.2. The nature of the change

The central objective of the SMP has been to abolish QRs on transport (with the exception of rail) between Member States and to establish cabotage rights. The liberalization of market access has been accompanied (usually preceded) by price deregulation. In maritime transport measures have also been introduced to liberalize shipping with third countries by doing away with requirements that only national flag ships can transport some cargoes and eliminating cargo-sharing agreements.

As in financial services, the liberalization of market access has been accompanied by measures to harmonize the regulatory regimes of the Member States. This has covered such issues as access to the profession, safety, social conditions, the transport of hazardous goods and the application of competition rules.

7.2.3. Direct implications for third countries

The implications for third countries of the SMP in transport services differ widely:

(a) among sectors, because of restrictions on foreign ownership (see below and Table 7.1); and

(b) between third countries, because of their proximity or lack thereof.

The opportunity for third-country firms to benefit from the SMP is limited by two requirements:

(a) in each transport sector, the full benefits of the single market are available only to firms established in the EC;

(b)   in several sectors – marine transport, inland waterways and air services – there are also ownership requirements, which restrict the ability of firms controlled by third-country nationals to provide transport services.

In carrying out cabotage services on inland waterways carriers may only use vessels belonging to:

(a)   either natural persons domiciled in a Member State and nationals of a Member State;
(b)   or legal persons with their registered office in a Member State and in which Member State nationals have a controlling interest.

Provided it consults the Commission, a Member State may waive this stipulation.

The provision of marine transport services between two Member States is restricted to Member State nationals or to third-country shipping companies using ships registered in a Member State and controlled by Member State nationals. The stipulations for the provision of marine cabotage are even more stringent. Only EC ship owners using ships registered in a Member State, flying the flag of that Member State and registered in the European Register of Shipping may provide cabotage services. In the absence of multilateral rules and principles, the EC has adopted its own trade policy instruments in marine transport with respect to unfair pricing and for coordinated action against countries that restrict or threaten to restrict access to cargo transports (WTO, 1995:144). Japanese pricing practices in maritime trade gave rise to one of the few investigations carried out to date under the 'New Commercial Policy Instrument'. No action was taken as the controversial practice was discontinued.

In air services, only airlines controlled by Member State nationals may exercise the freedoms provided by the SMP. In addition, reciprocity provisions pertain to airport slot allocation and computer reservation systems (CRS), although neither had been invoked as of November 1995 (WTO, 1995:113). The EC listed a most-favoured-nation exemption from its commitments in air transport services under GATS[19] with regard to CRS and the marketing of air transport services (WTO, 1995:136).

The creation of a single market in the different transport sectors also has varying effects in different extra-EC regions. Developments in road and inland waterway transport, for example, are of direct concern only to operators from Central and Eastern Europe. Only in air services and marine transport do SMP measures have the potential to affect a wide range of countries.

7.2.4.   Indirect implications for third countries

It is possible that being able reduce costs through taking advantage of cabotage and international transport within the EC might increase the competitiveness of EC operators in respect of transport to and from third countries. How significant this gain might be is unclear. Early indications from the road haulage sector indicate that very few hauliers have taken advantage of cabotage rights, although this number has been increasing (Committee of Enquiry, 1994). A similar picture exists in marine transport, where only 6% of liberalized cargo is transported by operators from another Member State (CEC, 1996a). On the other

---

[19]   In air services the GATS covers only aircraft repair and maintenance, the selling and marketing of air services, and CRS services.

hand, US sources have anticipated that the liberalization of the EC's air services market would improve the competitiveness of EC carriers and thus lead to increased competition on trans-Atlantic routes (US Chamber of Commerce, 1993). The emergence of a web of alliances between US and EC carriers covering issues such as code sharing, however, might mitigate this competition.

There may be indirect effects of the SMP on the relative competitiveness of European and foreign firms. The liberalization of EC transport has the potential to benefit firms exporting to the EC, particularly those whose target markets are far from ports or airports, by lowering transport costs. But reduced transport costs could be expected to have a greater impact on the competitiveness of firms established in the EC, since this will also affect the final cost of all of their inputs.

Another indirect effect of the SMP is that it creates the possibility of negotiating market access agreements with third countries. For example, an agreement on market access in inland waterway transport was reached in early 1996 with some of the countries of Central and Eastern Europe, and 'open skies' negotiations are being conducted with several countries, including Switzerland, and may eventually be opened with the USA.

7.3. Capital movements and foreign direct investment

SMP measures affecting foreign direct investment (FDI) may have implications for the conditions of access of third-country products on the European market. This would be the case if the FDI-related measures facilitate, or hinder, trade in goods and services. But because the relationship is indirect, the conceptual and empirical uncertainties concerning the relationship between trade and investment have to be added to those associated with the role of the SMP as opposed to the many other factors affecting FDI trends.

Among the findings of the study on FDI undertaken as part of the programme of work on the SMP are the following (EAG, 1996):[20]

(a)   the period 1984–93 has witnessed a substantial increase in inward FDI flows into the EC, part of which may be attributable to the SMP;

(b)   the evidence strongly suggests that FDI and trade are complementary, with some estimates suggesting that as much as one-third of all trade is intra-firm, in effect linking the foreign investments of multinational enterprises to exploit the advantages of internalization;

(c)   the trade/FDI relationship has been more oriented towards trade in the technology-intensive sectors than in the less technology-intensive sectors;

(d)   the complementary nature of FDI and trade is most true for downstream services.

The growth of FDI over the period 1986-92 is illustrated in Figure 7.1. Although the surge in FDI at the end of the 1980s was partly from EC sources, there was also a significant rise in non-EC investment.

---

[20]   Forthcoming in *The Single Market Review*, Subseries IV, Vol. 1: Foreign direct investment, Luxembourg: Office for Official Publications of the EC and London: Kogan Page/Earthscan, 1997.

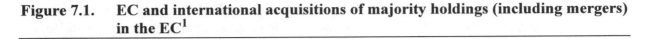

Figure 7.1.   EC and international acquisitions of majority holdings (including mergers) in the EC[1]

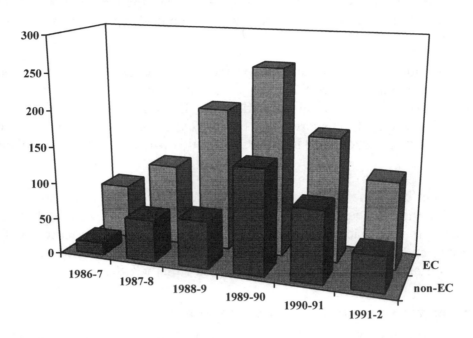

[1]   In 1994 the Commission (CEC, 1994d) began reporting acquisition data that had been gathered in a different fashion from those used in this graph. Those data cover the period only from 1987–88, and so do not clearly illustrate the change that took place in the wake of adoption of the SMP. The data gathered under the two methods are not directly comparable, but for the period of overlap (1987–88 to 1991–92) reveal similar trends. The most significant difference is that the new data collection method captures relatively more international activity. The data indicate that in 1992–93 both international and intra-EC cross-border investment stabilized at roughly the 1991–92 level.
Source: EC, 1988; 1993; 1994d.

Some work suggests that the EC's pre-SMP trade policy favoured outward processing *vis-à-vis* 'direct' trade and FDI (see, for example, Corado, 1994). If true, then the effects identified in Chapter 5 should favour FDI and direct imports of products.

One implication of this analysis is that inward investment as a result of the SMP may have encouraged imports from affiliates of the enterprises implanted in Europe. This may have had the effect not only of increasing imports, but of doing so in a way that tended to favour trade with countries that were the source of the inward investment relative to those that were not. This is important because the inward investment is highly concentrated in terms of country origin. Of the inward FDI into the EC in 1993, for example, over one-quarter was sourced in the USA, Japan and the EFTA states, in addition to the 60% originating in the EUR-12. Only one-eighth came from the rest of the world.

There have been no new national barriers to foreign investment as a result of the SMP, although the EC as a whole can adopt restrictions. But those prohibitions or restrictions at national or EC level relating to third countries which were already in place on 31 December 1993 are untouched. Perhaps the main advantage for third countries is that the decision rules adopted in the Treaty on European Union make it easier for the EC to liberalize the treatment of third countries than to impose new restrictions.

7.4. Summary of findings

Many of the changes covered in this chapter relate to the freedom of foreign-owned firms to establish and operate inside EC states. They do not, therefore, directly relate to the objective of this study, which is to assess conditions of access on to the European market for third-country products (defined to include goods and internationally traded services). Nonetheless, there are some implications for the study.

In the absence of the SMP the most reasonable counterfactual is that the pre-existing barriers to non-EC (as well as non-national EC) service providers would have continued. Hence, it is reasonable to attribute most of the improvements as direct SMP effects.

One of the most important features of the SMP is that it has opened up the possibility of providing services across borders, i.e. without establishment in the target market. Since the SMP measures benefit third-country firms in much the same way, and to the same extent, as non-national EC firms, they increase the scope for internationally traded services to be provided. It will still be necessary for foreign firms to be established in at least one Member State, but this then provides access to a much larger market with relatively little increase in regulatory burden. To the extent that they include an imported element, locally provided services provide a bridge for intra-firm trade and, hence, relate to market access for externally supplied products.

In the case of transport services, the direct implications for third-party suppliers of the SMP are much more limited. There remain restrictions on foreign ownership in some transport sectors, while in others geographical proximity to the EC is required for foreign parties to benefit in practice.

The changing relationship between the capacity to provide services from locally established companies and access to trade will contribute, with changes in the regulatory regime for goods, to an evolution in the relationship between FDI and trade. However, a serious investigation of this relationship is outside the scope of this study.

8. Changes to the business environment

The SMP includes a number of measures relating to the legal framework in which companies in Europe operate. Most relate only to companies established in Europe and apply equally to EC and non-EC own firms. Hence their implication for market access of third-country products is limited, although they are relevant to the broader aims of the study. Intellectual property rights protection and some provisions regarding audio-visual services affect companies not established in the EC. The EC Directive on television services explicitly favours 'European works' over those produced elsewhere (see below).

8.1. Company law

8.1.1. The *status quo ante*

In the absence of a European Company statute, companies from different Member States have been unable to merge without pursuing complex and costly arrangements.

8.1.2. The nature of the change

Relatively few measures have been adopted in this sphere so far as a result of the SMP. Those that have been adopted largely concern the approximation of national laws on the protection of shareholders, creditors and third parties. The crucial European Company statute is still pending.

8.1.3. Implications for third countries

To the extent that these measures when implemented reduce differences between the Member States they will facilitate investment decisions by third-country firms. As with several other elements of the SMP, the *status quo ante* discriminated both against non-national EC and third-country firms. Hence, the new rules will not necessarily affect third countries as a group differentially, save to the extent that firms from some third countries (e.g. other OECD states) are more likely to be able to establish in one Member State and, in the future, extend their operations to other Member States than will firms from other third countries (e.g. developing states).

8.2. Intellectual and industrial property

As with many other elements of the SMP, the principal forces affecting third parties are provided under other agreements. In this case, it is primarily the GATT provisions on trade-related intellectual property rights. The study in the overall programme on industrial property rights protection reports that no third-country operators have complained of any discriminatory treatment.[21]

---

[21]   In *The Single Market Review*, Subseries III, Vol. 4: Industrial property rights, Luxembourg: Office for Official Publications of the EC and London: Kogan Page/Earthscan, 1997.

8.3. Taxation

8.3.1. Indirect taxation

The Commission's objective is to ensure fiscal neutrality in commercial trade and thereby create a genuine single market (CEC, 1996a:39). There are, however, numerous problems associated with implementing the requirements of the tax system. The Commission has concluded that these deficiencies can be resolved only through a new framework, and is preparing a definitive VAT regime (CEC, 1996a:39).

One point that will have to be taken into account by the definitive VAT system is equal treatment and neutrality of taxation for domestic and intra-EC transactions. As the EC VAT system applies equally to EC and non-EC firms established in a Member State, third-country firms established in the EC will benefit from the further approximation of indirect taxation alongside their EC competitors. US reactions to the approximation of indirect taxation have been positive, as it believes that this will facilitate cross-border trade (USITC, 1993:148).

8.3.2. Direct taxation

In the Commission's view, divergent national direct taxation is becoming an increasingly important obstacle to the smooth functioning of the single market (CEC, 1996a:40). In particular, tax competition for business activities and capital poses a threat to the international tax system and to Member States' tax revenues. The Commission has focused its efforts on:

(a)   eliminating double taxation on cross-border income and gains;
(b)   introducing a more neutral system of taxation of savings;
(c)   realizing a neutral system for the taxation of insurance services;
(d)   addressing the problems of individuals who are resident in one Member State but earn their living in another;
(e)   the improvement of the fiscal environment of small and medium-sized enterprises (CEC, 1995b:113).

US reactions to the harmonization of indirect taxation have been positive, as it is believed that this will facilitate cross-border trade (USITC, 1993:132).

The proposed changes in company taxation strongly appeal to US firms having operations in more than one Member State (USITC, 1993:148).

8.4. Media

The crucial measure in audiovisual policy as far as third countries are concerned is the 'Television without Frontiers' Directive (89/552/EEC). It both harmonizes and liberalizes single market conditions and encourages the production and consumption of 'European works'. It is the second objective that presents problems for third-country firms.

The Directive requires that 'wherever practicable' a majority of broadcasting time be reserved for 'European works'. These are defined as works created by persons located in a member state of the Council of Europe. The Commission's 1995 proposed amendment leaves essentially unchanged this requirement which effectively perpetuates pre-SMP national policies (Hoeller and Louppe, 1994:34).

According to the Commission, nearly two-thirds of the channels complied with the required European-content provisions of the Directive in 1991–92 (CEC, 1995a:145). Even those that did not do so revealed 'an overall upward trend'. All Danish, Dutch, Irish and Portuguese channels, and all British and French terrestrial channels, complied with the Directive.

Although the USA has complained most loudly about the European-content requirement, other third countries (excluding the non-EC members of the Council of Europe) may well be squeezed out by US dominance of the non-European allocation. The WTO has raised doubts about the longer-term sustainability of the quota, given the ascent of new transmission modes (satellite and video) and of international co-productions, the origin of which is difficult to determine (WTO, 1995:145).

Another potentially contentious issue concerns media ownership. The Commission is planning to bring forth a proposal that would increase the diversity of ownership in the Member States. Unless it explicitly excludes ownership by third-country firms or individuals, this would probably serve to open the broadcast market to non-EC firms.

8.5. The free movement of persons

Since this study is focused exclusively on trade in products, the SMP measures relating to the free movement of persons are not of major concern. However, to the extent that the changes make it easier for companies to operate in different national markets, they may be said to contribute to an improvement in the business environment. The goal of the free movement of persons is to be achieved through:

(a)   abolition of controls on people at international frontiers and the removal of border posts;
(b)   rights of residence;
(c)   mutual recognition of qualifications.

Changes in relation to movement across borders and rights of residence will affect the capacity of firms to use third-country nationals in their operations. In 1995, the Council adopted two Regulations with potential effect in this area. One established a list of third countries whose nationals need a visa in order to cross the external frontiers of the Community. In the case of third countries not on this list, the Member States will remain free to decide whether or not to require a visa. The other Regulation establishes a uniform format for visas.

The net effect of these changes, together with the removal of controls on the movement of people at internal borders, is likely to make it easier for nationals from countries not requiring visas, and for the firms that employ them, to operate effectively as economic agents in the Community. By the same token, nationals from countries that require visas may face relative disadvantage.

The measures being taken (but not yet fully in force) to achieve mutual recognition of diplomas and other qualifications will also tend to facilitate the effective use of economic operators across borders.

8.6. Summary of findings

There are relatively few changes to the business environment with direct implications for market access for third-country products. However, in broad terms the SMP can reasonably be said to have made business operations easier in the Community, and as more elements of the programme are fully implemented this will continue. To the extent, therefore, that improvements in the business environment feed through into access conditions for imports (for example, by facilitating intra-firm trade of foreign-owned companies established in the EC), then the SMP measures may be relevant to this study.

Those elements of the SMP that have provoked international concern, such as the requirement about the proportion of media broadcasting time reserved for 'European works', tend to be the exceptions.

9. Removal of barriers to public procurement

This chapter and the next review SMP changes in relation to markets that are subject to close government control. Between them they cover both the general issue of government procurement and the specific industry situation in relation to telecommunications and energy.

9.1. The *status quo ante*

9.1.1. Public procurement practice

The removal of barriers to the direct or indirect implementation of public procurement contracts by foreign parties could, in principle, bring significant gains. The study on public procurement, undertaken as part of the overall programme of work on the SMP by EuroStrategy Consultants, included a review of Member State public procurement practice. It found that, in general, purchases of foreign origin appeared to account for a smaller share of public sector than of private sector purchases.[22] Hence, changes that reduce the scope of public authorities to favour domestic suppliers have the potential to raise the level of foreign supply, at least for some activities, closer to that already experienced in the private sector.

9.1.2. Non-SMP changes

The conditions of access to the European market for external supplies have been strongly influenced by events that fall outside the SMP. These include the creation of the EEA, the negotiation of the WTO Agreement on Government Procurement (GPA), bilateral agreements with the USA and other countries, and association agreements with Central and Eastern Europe. As in many other cases, therefore, it is difficult to disentangle in a wholly objective fashion any changes in the access of third-country products to the European market that result directly from the SMP and those that are consequent upon both the SMP change and the general context within which the SMP has been implemented.

The relationship between the two sets of factors also has importance for the distinction made in this study between differential effects between third countries, on the one hand, and EC producers, on the other, and between one set of third parties and another. Because the conditions of access of third-country products in relation to public procurement are heavily influenced by other agreements, such as the EEA and the GPA, there is a differential impact between those third parties that are covered by the agreements and those that are not.

9.2. The SMP

9.2.1 The SMP provisions

Negotiation of the multilateral and bilateral agreements took place during or shortly after the development of the EC's public procurement regime. This regime consists of measures regulating works, supply, and services contracts of public bodies (each governed by its own Directive(s)) and a separate Directive on purchases by utilities, whether publicly owned or not.

---

22 This section draws on the findings of the public procurement report by EuroStrategy Consultants (forthcoming in *The Single Market Review*, Subseries III, Vol. 2: Public procurement, Luxembourg: Office for Official Publications of the EC and London: Kogan Page/Earthscan, 1997).

The measures regulating purchases by public bodies do not specifically mention third-country goods, services or service providers. Thus the EC measures neither discriminate nor prohibit discrimination against them.

The situation, therefore, is that on the face of it the *status quo* is not necessarily strongly different from the *status quo ante*, since the Directives do not of themselves prevent Member States from excluding such products. However, they do prohibit the application of a price preference against such products, since the origin of the products is not a permissible award criterion. The requirement that contracting authorities must give preference to international standards over European standards (where different from international ones) and national ones should make it easier for third-country firms to compete for public procurement contracts.

The Utilities Directive, however, does discriminate against third-country suppliers. In Article 36 it provides that purchasers:

(a)   may reject third-country offers, defined as those offering products of which more than 50% originates in certain third countries;

(b)   must reject such offers where their price advantage over the next-best offer is less than 3%, provided that the next-best offer is equally advantageous in features other than price.

Although the Public Sector Directives do not of themselves forbid the exclusion of third-country goods, and the Utilities Directive expressly allows it under certain conditions, it has been argued in the EuroStrategy Consultants report that practical limitations apply to Member States making use of this discretion. These are to be found in the provisions for the free movement of goods and services under the Treaty and provisions giving the Community power in external trade relations. Even though a degree of discrimination against third parties is permitted, the SMP provides some restriction to the scope of that discrimination. As a result, the EC's public procurement regime should provide better access for foreign companies than did the pre-SMP national preference regimes (Hoeller and Louppe, 1994:34).

9.2.2. Implications for third countries

Since the *status quo ante* discriminated against both non-national EC and third-country firms, change will not necessarily result in any clearly identifiable differential effects on the latter as a coherent group. But by opening up tendering to non-national companies the Directives create significant new opportunities for firms both from third countries and from other EC states, even given the disadvantages that the former face under the Excluded Sectors Directive. The impact of the Excluded Sectors Directive is hard to assess as its discriminatory article is waived for some countries on the basis of bilateral market access agreements. For example, it does not apply to US firms in the electricity sector or to Israeli firms in telecommunications.

The direct impact of the changes in public procurement are likely to be relatively small. The EuroStrategy report has calculated public sector import penetration in 1994. It found that an estimated 96–98% of total EC public sector purchases were procured from domestic suppliers. When indirect foreign purchases were included (i.e. via a domestic supplier such as a subsidiary or importer) this proportion fell to an estimated 87–93%. However, the vast majority of 'foreign purchases' are procured from other Member States. Third-country suppliers accounted for less than an estimated 0.5% of the total.

The majority of public sector purchases of foreign origin were in the areas of: paper and stationery, office machinery, medical equipment, motor vehicles, and uniforms.

US suppliers and procurement experts believe that the EC 1992 procurement programme will eventually open European public sector markets, and increase awareness of contract opportunities, thus creating competition (USITC, 1993:90). However, there is also agreement that short-term effects are likely to be small considering procuring authorities will continue to favour local suppliers. Enforcement will therefore play an important role in determining whether the new laws are implemented effectively.

US-EC tension has mainly arisen about the ratification of the Utilities Directive. There was US concern about the 50% rule in the Directive restricting US suppliers' ability to take advantage of more open procurement. Moreover, it was claimed that the rule would result in an unpredictable bidding situation and could have the effect of requiring US firms to invest in the EC in order to win procurement contracts. Public procurement liberalization will benefit unambiguously EC-based subsidiaries of foreign firms.

9.3. Summary of findings

Changes to public procurement are unlikely to have major effects on the conditions of access for third-country products in the short term, but might have more substantial effects in the future. There has been some improvement in absolute access for third-country suppliers of products. However, this absolute improvement may be less important than a relative deterioration *vis-à-vis* non-national EC suppliers, for whom barriers have been lifted more substantially. Third-party supplies currently form an extremely small share of public procurement, and there is no reason to suppose that this situation will change dramatically in the short term.

10. Removal of barriers in regulated industries

In addition to introducing a common regulatory regime in many industries, the SMP also includes measures to liberalize the national telecommunications and energy markets of the Member States. Many of these steps are relatively recent and some are still pending. Both sectors are, however, of significant interest to third countries.

10.1. Telecommunications services

10.1.1. The *status quo ante*

Until recently the national markets for telecommunications services were dominated by one, usually state-owned, supplier and in many cases they still are. The segmentation in service provision was paralleled by divergent national standards for telecommunications equipment. Developments in this area are addressed in general terms in Chapter 6 on the removal of technical barriers to trade.

10.1.2. The nature of the change

The SMP is expected to have the greatest impact in value-added and basic telecommunications services. The provision of value-added services and data services has been opened to competition. In March 1996 the EC adopted a Directive on the liberalization of telecommunications services, including voice telephony (96/19/EC). The target date for full liberalization of all telecommunications services is 1 January 1998, although Greece, Ireland, Luxembourg, Portugal, and Spain have been granted longer transition periods.

With regard to network access, Member States may at present maintain exclusive public networks, but must establish objective, transparent and non-discriminatory access conditions. No distinction is made between conditions for non-national firms, whether they be based in other EC states or outside the EC. The Council has endorsed the general principle of full infrastructure liberalization from 1 January 1998, with the same derogations as apply in telecommunications services.

10.1.3. Implications for third countries

The Directives liberalizing the provisions of telecommunications services do not draw a distinction between EC and non-EC firms. But the Council has mandated that measures governing the liberalization of infrastructure include reciprocity provisions ensuring 'comparable access' to foreign markets (WTO, 1995:132-3).

The US has requested that the EC ensure that non-EC competitors have access to reserved services on an equal footing to EC competitors once the services are liberalized (USTR, 1996:112). The Commission's proposals for third-country access to the market for many of these services are linked to the treatment agreed in the GATS negotiations on basic telecommunications (USTR, 1996:113). Pending the conclusion of these negotiations, the EC and Member States are bound by the obligations listed in the Annex on telecommunications, which include the granting of access to, and use of, public telecommunications networks and services 'on reasonable and non-discriminatory terms and conditions' (WTO, 1995:133).

In the USTR's view, the EC's initial negotiating position:

(a)   safeguarded discriminatory provisions against non-EC investors in Belgium, France, Italy, Portugal and Spain;

(b)   provided for deferment of foreign companies' market entry rights in Portugal and Spain;

(c)   included a carve-out that would allow denial of virtually any market access by Belgium;

(d)   maintained restrictions on international services in Belgium;

(e)   maintained restrictions on telex and telegraph services in some Member States (USTR, 1996:113).

The USA fears that unless the negotiations are concluded promptly access to service sectors in Europe may be tied to service opportunities offered to European providers in the USA (USTR, 1996:113).

The USA is also concerned by a Commission proposal that companies wishing to benefit from mutual recognition of licences for the provision of satellite network or communications services be 75% owned by EC nationals (USTR, 1996:109).

10.2. Energy

10.2.1. The *status quo ante*

Although restrictions on the free movement of petroleum and coal had been liberalized by direct application of the Treaty of Rome, the national electricity and gas markets remained tightly regulated. Often they were government owned. Consequently, they were largely independent of each other. The Member States also controlled access to their national natural energy resources.

10.2.2. The nature of the change

In energy, as in telecommunications, one of the important first steps towards the creation of a single market is liberalization of the national markets. In June 1996 the Council agreed a common position on the liberalization of electricity. The new rules foresee the continued operation of transmission networks by single operators, subject to certain negotiation arrangements. The common position provides for 'eligible' consumers, initially large industrial consumers and potentially distributors, to source electricity in other Member States. There is also greater scope for entry into the distribution and generation sectors.

Progress has been more rapid with respect to exploitation. All entities established in the EC must receive equal treatment regarding prospecting, exploration and production of hydrocarbons. Before 1 January 1997, Member States must abolish all existing provisions which reserve to a single entity the right to obtain authorization in a specific geographic area.

10.2.3. Implications for third countries

With regard to the liberalization of the energy markets, the most direct impact is likely to be for non-energy industries established in Europe. Like non-national EC firms, they will have potential access to cheaper sources of energy. There may also be increased opportunities for non-EC firms to enter the distribution and power generation sectors.

It is only in energy exploration that there are potentially discriminatory clauses concerning third-country firms. For national security reasons Member States may exclude from access to their national energy sources entities established in the EC but controlled by third countries or third-country nationals. Access for firms not established in the EC is subject to reciprocity.

10.3. Summary of findings

The liberalizations of the telecommunications and energy markets are unlikely to have major effects on the conditions of access for third-country products in the short term. However, they might have substantial effects in the future when complete liberalization could provide opportunities for third-party suppliers to enter the telecommunications and energy industries.

By and large, foreign firms will have to establish themselves in the EC in order to take advantage of these opportunities. Thus these changes are not the focal point of our study. Moreover, it is not easy to assess the likely impact of the liberalization measures as many have been adopted only recently and much remains to be done.

11.   Concluding remarks

11.1. Diversity of effect

This chapter is not labelled 'Conclusions' because the nature of the subject does not lend itself to a small set of clear, overall findings. Rather, the conclusions are to be found in the sum of the final sections of the main chapters, each of them labelled 'Summary of findings'.

With this caveat, it may be helpful to recapitulate the findings on the various SMP measures that would enable a broad order of priority to be established. This prioritization is based upon a mix of quantitative and qualitative data to establish a broad order of probabilities.

11.1.1. Immediate effects

In terms of the immediacy and directness of its effect on market access for products from external sources, the most important aspect of the SMP must be the sharp reduction in national differences in the treatment of traded goods. This was achieved by the elimination of formal national trade barriers, the elimination of customs formalities at national borders, and the fact that these controls were replaced only very partially by Community-level instruments with sub-Community effect.

The direct benefits of these changes are likely to be significant, but only for a relatively small number of states. Except in the area of textiles and clothing (where the MFA is probably a more substantial influence on trade patterns), most of the national QRs were applied by a relatively small number of states in relation to each product and targeted a small number of suppliers. Nonetheless, there is evidence to suggest that they had a significant effect on imports of the product in question from the targeted source.

For those third parties that were not subject to national QRs (or were beneficiaries of them), the substantial erosion of sub-Community trade policies will not necessarily have been beneficial. The improvement in absolute access for formerly restricted suppliers, together with no change (as a result of this aspect of the SMP) for other suppliers, will have produced a relative deterioration in access terms for the latter group. However, quantification of this differential effect between third parties was not a priority for this study.

11.1.2. Broader, direct effects

In a broader and longer-term perspective, the erosion of technical barriers to trade may turn out to have the greatest importance for third-party suppliers of goods. Certainly it is an area of SMP change that has attracted particular interest by foreign suppliers, notably those in the USA.

In many cases, the SMP changes are unambiguously beneficial for third parties, although the greatest gains will tend to go to those states with the greatest supply capacity. This differential impact is likely to be even more marked in the minority of cases in which the gains are ambiguous, since they are subject to potentially onerous compliance requirements. The strong balance of probabilities, though, is that trade in the products for which gains will be unambiguous is much larger than in products which may be subject to new restrictions as a result of SMP measures.

The relaxing (but not the removal) of restraints on extra-EC firms bidding for government procurement may improve access conditions for extra-EC supplies. However, this is likely to be very small in the short to medium term, not least because the relaxation of restrictions has been greater for non-national EC firms than for those from outside the Community, so that the latter have experienced a relative deterioration in their terms of access compared with the former.

11.1.3. Indirect and longer-term effects

Many of the other aspects of the SMP could affect access conditions for products from third countries, but in most cases this will be an indirect consequence of changes that make it easier for foreign-owned companies to establish themselves and do business within the Community. Given the high proportion of international trade accounted for by intra-firm transactions, this indirect effect could be quite substantial. However, it is not easy to establish a firm basis for according it a particularly high priority in terms of SMP effects on access conditions.

Measures in respect of financial services, taxation, freedom of movement of persons, and protection of intellectual and industrial property appear most likely to produce tangible gains in the short to medium term.

The improvements in access for telecommunications products will depend upon both the nature and progress of moves towards liberalization and the application of requirements for reciprocity. The SMP is expected to have the greatest impact in value-added telecommunications services. In energy, the main gains in the medium term are likely to accrue to firms consuming energy products (EC and non-EC alike) rather than to foreign suppliers.

11.2. A different perspective

An alternative way of cataloguing the SMP changes with potential implications for access conditions is to distinguish between measures in which there is identical treatment of third-country and non-national EC operators and those in which there are explicit effects on third-country operators alone. The measures that are catalogued in this way are all those that have been described in the preceding chapters, but by presenting them according to this new two-way classification their relative importance may be seen in a different perspective.

11.2.1. Measures involving equal treatment

Among the SMP measures designed to promote trade are many that affect third-country and non-national firms in the same way. These include, for example, the abolition of customs and fiscal frontiers to cross-border trade, some aspects of the liberalization of government procurement, and the removal of technical barriers to trade.

In many cases, third-country suppliers not established in the EC will benefit equally with non-national EC firms from the removal of controls. This would be the case, for example, in relation to those aspects of the removal of technical barriers to trade that have been identified as being unambiguously beneficial.

In other cases, however, the gains for European suppliers may be greater, so that absolute improvements for third-party suppliers may also represent a relative deterioration. This would be the case for some aspects of technical harmonization with ambiguous effects on third parties, together with any difficulties created by the reinforcement of external borders consequent upon the breaking down of internal borders.

To the extent that the SMP has facilitated establishment within the EC, then intra-firm trade with foreign-owned companies would benefit from both sets of changes. However, these gains are likely to have differential effects on third parties given the different propensities of firms from rich and poor states to establish themselves in the EC. Many of the potential gains identified, for example, by US firms are predicated on establishment within the Community. Since the impact of the SMP on conditions of access for traded services is likely to be closely associated with rights of establishment, it is likely that this differential effect will be particularly marked.

11.2.2. Measures involving unequal treatment

Some aspects of the SMP affect third-country suppliers relatively, and in some cases absolutely. This differential treatment may be discriminatory as between third parties. This is the case, for example, in cases where the discrimination takes the form of requiring reciprocity. In others, such as the Excluded Sectors Directive, it is an absolute discrimination against third parties.

In other cases, however, changes have been targeted favourably on third-party supplies. The elimination of national QRs and the suppression in practice of Article 115 benefit third parties but do not affect European suppliers. Hence, there has been a relative improvement in the market access of the former.

11.2.3. The balance of probabilities

In terms of an overall prioritization, the balance of probabilities is that the gains for third parties outweigh the potential losses by a wide margin. In the case of measures affecting European and foreign suppliers equally, in most cases absolute improvements in access have not been offset by relative declines because European suppliers benefit more. Whilst some aspects of the SMP do discriminate against third-party suppliers, these appear to be less important than those from which third-party suppliers benefit. Moreover, in the case of national trade barriers the differential effect has been in favour of third-party suppliers.

Because of the diversity of SMP measures, and of the pre-SMP situation as it affected particular suppliers, the actual impact of change will vary widely, depending upon the precise characteristics and circumstances of the product and supplier in question. Hence, it is perfectly possible that the overall conclusion of third-party gain is compatible with the existence of cases in which particular third parties have suffered a clear absolute and relative deterioration in access for some products.

APPENDIX A

Trade associations' views on obstacles to a single market

Trade association	Business sector	Page ref.	Existing obstacles to the establishment of a single market
EURELECTRIC	Electricity generation and distribution	10	Await functioning regulatory framework
International Minerals Association	Physical industrial minerals	32	High intra-EC export administration Customs procedures cumbersome Poor control of extra-EC imports
EUROFER, EISA	Iron and steel	35, 36	State subsidies obstacle to competition Lack of economic and monetary union
CET, CIELFFA, CIPF, EBA, European Profiles and Panels Producers Federation	First processing of steel	43, 47	Exchange rate fluctuations No harmonized payment conditions Intrastat not satisfactory
EUROMETAUX	Non-ferrous metals	50	Cross-border shipping restriction
EUROALLIAGES	Ferro-alloys	52	Energy price differences National waste treatment discrepancies
CEMBUREAU	Cement	57, 58	Clarification of competition issues (dumping, subsidization) and energy/environment factors needed
CEPE	Paints, varnishes and printing inks	67	French translation needed for all label information
APAG	Oleochemicals and allied products	75, 76	Total dedication of ocean vessels considered expensive and unnecessary
ECPA	Agrochemicals	77, 79	Environmental measures insufficiently scientifically-based No real free movements of goods
EFMA	Fertilizers	81, 82, 83	Internal barriers to trade remain (Regulation on ammonium nitrate) Differences in environmental legislation remain Administrative burden imposed by the transitional VAT system Further concentration of production constrained by transport costs Risk of disruption of the fertilizer market if unharmonized CO_2-tax implemented
AIS, COLIPA	Soaps and detergents, personal care products	84, 86	Obstacle posed by road transport problems (limited cabotage) Lack of mutual recognition due to the prevalence of national rules EC companies disadvantaged by many services' high costs
	Non-prescription pharmaceuticals	87, 89, 90	Marketing authorization still needed in all the countries in which they operate Companies should be allowed to advertise a product which has the same label as a prescription medicine VAT rate differences between reimbursed and non-reimbursed products Impossible Europe-wide advertising and selling Problem with trade mark

Trade association	Business sector	Page ref.	Existing obstacles to the establishment of a single market
ORGALIME	Metal products	91	Internal barriers remain (due to differences of national laws transposing European Directives)
CECT	Boilers and metal containers	101	Removal of barriers to free movement of goods needed
CEO	Hand tools	103	EC Regulations should be enforced and applied in all Member States
SEFEL	Light metal packaging	105	Harmonization of regulations needed
CEMATEX	Textile machinery	115	National environmental protection measures cause internal barriers
EUCHEMAP	Chemical machinery	120	Negative impact of the SM on profitability as it has led to more bureaucracy
COPAMA	Plastics and rubber Machinery	124	National standards become internal barriers to free intra-EC trade
FEBMA, EUROTRANS	Bearings and transmission equipment	128	Member States should only act in accordance with the European competition regulations
ORGALIME	Electrical engineering	135, 136	National environmental protection hinders trade and economic relations Adoption of EC legislation should be completed quickly to avoid problems and delays in Member States' full acknowledgement of the European standard regulation
ELC	Electric lighting	150	Opening of public procurement markets still to be completed
EUROBIT	Computers and office equipment	154	Fully homogeneous market still to be created Barriers remain: VAT system, lack of technical harmonization, problems of cross-border payments and export controls
	Transport equipment	161	Further harmonization needed in : public procurement, indirect taxation and cross-border payments Competition and environmental policy to be implemented taking into account the situation at world level to avoid a deterioration of the competitiveness of the EC transport equipment industry
ACEA	Motor vehicles	163	The SMP should be fully applied to car distribution within the EC (the distribution of motor vehicles in the EC still operates within the basic framework of Regulation (EEC) No 123/85 which allows a system of exclusive dealership)
EBMA	Bicycles	173	Mutual recognition of rules needed
CIAA	Food and drink	190	Internal barriers remain due mainly to Member States' legislation
FEDIOL, FEDOLIVE, IMACE	Oils and fats	193	Remaining internal barriers due to differences in control implementation and VAT levels
UEA, AVEC, CLITRAVI	Meat	194, 195	VAT level differences Production techniques standards differences

Trade association	Business sector	Page ref.	Existing obstacles to the establishment of a single market
OEITFL	Fruit and vegetable processing and preserving	198	Harmonization of technical and hygiene legislation needed Clear definitions of some products needed Differences between fiscal structures and taxation rates
FAFPAS	Deep frozen products	202	Further harmonization needed (in temperatures of transport, warehousing and storage of quick-frozen foodstuffs, procedures of control)
EUROGLACES, CAOBISCO	Cocoa, sugar confectionery and ice cream	211, 212	Harmonization of taxation needed (indirect taxation, VAT) Remaining internal barriers linked mainly to interpretation of labelling and packaging legislation
CEPS, UEPA	Alcohol and spirits	220	Remaining internal barriers linked to different advertising legislation, different taxation regimes, lack of common technical standards and different levels of excise
Comité Vins	Wine	222	Harmonization of advertising legislation needed Fiscal harmonization needed
EUROMALT, CBMC	Brewing and malting	223	Harmonization of indirect taxation levels needed (VAT and excise) Harmonization of advertising legislation needed
UNESDA	Soft drinks and mineral waters	227	Harmonization of VAT needed Prevention of new national barriers connected to the environmental issues needed Implementation of labelling norms required EC currency necessary
COMITEXTIL	Textiles	230, 232	Lack of mutual recognition of certification rules
CEC	Footwear	238	Recent establishment of non-tariff barriers
CEI-BOIS	Wood processing	244	Restrictive Commission interpretation of Construction Products Directive (89/106/EEC) helps existing barriers to free trade to continue
CEPI	Pulp, paper and board	248	Currency instability Environmental and technical obstacles
CITPA	Paper and board Converting	251	Lack of harmonized direct taxation Lack of harmonized environmental standards
INTERGRAF, ENPA	Printing and publishing	254, 255	VAT differences No clear guidelines on some postal charges Lack of harmonized advertising regulations Uncertainty linked to the definition of cross-media ownership
BLIC	Rubber products	257	EC legislation unclear on waste management
UEA	Furniture	260, 261	No EC market for public procurement contracts Inconsistent application of EC legislation re competition and advertising
CIBJO	Jewellery	263	Lack of harmonization regarding the marking of precious metals
TME, FEJ	Toys	267	Lack of harmonization of rules for television advertising and infant safety requirements Differential interpretation of EC legislation
FESI	Sporting goods	270	Inequalities in indirect taxation

Trade association	Business sector	Page ref.	Existing obstacles to the establishment of a single market
FIEC	Construction	273	Slow implementation of EC Directives
	Tourism	279	Absence of tax harmonization Lack of progress toward economic and monetary union
EAZA	Recreation parks	288, 290	Lack of direct tax harmonization Lack of indirect tax harmonization Lack of social security cost harmonization Poorly implemented state aid regulations No economic and monetary union
ECTAA, IFTO, ETOA,	Travel services	293	Need further easing of passport control Need even implementation of SMP measures
UITP	Public transport	302	Inability of current legislation to create a level playing-field for inter-modal competition
IRU	Road passenger transport	305	Lack of VAT harmonization Regulations poorly enforced
IRU	Road freight transport	308	Poor enforcement of existing regulations Excise duty harmonization
Union internationale de la navigation fluviale	Inland waterways transport	311	National state subsidies providing for unfair competition Lack of homogeneous infrastructure
ECSA	Shipping	313	High administration costs
ACE	Air transport	314, 316	Unfair competition due to state subsidies Liberalization of assistance services at airports Differential tax rules
AEA	Air transport	319	Cost effect of the Schengen Agreement No harmonized air traffic control system
ERA	Air transport	320, 321	State subsidies to rail networks
EEO	Postal and express services	325	Need to liberalize cross-border mail Incoherent indirect taxation rules
POSTEUROPE	Postal and express services	328	Different customs clearance formalities Need to liberalize transport services
Port of Rotterdam	Sea ports and other sea transport facilities	331	Need to deregulate transport sector Abolish state aids that distort competition
ACI	Airports	335	Suppression of identity checks needed
	Financial services	337	Lack of harmonization of taxation rules Need efficient adoption of EC measures into national law
FBE	Credit institutions	339	Lack of economic and monetary union Balance sheet requirements
EUROFINAS	Credit institutions	341	Lack of economic and monetary union Differential interpretation of EC legislation
EMF	Credit institutions	342, 343	Lack of tax harmonization Unsatisfactory provisions of the Second Co-ordination Banking Directive (89/646/EEC) Obstacles to cross-border mortgage activities Lack of economic and monetary union
CEA	Insurance	345	Differences in contract law Differences in taxation Exchange rate fluctuations

Trade association	Business sector	Page ref.	Existing obstacles to the establishment of a single market
FESE	Financial intermediaries	347	Lack of economic and monetary union Continued fiscal and administrative barriers
FIABCI	Real estate	349	Lack of mutual recognition of diplomas Different requirements for licences
EAAA, FEDIM	Advertising and direct marketing	353	Lack of tax harmonization Considerable regulatory differences between states High national market protectionism No harmonized form of cross-border payments Lack of economic and monetary union
FEE	Accountancy services	361	Restrictions to the freedom to provide accountancy (and related) services Lack of mutual recognition of diplomas Problems with cross-border ownership Lack of tax harmonization
CEEC, AEEB	Construction economists	372	Lack of qualification and training harmonization
EFCA	Engineering constancy services	375	Continued state subsidies Lack of opening up of the public procurement market
CEOC	Inspection and quality control	376	Need more technical harmonization Need improved mutual recognition of diplomas
CLGEE	Geodetic surveying	378	Differential regulations (Semi) public officers still have monopolies in some states
ELCA	Landscaping	380	Bidding rules too complicated and therefore exclude small and medium-sized enterprises
Federation of European Publishers	Publishing services	384, 385	Different levels of VAT Problems regarding copyright law
CIETT	Temporary work services	386	Unfair competition due to unequal access to information
COESS, ESTA, LISS	Security services	392	Recent creation of state laws hampering cross-border trade
ECATRA	Car rental	393, 394	General lack of standardization and harmonization within the sector Differences in indirect taxation
LEASEUROPE	Leasing	397	Lack of harmonization of the legal, fiscal, and accounting frameworks
EFF	Franchising	399	No economic and monetary union
EIIA, EUSIDIC	Electronic information services	405	Need to harmonize legislation in the fields of copyright, legal protection and databases, privacy and data security, access to government information and codes of conduct for trains-border Audiotex Need deregulation of telecommunications industry Pan-European toll-free numbers need to be established

Trade association	Business sector	Page ref.	Existing obstacles to the establishment of a single market
ETNO	Telecommunication services	408	Problems of technical harmonization
HCEC	Hospitals	413	Need harmonization of VAT regimes
	Audio-visual services	423	No common European audio-visual standards

Source: DRI, 1995.

PART II: Quantitative analysis

12. Summary

12.1. Objective of Part II of the study and terms of reference

The main purpose of Part II was to provide a quantitative assessment of the effect of the single market programme on the access of third-country suppliers to the European Community (EC) market. Specifically, the terms of reference required the estimation of the effects of two different consequences of the single market:

(a)   the replacement of national quotas or other quantitative restrictions (QRs) by full liberalization of access to the EC market;

(b)   the replacement of national QRs by Community-wide QRs.

The terms of reference required the construction and application of a partial equilibrium model similar to those that have been used previously for the purpose of analysing constrained imports. The main objective of the model is to quantify the impact of the SMP on exporters to the EU, distinguishing between those who were constrained before the change and those who were not. For this purpose, two sectors were to be selected as exemplars of the two possible outcomes (liberalization or the erection of Community-wide QRs). The study was not, however, expected to produce an overall analysis of trade flows as that is the subject of a different study within the overall Single Market Review.

12.2. Approach and main findings

Following discussions with Commission officials, the two sectors selected for study were clothing, where the SMP has led to the replacement of national QRs by a Community-wide regime; and footwear where liberalization has occurred except for the introduction of a restriction on imports from just one supplier, China. Both sectors are characterized by competitive, rather than oligopolistic market structures.

To assess the impact of the SMP, three complementary empirical exercises were undertaken:

(a)   First, an examination of trends in 'apparent consumption' – the sum of domestic production and imports, less exports – to establish the extent to which demand in each Member State had been supplied by indigenous production, intra-EU imports and third-country exporters. This analysis produced clear evidence that the share of imports from partner countries and third countries alike had risen substantially. Although there are inevitable differences between Member States in the composition of apparent consumption, the sharp increase in the extra-EC import share points to improving market access. A comparison with the (pre-1995) EFTA countries reinforces this view since, in spite of the switch to Community-wide restrictions on clothing, the growth of imports into the EC was higher than into EFTA from outside their respective trade zones.

(b)   Second, a detailed examination of quota utilization in the two sectors. The terms of QRs vary according to the particular commodity, the partner country and the Member State imposing the restraint, and are subject to various rules about when an allocation could be modified. By relating actual outcomes to nominal restrictions, the degree to which quotas had been binding (and, thus effective in restraining imports) can be ascertained. Setting a benchmark to judge when a quota becomes binding is, in essence, arbitrary, and although a figure of 90% was used for this purpose, the interest of the exercise lay as much in shedding light on what was happening as the SMP was implemented. The analysis revealed a mixed picture. In many market segments, quotas do not appear to have been much of a constraint on third-country exporters. Moreover, as the '1992' deadline approached, exporters seem to have taken advantage of the growing liberalization of the market to increase sales relative to quotas. Indeed, several quotas have regularly been exceeded.

(c)   The third exercise was the construction and use of partial equilibrium models for the two sectors. These were calibrated for two years, 1988 and 1994, and used to simulate either (for 1988) a change to the new regime or (for 1994) the reimposition of QRs as they existed prior to the SMP. In this way, two different perspectives on the impact of the SMP could be appraised. In the construction of the model, use was made wherever possible of secondary information on elasticities and other key parameters. Sensitivity analysis was carried out to verify that the imposition of parameter values did not distort the results. The simulations showed that where the change is to complete liberalization, market access is greatly improved, but also that EC consumers benefit substantially. The simulations of a move to a Community-wide QR in place of national QRs produced little change in market access, but a significant redistribution between Member States. Member States which previously imposed the most restrictive QRs see the greatest increase in extra-EC imports but gain from lower prices, whereas prices rise in relatively unrestricted destinations.

12.3. Conclusions and policy implications

The main conclusion of Part II of the study is that, in both sectors, access for third countries has improved as the SMP has been implemented. This suggests that in other sectors in which similar changes in the trade regime occurred as a direct result of the SMP, the effect on access for extra-EC suppliers will also have been favourable. There may, however, be indirect effects on the competitiveness of EC producers that may alter their ability to defend their market share in future.

13. Introduction

13.1. Terms of reference and approach

The terms of reference for this contract required the consultants to carry out a quantitative evaluation of the impact of the single market programme (SMP) on market access conditions for third-country suppliers. While recognizing that the impact of the SMP on third-country suppliers has been multifarious, it has been necessary to focus on the effects on third-country suppliers of the elimination of quantitative restraints applied at the Member State level. The removal of internal borders has rendered inoperable the enforcement of quantitative limits on imports from third countries which are specific to a single Member State. Thus, the provisions contained in Article 115 of the Treaty of Rome allowing countries to suspend the free circulation of products in order to prevent national quotas/voluntary export restraints from being circumvented have become unenforceable. As stated in the terms of reference, these are the effects which most readily lend themselves to quantitative measurement.

13.1.1. The research team

The principal authors of Part II of this report are Iain Begg, Nigel Grimwade and Tannis Seccombe-Hett (European Institute, South Bank University). Professor Ian Wooton of the University of Glasgow provided overall guidance and help in constructing the simulation model presented in Chapter 16. Volker Stabernak of World Systems supplied trade and production data and Dr Peter Holmes provided advice.

13.1.2. Methodology

As stipulated in the terms of reference, the methodology employed has been that of partial equilibrium analysis. That is to say, only the direct impact of the SMP changes on the sectors under consideration is measured ignoring any feedback effects from changes brought about in other sectors of the economy. The methodology used combines descriptive analysis with formal modelling. In the descriptive part, the impact of the SMP on trade flows is examined at both an aggregated and more disaggregated level. Changes in the share of imports in apparent consumption are set out and analysed for each sector. Next, quota utilization percentages are calculated for individual product groups to determine the extent to which quotas have actually been binding and the trends in these ratios are used to assess whether or not the removal of internal barriers has enabled third-country suppliers to use their EC-wide quotas more efficiently. The formal model employed is a relatively simple, partial equilibrium model which treats clothing and footwear as homogeneous goods and is used to simulate the policy changes taking place in both sectors.

The terms of reference requested a quantitative analysis of the effects of the SMP on two sectors. Following consultations with the Project Evaluation Committee, the two sectors chosen to provide a quantitative assessment of the impact of the SMP on market access for third countries were clothing and footwear. Several characteristics justify their selection. First, and most important, they have been subject to the kinds of quantitative restrictions that have to change as a result of the SMP. The sectors are two which have, in the past, been most subject to Article 115 restrictions and clothing has also been covered by successive MFA agreements. Over the period 1980–90, 1,715 requests to suspend the free circulation of goods (75% of the total) were accepted by the Commission. Of these, 1,179 related to textiles and clothing (69%

of the total). There were a further 30 cases involving leather and footwear products with electronics, vehicles and motorcycles among non-agricultural goods accounting for the remainder (GATT, 1991). The choice of the above two sectors was in part influenced by the desire to examine two sectors where different changes have occurred. In the case of clothing, national quantitative restraints have largely given way to EC-wide measures, whereas, in footwear, both national and EC-wide quotas were (with the exception of one supplier) eliminated altogether.

Second, they are sectors in which there are large numbers of suppliers, rather than an oligopolistic market structure. This makes it easier to deploy the tools of partial equilibrium analysis without having to resort to unrealistic assumptions about the nature of the products. Moreover, useful insights can be gleaned from previous studies on such matters as model specification or parameter values.

13.2. The two sectors

It is useful to set out a few basic statistics about the industries in order to place them in context. Although both sectors are generally considered to be industries in decline, they continue to provide substantial employment in the EU, especially in some of the Mediterranean Member States. According to the most recent annual enquiry into the *Structure and Activity of Industry 1989-92*, employment in clothing and footwear (together – NACE industry 45) accounted for 5.3% of total EUR-12 industrial employment in 1991 (in 1985, it was 5.5%), but only 4.6% of value-added (4.9% in 1991). Estimates in the latest *Panorama of EU Industry* (1995/6) put the 1994 share of clothing in total manufacturing employment at 4.0%, and footwear at 1.1%, illustrating that the decline in employment continues. The clothing and footwear industry as an aggregate had the lowest apparent productivity of all two-digit NACE industries in every Member State except Denmark.

Both sectors are heavily traded, and the volume of trade has comfortably outpaced production. The volume of trade rose by 79% between 1988 and 1994 in clothing and by 59% in footwear. In 1994, according to *Panorama* the industries accounted for 1.9% (clothing) and 1.0% (footwear) of extra-EC exports, and 5.2% and 1.3% of extra-EC imports. Table 13.1 shows how the value of extra-EC imports has risen from below half the total to 60% between 1988 and 1994.

Table 13.1.   EC imports of clothing

(% of total imports by value at current prices)

	1988	1989	1990	1991	1992	1993	1994
Intra-EC	50.3	49.6	49.7	47.2	47.4	40.3	39.7
Extra-EC	49.7	50.4	50.3	52.8	52.6	59.7	60.3

Source: Eurostat.

The main extra-EC suppliers of clothing (Table 13.2) in the late 1980s were Hong Kong, Turkey, Korea and China, but China has progressively increased its share such that it is now easily the biggest exporter. The decline in the shares of Korea and Hong Kong have been so substantial and seem to coincide so closely with the rise in Chinese exports that there must be a suspicion that the explanation lies in a relabelling of exports. It is also noteworthy that the shares of some other major exporters, some of which were subject to MFA restrictions, have broadly been maintained in the period observed.

Table 13.3 shows that footwear has also exhibited a steady tendency towards a higher extra-EC share, with the intra-EC share dropping from nearly two-thirds to just over a half between 1988 and 1994.

Table 13.2.   Main extra-EC exporters of clothing to the EC

(% of extra-EC imports by value at current prices, ranked by 1994 shares)

	1988	1989	1990	1991	1992	1993	1994
China	7.0	7.5	9.9	13.2	12.8	13.4	13.5
Turkey	8.2	9.5	9.9	9.1	10.2	10.0	9.6
Hong Kong	16.6	15.1	12.6	11.4	10.2	10.4	9.4
Tunisia	4.0	4.4	5.1	4.5	5.1	5.1	5.5
Morocco	4.1	4.8	5.5	4.9	5.1	5.2	5.4
Poland	2.0	2.0	2.6	3.1	4.0	4.6	5.2
India	4.0	4.6	4.8	3.8	4.0	4.4	4.9
EFTA	7.1	6.4	5.7	5.0	4.9	4.3	3.9
Indonesia	1.4	2.0	2.4	3.1	3.7	3.6	3.6
South Korea	7.6	5.9	4.0	4.0	3.0	2.3	1.8
Other	38.0	38.0	37.5	37.7	37.1	36.7	37.2

Source: Eurostat.

Table 13.3.   EU imports of footwear

(% of total imports by value at current prices)

	1988	1989	1990	1991	1992	1993	1994
Intra-EC	64.9	64.6	64.6	59.6	58.9	54.5	54.6
Extra-EC	35.1	35.4	35.4	40.4	41.1	45.5	45.4

Source: Eurostat.

Turning to individual suppliers, the market is more concentrated. Up to 1991, Korea and Taiwan were the dominant external suppliers, but have since been replaced by China (Table 13.4). As in clothing, the rise of China coinciding with the decline of its close neighbours gives grounds for suspicion about the true origin of the exports. Despite the decline, for obvious reasons unrelated to the SMP, in the share of Yugoslavia, other areas have also increased their shares markedly, such as Thailand and Romania, all of which testifies to a comparative easing of market access.

The most recent index of production figures shows that between 1989 and 1995, output of clothing has declined in all but three (Belgium, Denmark and Italy) of the Member States – see Table 13.5. In footwear and leather, the picture is broadly similar with two of these same countries (Denmark and Italy) standing out, and, to a lesser extent, Portugal. An index of specialization in clothing and footwear (Table 13.6) reveals that both industries are especially prominent in Portugal and Italy.

Table 13.4. Main extra-EC exporters of footwear to the EC

(% of extra-EC imports by value at current prices, ranked by 1994 shares)

	1988	1989	1990	1991	1992	1993	1994
China	6.1	7.2	7.8	11.6	15.9	17.9	17.3
EFTA	11.0	10.3	9.4	7.3	7.0	7.8	7.2
Thailand	3.0	4.3	6.5	7.2	7.3	7.3	7.0
India	4.5	4.4	5.5	4.7	4.4	5.3	5.9
South Korea	18.4	16.4	17.6	16.7	13.8	8.2	5.1
Brazil	8.0	8.2	6.1	5.9	5.5	5.8	4.4
Yugoslavia	8.6	9.1	8.5	6.9	2.4	4.6	4.2
Romania	1.6	1.1	1.2	1.2	1.6	2.8	4.1
Taiwan	18.9	17.4	11.1	9.5	6.0	4.0	3.1
USA	3.6	2.9	3.4	3.0	2.9	2.7	2.5
Other	16.4	18.5	22.8	25.8	33.2	33.5	39.2

Source: Eurostat.

Table 13.5. Production trends of clothing and footwear

(index 1990 = 100)

	Clothing			Leather and footwear		
	1989	1992	1995	1989	1992	1995
Belgium	90.9	108.3	114.1	102.7	82.4	41.7[1]
Denmark	100.6	104.4	107.4	94.1	116.8	130.3
Germany	102.6	84.4	58.5	102.1	83.2	59.9
Greece	87.9	99.5	75.1	126.0	89.0	83.3
Spain	98.1	84.5	82.3	103.5	89.8	76.5
France	104.5	87.7	75.6	98.4	89.1	79.4
Ireland	98.3	83.8	70.2[1]	103.6	77.5	na
Italy	101.2	98.4	109.1	99.5	94.7	112.0
Luxembourg	na	69.4	21.1	na	na	na
Netherlands	94.8	91.6	88.6	98.0	90.0	83.1[1]
Portugal	90.6	98.7	79.0[1]	96.8	97.2	99.3[1]
UK	100.2	91.7	93.9	113.9	83.2	84.6
EUR-15	na	91.7	86.6	na	90.9	93.9

[1] These figures were part estimated.
Source: Eurostat.

Table 13.6. Specialization index for clothing and footwear

(share of sector in manufacturing value added compared with EC)

	Clothing, 1993	Footwear, 1993
Belgium	1.14	na
Denmark	0.54	0.71
Germany	0.75	0.41
Greece	2.20	1.26
Spain	1.32	1.28
France	0.89	0.79
Ireland	0.59	0.10
Italy	1.82	2.89
Luxembourg	0.22	0.00
Netherlands	0.25	0.19
Portugal	4.27	7.27
United Kingdom	0.82	0.63

Source: Panorama of EU Industry 1995/96.

13.3. Structure of the report

The next chapter summarizes relevant background material, focusing on the characteristics of the trade regime and previous empirical research on market access and the SMP. The following two chapters present the results of the empirical work while a concluding chapter discusses the main findings, and draws out the policy implications. Appendices contain more detailed background material and tables of results.

14. Institutional context and previous empirical work

This chapter presents an overview of relevant background material that bears on the subsequent empirical work. This material is presented in more depth in the appendices. First, we summarize the main characteristics of the trade regime that applies to clothing and footwear, and discuss the consequences of the SMP for market access. The second part of this chapter reviews previous research into market access and the analysis of trade flows.

14.1. Summary of the main consequences of the single market for market access

The move to complete the single market has resulted in a number of changes in the conditions under which third countries have access to the EC market. In this section, we provide a summary of the relevant changes in market access conditions and assess their expected consequences for the two sectors. Appendix A to Part II provides a detailed review of the EC import regime for the two sectors, clothing and footwear, covered by this study and of the changes to the regime directly brought about by the realization of the single market.

14.1.1. Single market measures which affect trade

A thorough examination of the range of SMP measures which have had an impact on market access conditions for third-country suppliers is provided by the qualitative evaluation carried out for Part I of this study. This provides a typology of SMP changes which seeks to describe the potential effect of these changes on external suppliers. Using a system of classification employed by the European Commission, seven categories of measures are described:

(1) The removal of quantitative restraints (QRs) on imports or their replacement with Community-wide measures.
(2) The removal of physical barriers between Member States (e.g. border controls).
(3) The elimination of technical barriers through a mixture of harmonization and the application of the principle of mutual recognition.
(4) Measures to remove barriers to the provision of services, to enforce the right of establishment and ensure free movement of capital.
(5) Measures to remove barriers in the business environment (e.g. intellectual and industrial property, company law, taxation and media).
(6) Measures to eliminate discrimination in public procurement.
(7) Measures to remove barriers in regulated industries such as energy and telecommunications.

All of these measures were found potentially to affect external suppliers, in most cases in a favourable manner. In some cases, the nature of the external effect is a complex one and not straightforward. Moreover, in most cases, the precise effect is not susceptible to measurement. The only one of these changes which can in any meaningful sense be made subject to quantitative measurement is the first one. This is because QRs have effects on prices similar to those of tariffs and these effects can, with some difficulty, be measured. These changes are, therefore, those which this study has primarily focused upon. It should, however, be pointed out that quantifying the impact of these measures necessarily fails to capture the full extent of the SMP on third countries.

14.1.2. The import regime

Before discussing these effects, we begin with a simple description of the import policy regime with specific reference to clothing and footwear as it operated before the completion of the SMP. In the case of clothing, the main barriers to access impeding imports from third countries were import quotas applied at both the Community level and Member State level. Following the implementation of the tariff reductions agreed in the course of the Tokyo Round of multilateral trade negotiations (1973-79), the EC's weighted average Most Favoured Nation (MFN) tariff on clothing imports stood at 13.2%. Although this was higher than for manufactured products in general, of greater impediment were the various kinds of quantitative limits which the EC, along with other Western industrialized countries, applied to imports coming from the developing countries. Some 19 major suppliers of clothing products to the EC were subject to bilaterally negotiated quantitative limits under the Multi-Fibre Arrangement (MFA). A few other countries which were not signatories of the MFA were subject to MFA-type agreements, while suppliers from state-trading countries faced unilaterally imposed quotas (the so-called autonomous restrictions). The only countries which enjoyed quota-free access to the EC market were other advanced industrialized countries (e.g. the USA) and those countries which had signed preferential trading agreements with the EC (members of EFTA and the Mediterranean countries, although imports from the latter were closely monitored with provisions for safeguard arrangements in the event of the EC market being disrupted).

Taking textiles and clothing together for the moment, it was estimated that, in 1988, roughly one-half of all imports entered the Community under some sort of quantitative limitation (or preferential surveillance), about one-quarter were subject to the so-called 'basket exit mechanism' but not restricted (see Appendix A to Part II) and that about one-quarter of MFA products were not covered by any form of arrangement (CEC, 1993b). In all cases, EC-wide quotas were broken down into individual Member State quotas.

In the case of footwear, while being rife in the late 1970s and early 1980s, QRs were much less important by the mid-1980s, the time of the launching of the SMP. Moreover, unlike clothing products, such quotas as did exist were operated at the Member State level. Most imports from state-trading countries were subject to autonomous restrictions analogous to those applied to clothing imports. However, in 1988, the EC negotiated with Taiwan and South Korea (the two major suppliers to the EC) voluntary export restraint (VER) agreements with respect to the French and Italian markets. In July 1990, this was replaced with one of the first ever EC-wide VERs regulating imports from these two countries to the entire EC market. As with clothing, third-country suppliers also faced a relatively high MFN tariff of some 13.5% measured on a weighted average basis. Further possible barriers to market access affecting suppliers in both sectors could rise from the application of anti-dumping measures (although there were none applying at this point in time) and the application of surveillance measures which, while not restricting imports, may herald the threat of quantitative restrictions and, as such, deter exporters.

To prevent national quotas from being undermined by imports being deflected through another Member State, Article 115 of the Treaty of Rome allowed a Member State, at any time, to request authorization from the Commission to intervene temporarily at the internal frontier and to suspend such products from Community treatment. The European Commission was empowered to consider any such applications and to grant the necessary approval as well as to set time limits on the application of any such measures. The abolition of internal frontiers, however, has rendered Article 115 unenforceable. Prior to the abolition of internal frontiers on 1 January 1993, the Commission began a progressively stricter application of Article 115. In consequence, the number of protective measures under these provisions fell progressively over the five years leading up to 1992. The use of Article 115 was largely confined to a small group of products most subject to QRs. Of the 1,715 acceptances over the period 1980-90, 1,179 were accounted for by textile and clothing products and 64 by agricultural products. Other important products included electronics, vehicles, motorcycles and leather and footwear (GATT, 1991).

The fact that Article 115 could no longer be enforced once internal frontiers were dismantled necessitated either the abolition of all national controls or their replacement with Community-wide restrictions. In reality, examples of both approaches exist. In the case of textiles and clothing, the allocation of Community-wide quotas to individual Member States ended in October 1993, although there are provisions for the re-establishment of regional quotas in the event of 'excessive concentration' leading to market disturbance in individual Member States. (The new wording of Article 115 appears to give the Commission more power to prevent national measures.) Likewise, in July 1991, the various VERs/quotas which the Member States applied to imports of Japanese automobiles were replaced with a new EC-wide VER to last up until the end of 1999. In the case of footwear, as mentioned above, an EC-wide VER applying to imports from Taiwan and South Korea had already come into being. However, it was allowed to expire at the end of 1992. Indeed, footwear largely fitted the model of total liberalization as opposed to the mere replacement of national with Community-wide measures to be found in textiles and clothing and automobiles. In March 1994, the Council of Ministers announced the elimination of a further 6,700 national restrictions on a wide variety of products including footwear. Only in the case of certain products (mainly from China) were these national quotas replaced with Community-wide measures.

14.1.3. Other influences on trade

The difficulty faced in making any quantitative assessment of the effects of these SMP-related changes in the import regime is the need to isolate these effects from those caused by changes not related to the SMP which were taking place at the same time. Table 14.1 summarizes the main changes in legislation affecting market access taking place over the period from 1986 to 1995 including both SMP-related changes and those which were not the consequence of the SMP. With regard to the latter, the most important changes affecting third-country access to the EC market were the accession of new members to the EC (Spain and Portugal in 1986 and Austria, Sweden and Finland in 1995), the signing of the Europe Agreements granting preferential access to the EC market for the former Communist Central and East European countries (CEECs) and the completion of the Uruguay Round of multilateral trade negotiations. Of these, the most important changes pertain to the period after 1995. The second of the two enlargements took place on 1 January 1995, while the measures contained in the Uruguay Round Final Act (including those which provide for a phasing out of the MFA) similarly took effect from the same date. With regard to the Europe Agreements, certain of the Interim Agreements commenced in March 1992. However, the timetable for removing barriers on imports from the CEECs was more protracted for the sensitive goods sectors such as clothing and footwear.

Table 14.1.   Changes in legislation affecting market access, 1986–95

Date	Clothing	Footwear
1986 - January	Accession of Spain and Portugal to the EC (five-year transitional period)	
-September	Launching of Uruguay Round	
	Council Regulation on OPTs	
1987 - January	New Multi-Fibre Arrangement (MFA4) commences	
1988 - January	Bilateral agreement with China commences	
		EC negotiates VERs on imports with South Korea and Taiwan for the French and Italian markets
1989 - November	Liberalization of QRs under Uruguay Round 'Roll-back' provisions	
1989 - December	New Lomé Agreement signed (Lomé 4)	
1990 - January	Bilateral agreement with Soviet Union	
		Suspension of UK VER on Poland
- July		EC-wide arrangement covering footwear imports replaces French and Italian VERs on South Korea, Taiwan (valid until end of 1992); surveillance introduced
1992 - March		France imposes quotas on shoe imports from China for one year
	Interim Europe Agreements with Czech and Slovak Republics, Hungary, Poland	
1993 - January	**Single market created**	
	EEA created to replace existing free trade agreements between the EU and EFTA	
	Phasing in of Europe Agreements begins	
- May	Interim agreement with Romania	
- December	Interim agreement with Bulgaria	
1994 - February	Full Europe Agreement with Hungary, Poland takes effect	
- March	Council Regulations introduced which eliminate national restrictions; a limited number of Community quotas are introduced in their place	
- July	Free Trade agreements negotiated with Estonia, Latvia, Lithuania	
	Regional OPT quotas replaced by EC-wide quotas	
1995 - January	Accession of Austria, Finland, Sweden to the EC (Finland allowed three-year period to harmonize all external tariffs)	
	Revised GSP takes effect	
	MFA4 superseded by ATC (Uruguay Round Agreement on Textiles and Clothing)	
- February	Full Europe Agreement with CSFR, Romania takes effect	
- March	Quotas (from March 1994) revised upwards to take into account accession of new members, and to increase the levels in real terms	

14.2. Previous studies of the impact of the single market on third-country suppliers

This section gives a brief summary of the type of methodology that has been used in previous studies of the impact of the single market on third-country suppliers, and the types of assumptions this work has involved. The two questions relevant to us here are: what are the potential effects of (i) trade liberalization and (ii) completion of the single market, or quota unification. A detailed summary of the literature and the main empirical results may be found in Appendix B.

One of the most basic issues to address in modelling the effects of quantitative restrictions is that of market structure. For both the clothing and the footwear sectors, all previous empirical work has modelled the two sectors as perfectly competitive. The number of different producers and lack of significant market power by any group of firms or countries justifies this assumption. Less obvious, however, is how to address the question of product homogeneity or heterogeneity. Empirical evidence suggests something less than perfect substitutability between both suppliers and markets in both sectors. Modelling heterogeneity, however, requires assumptions about a range of elasticity parameters. Because these are not always accurate, and because heterogeneity appears to be relatively mild, it is not clear that one approach should be strictly preferred to the other. As a result, both approaches have previously been used to model the sectors in question.

A substantial amount of literature now exists on the effects of quantitative restrictions on trade. Prominent in this area are simple partial equilibrium models which quantify the effects of VERs by converting them into import tariff equivalents (MTEs). Their welfare effects may then be estimated in a manner similar to studies of tariffs. This process is theoretically straightforward. Empirically, however, it may be difficult to achieve, since the size of quota rents cannot be directly observed. Instead, it must be estimated using variables such as the prices of export licences (where such licences may be traded), the unit value of imports into restricted versus unrestricted markets, or the change in exporters' prices following the introduction of restrictions. None of these measures is ideal; however, in the sectors relevant to this study significant empirical work has been conducted to estimate these values. Estimates range from 13 to 33% for the European clothing sector and from 16 to 28% for footwear (depending on the country and the year).

Other accounts of the restrictiveness of VERs have concentrated on deriving quota-utilization ratios, and trends in variables such as the number of products or percentage of trade covered by restrictions. This approach has been especially important in studies of the MFA, and can be particularly useful in enlightening the difference in restrictiveness between European countries and the importance of trade diversion.

Empirical work applying all of these approaches to the clothing and footwear sectors demonstrates that the potential effects of trade liberalization are significant and positive for all European countries. Studies of the effects of quota unification, however, have produced differing conclusions depending on the assumptions about the existing degree of market segmentation, product heterogeneity and market structure. In sectors which may be treated as perfectly competitive, it may be demonstrated that quota unification will never harm the union as a whole, and can usually be expected to benefit it. However, the costs and benefits of this process will be unevenly distributed between Member States and between producers and consumers.

Studies of the effects of these processes on external suppliers, as opposed to the domestic markets, are not as common. However, examinations of recent trends in the clothing and footwear sectors show strong evidence of external trade creation.

15. Empirical analysis

15.1. Overview

The conceptual framework adopted in Part II of this study involves three separate yet related exercises. The first examines changes over time in the share of extra-area and intra-area imports and domestic production in apparent consumption for both clothing and footwear. (Apparent consumption is defined as domestic production plus imports minus exports). The use of shares analysis to analyse *ex post* the effects of integration on trade flows has a well-established pedigree (see Sapir, 1995, discussed above). Since the SMP has involved a progressive removal of internal barriers culminating in the abolition of internal borders on 1 January 1993, changes in these shares resulting from the SMP should be discernible at an early stage in the time series. The second exercise observes the impact of changes in the EC's import policy regime for clothing and footwear at a more disaggregated level by focusing on the extent to which quotas have been more fully used by third-country suppliers. The procedure is to calculate quota utilization ratios (the ratio of actual imports to quota constrained imports) for relatively narrow product categories and to examine trends in the average ratio for individual Member States, the Community as a whole and individual supplier countries over time. The purpose of the exercise is to determine which quotas have been binding and whether or not quotas have become more binding over time. Finally, the third part employs a more formal yet simple partial equilibrium for each of the two sectors calibrated separately for two years and then simulates various policy changes. The first counterfactual entails the replacement of individual national quotas with exactly equivalent EC-wide quotas. The second simulates the effects of quota abolition (total liberalization).

15.2. Share of imports in apparent consumption

A broad indication of the evolution of market access can be obtained by looking at trends in the sources of supply of 'apparent consumption', i.e. the demand for the goods in question. Consumers in any country can obtain goods from indigenous producers, from EU partner countries or from third countries, so that a comparison of the market shares of these three suppliers provides a measure of developments in market access.

The calculation of apparent consumption for any Member State is straightforward:

$$AC_i = (P_i - X_i) + M_{in} + M_{ix}$$

where AC_i is apparent consumption of country i, P_i is the total production of country i, X_i is exports from country i, M_{in} is intra-EC imports of country i and M_{ix} is extra-EC imports of country i. The focus of interest is in whether the respective shares of the three main sources of supply change as a result of the SMP. For the EC as a whole, internal trade counts as domestic production, so there is no M_{in} term.

15.2.1. Apparent consumption in the EC in aggregate

Aggregate figures for the EC have been presented in successive issue of *Panorama of EU Industry* and are reproduced here for clothing and footwear as Table 15.1. For clothing, the table shows that the share of extra-EC imports in apparent consumption has risen consistently since the SMP was launched in the mid-1980s. In 1984, imports only provided 7.69% of demand, but by 1993, the last year for which full data are available, the proportion had risen to 25.57%. Estimates produced by DEBA and OETH for 1994 and forecasts for subsequent years show the share of extra-EC imports continuing to rise. This has been associated with a steady deterioration in the extra-EC trade balance which went from a deficit of just over 5% of apparent consumption in 1984, to 10.2% in 1990 and up to 15.5% by 1993. The forecasts anticipate a further deterioration.

Table 15.1.   Shares of imports and domestic production in apparent consumption

(million ECU)

Clothing	1984	1988	1989	1990	1991	1992	1993	1994e	1995f	1996f	1997f
Apparent consumption	49,171	60,475	63,408	68,525	73,749	76,040	70,336	69,200	69,500	70,700	72,700
Production	49,630	55,172	57,689	61,471	63,747	66,301	59,438	57,100	56,000	55,500	55,500
Extra-EC exports	4,240	5,093	6,218	6,727	6,682	6,853	7,086	7,300	7,500	7,900	8,200
Domestic supply	45,390	50,079	51,471	54,744	57,065	59,448	52,352	49,800	48,500	47,600	47,300
Imports from extra-EC	3,781	10,396	11,937	13,781	16,684	16,592	17,984	19,400	21,000	23,100	25,400
Domestic supply, %	92.31	82.81	81.17	79.89	77.38	78.18	74.43	71.97	69.78	67.33	65.06
Imports from extra-EC, %	7.69	17.19	18.83	20.11	22.62	21.82	25.57	28.03	30.22	32.67	34.94

Footwear	1984	1988	1989	1990	1991	1992	1993	1994e	1995f	1996f	1997f
Apparent consumption	11,297	13,421	14,240	15,678	17,472	17,317	16,718	17,344	18,070	18,600	19,240
Production	13,297	13,881	15,139	16,548	16,991	17,029	16,270	17,291	18,000	18,500	19,100
Extra-EC exports	3,643	3,192	3,923	4,116	3,938	4,176	4,349	5,173	5,500	5,700	6,100
Domestic supply	9,654	10,689	11,216	12,432	13,053	12,853	11,921	12,118	12,500	12,800	13,000
Imports from extra-EC	1,643	2,732	3,024	3,246	4,419	4,464	4,797	5,226	5,570	5,800	6,240
Domestic supply, %	85.46	79.64	78.76	79.30	74.71	74.22	71.31	69.87	69.18	68.82	67.57
Imports from extra-EC, %	14.54	20.36	21.24	20.70	25.29	25.78	28.69	30.13	30.82	31.18	32.43

Note: Figures for 1994 are part estimated; figures for 1995–97 are forecasts.
Source: Panorama of EU Industry 1995/96.

In footwear, a rise in the share of extra-EC imports can be also seen, although because the initial market share for imports was higher, the growth is not so rapid. Once again, the forecasts produced by DRI suggest that the import share will continue to rise, and that this will result in a worsening of the trade balance. Between 1984 and 1993, this moved from a surplus of 17.8% of apparent consumption to a deficit of 2.6%.

In both industries, an initial growth in the share of imports occurred in the mid-1980s, and the advent of the single market seems to have coincided with a further jump in market share from 1991/92 onwards. Factors other than the completion of the single market are, however, bound to have influenced the degree to which import penetration of the EC market increased during the period 1988-94. Without constructing a fully specified trade model, the effects of other variables cannot be assessed with precision, and it is for this reason that the comparison with the EFTA countries is valuable. Among the other factors that might have been expected to play a part, the most important are the external trade regime, exchange rate movements and other systematic influences on relative prices, possible shifts in patterns of consumption, the realignment of market power, product innovation or major shifts in consumption patterns.

In practice, the nature of the markets for clothing and footwear is such that many of these factors would not be expected to have much impact. As described above, the external trade regime was fairly consistent in the period in question. For clothing, MFA4 was extended because of the delays in concluding the Uruguay Round, and there were no major changes affecting footwear other than those which flowed directly from the SMP. New arrangements negotiated as part of the Uruguay Round changes only come in to effect after the period in question.

Exchange rate movements or similar changes in relative prices are more likely to have had some effect on the share of imports. Although the underlying assumption of product homogeneity cannot be sustained (a pair of Gucci loafers is far removed from cheap Chinese imports, even though both can be described as leather shoes), both sectors are characterized by ease of market entry, a lack of dominant suppliers and, thus, a market which comes closer than most to the stylized perfect market. For this reason, producers will nearly always be price-takers, so that the main effect of exchange rate changes will manifest itself in profitability rather than price. In clothing and footwear, most third-country exporters tend to regard the dollar as the numéraire currency, so that the comparative weakness of the dollar *vis-à-vis* the ECU may partly explain the rise in import shares. However, exchange-rate-induced gains would be expected to be transitory, so that this is belied by the consistency of the rise in imports.

While fashion is fast-moving, information on fashion trends is readily available to all suppliers and the basic nature of products (cotton shirts, leather shoes, woollen garments) is stable, and producers typically adapt rapidly to new trends. For these reasons and bearing in mind the fragmented supply side of the industries, neither technological advances nor product differentiation can reasonably be put forward as a very plausible explanation for changes in import shares.

15.2.2. Apparent consumption by Member State

To take this analysis further, trends in apparent consumption were calculated for individual Member States. The source for this work was the OECD Structural Analysis (STAN) database which provides harmonized data for a range of variables, including exports and imports, using a standard industry classification. Eurostat data on intra- and extra-EC trade for the two classes of goods were used to obtain the necessary split of the import data. The STAN database has the advantage of being harmonized and consistent, but does not have complete coverage of EC countries. To overcome this, additional data for Ireland were obtained from the VISA database. VISA data or statistics from national sources were also linked to the STAN data to provide estimates for 1994. STAN does, however, have the added benefit that it covers several of the pre-1995 EFTA countries, making possible comparisons between the EUR-12 and the EFTA countries.

Tables 15.2 and 15.3 show the results of this exercise. For clothing, the table shows that the share of imports in apparent consumption has risen in nearly all the Member States between 1986 and 1994. The exceptions are Belgium where the share of imports fell after 1992, and Greece and Portugal where the proportion fell slightly after 1989. Data for these latter two countries are, however, rather erratic so that not too much significance should be attached to their figures. The results for some of the smaller Member States are generally prone to be unreliable because of the unpredictable effects of re-exporting and OPT. Import shares in excess of 100% for the Netherlands – accentuated by the fact that Rotterdam is a principal port of entry for the EC – exemplify this phenomenon.

Table 15.2.   Imports as a proportion of apparent consumption: clothing

Import share, %	1986	1987	1988	1989	1990	1991	1992	1993	1994
Belgium	73.1	76.1	73.1	72.9	74.2	79.9	80.6	72.1	66.5
Denmark	87.2	93.5	94.5	96.4	106.1	123.7	118.0	127.3	123.5
France	27.5	30.9	31.9	35.1	37.8	39.9	42.2	42.2	43.7
Germany	51.7	54.3	54.9	57.1	59.4	63.8	64.1	64.8	66.2
Greece	*	*	93.5	158.5	71.0	113.9	184.7	96.3	99.1
Ireland	106.8	106.7	108.6	112.8	113.9	132.5	139.8	138.7	143.3
Italy	15.0	15.2	17.9	16.9	17.8	21.4	23.4	30.8	33.7
Netherlands	102.5	106.1	123.3	128.5	136.9	142.7	144.5	142.2	162.7
Portugal	*	*	*	32.5	25.1	26.2	27.3	24.3	24.3
Spain	7.6	10.1	12.5	16.4	19.6	24.5	30.2	26.6	28.8
United Kingdom	33.6	36.6	37.2	39.7	43.0	46.7	47.0	49.0	50.5
EC	**40.6**	**42.9**	**43.6**	**44.8**	**47.3**	**51.1**	**52.0**	**54.3**	**56.2**
Austria	83.9	86.6	86.6	89.3	91.4	94.8	98.1	97.8	98.0
Iceland	83.0	83.1	78.9	84.7	80.2	80.5	75.3	70.5	70.1
Finland	45.8	54.0	58.6	59.7	66.3	68.5	77.2	80.3	85.2
Norway	88.4	89.2	90.8	92.3	91.8	91.9	92.2	91.9	91.9
Sweden	92.9	93.5	92.2	93.7	96.4	95.8	96.3	101.9	97.8
Switzerland	69.2	69.9	72.7	79.2	79.0	77.2	76.8	73.2	70.4
EFTA	**77.2**	**78.9**	**80.2**	**83.5**	**85.2**	**85.5**	**87.4**	**86.6**	**85.0**

Extra-EC import share, %	1986	1987	1988	1989	1990	1991	1992	1993	1994
Belgium	10.1	12.3	14.0	15.1	17.3	20.4	22.0	21.4	22.5
Denmark	44.8	50.4	51.9	52.7	60.0	80.1	74.6	82.9	81.6
France	11.8	14.8	13.8	15.7	18.0	19.8	20.6	23.1	24.3
Germany	30.1	32.8	33.1	35.2	36.3	40.0	39.6	44.5	46.0
Greece	*	*	12.1	19.1	8.9	16.8	30.0	18.1	15.6
Ireland	18.4	19.7	10.3	12.1	12.4	14.7	14.3	18.2	20.8
Italy	7.6	8.5	9.9	9.2	9.2	12.0	13.6	19.6	21.9
Netherlands	32.9	35.5	44.8	49.4	52.9	57.4	64.2	85.3	96.7
Portugal	*	*	*	3.7	2.5	2.5	2.4	2.5	2.2
Spain	2.9	4.0	3.2	4.3	5.8	8.3	11.1	8.6	8.9
United Kingdom	19.1	21.9	22.4	23.9	24.9	28.9	29.3	36.1	36.4
EC	**19.3**	**21.6**	**21.7**	**22.6**	**23.8**	**27.0**	**27.4**	**32.4**	**34.8**
Austria	81.6	84.5	84.6	87.4	89.7	93.2	96.5	96.2	96.4
Finland	40.6	48.7	53.7	55.0	61.7	64.5	72.5	76.4	81.6
Iceland	74.6	74.9	71.0	76.2	73.7	75.3	71.3	67.0	66.6
Norway	72.1	75.0	77.3	80.9	82.7	84.3	85.2	86.0	91.9
Sweden	80.1	82.3	81.5	83.7	87.8	88.8	90.6	97.1	93.2
Switzerland	64.5	65.5	68.4	74.8	74.7	73.1	73.0	70.0	67.6
EFTA	**69.5**	**72.1**	**73.8**	**77.5**	**80.0**	**81.0**	**83.2**	**83.2**	**82.0**

* These figures have been suppressed because of erratic source data.
Source: Authors' calculations from Eurostat data.

Table 15.3. Imports as a proportion of apparent consumption: footwear

Import share, %	1986	1987	1988	1989	1990	1991	1992	1993	1994
Belgium	90.8	92.7	94.6	94.6	96.0	99.2	99.9	108.9	109.9
Denmark	89.2	89.4	95.7	88.8	85.1	86.2	85.8	90.3	93.3
France	41.5	44.7	51.3	52.7	52.6	54.8	56.6	57.6	61.0
Germany	47.8	50.0	53.5	58.2	61.4	67.5	66.4	65.8	67.4
Greece	18.3	22.2	26.9	41.8	37.1	39.4	40.0	34.8	39.8
Ireland	94.0	96.0	94.4	98.3	101.1	105.2	112.3	125.6	132.7
Italy	27.7	30.2	40.4	35.7	34.3	40.2	40.5	57.5	56.0
Netherlands	101.5	103.8	110.5	114.4	120.2	124.5	137.0	156.2	173.3
Portugal	*	*	*	40.5	26.8	22.8	25.5	36.6	55.9
Spain	9.2	17.7	16.9	15.0	19.6	24.7	29.2	42.9	72.3
United Kingdom	40.3	38.8	44.3	47.5	50.6	52.3	51.9	55.7	62.8
EC	**47.3**	**49.8**	**53.4**	**54.7**	**55.9**	**59.1**	**59.3**	**64.8**	**69.5**
Austria	64.5	64.6	65.4	69.0	70.4	68.3	77.2	84.1	82.4
Iceland	87.5	91.1	98.0	92.5	88.9	90.8	95.9	95.1	95.4
Finland	51.6	55.2	54.5	63.8	64.7	63.9	68.0	72.9	71.6
Norway	91.7	91.8	93.1	94.7	95.0	95.6	96.5	96.4	96.5
Sweden	91.1	93.6	97.3	99.1	100.0	98.6	98.6	100.2	99.8
Switzerland**									
EFTA	**84.9**	**85.0**	**85.1**	**89.1**	**90.2**	**86.8**	**94.1**	**104.7**	**100.7**

Extra-EC import share, %	1986	1987	1988	1989	1990	1991	1992	1993	1994
Belgium	8.1	11.2	15.4	14.4	14.9	19.9	22.0	28.4	27.1
Denmark	31.0	34.1	37.9	33.5	31.9	34.9	29.9	30.7	32.3
France	9.6	12.1	15.4	16.6	15.9	19.6	19.8	20.8	20.8
Germany	15.5	17.0	19.6	20.6	21.3	26.0	26.0	31.3	31.4
Greece	5.7	9.4	11.8	18.2	15.6	18.7	19.5	17.8	14.5
Ireland	16.1	18.5	10.7	13.2	19.3	27.2	48.4	67.5	58.9
Italy	16.9	19.5	26.2	24.6	22.0	27.5	28.6	42.9	42.5
Netherlands	20.3	23.5	30.9	32.5	36.1	43.1	49.1	69.6	83.7
Portugal	*	*	*	4.3	3.3	3.3	4.1	9.2	16.0
Spain	3.9	8.5	9.3	7.5	10.2	15.3	18.8	19.2	39.3
United Kingdom	12.0	14.2	18.3	19.7	22.2	25.3	23.3	25.1	27.2
EC	**13.4**	**15.8**	**18.8**	**19.4**	**19.8**	**23.9**	**24.4**	**29.5**	**31.5**
Austria	62.7	63.0	64.2	67.7	69.1	67.1	75.3	82.2	80.6
Finland	45.8	49.8	50.8	59.6	60.8	60.5	64.6	70.8	69.8
Iceland	78.6	82.1	89.8	84.6	81.0	83.0	90.7	91.7	92.2
Norway	74.8	77.3	77.6	82.4	84.7	86.0	87.2	87.7	87.8
Sweden	78.5	82.4	86.6	89.9	91.5	91.0	90.4	92.8	91.8
Switzerland**									
EFTA	**76.9**	**77.3**	**77.9**	**82.9**	**84.6**	**81.8**	**88.8**	**99.6**	**96.2**

* These figures have been suppressed because of erratic source data.
** Swiss production data cannot be disaggregated in an appropriate manner for footwear.
Source: Authors' calculations from Eurostat data.

In several countries, a high proportion of imports comes from EC partners. Nevertheless, the progressive elimination of Article 115 restrictions and the move towards Community-wide QRs seems to have been associated with a steady increase in the share of extra-EC imports in apparent consumption in all Member States except Portugal. Third-country penetration of the protected Italian and French markets has increased notably, while extra-EC sales into other major markets such as Germany and the UK have continued to climb. The overall figure shown in this table for the EC differs slightly from that in Table 15.1 above because of differences in estimation procedures and coverage.

For footwear, the share of imports in apparent consumption is generally high throughout the EUR-12 Member States, although similar caveats about possible distortions of the results as a consequence of re-exports apply. As for clothing, the share has been rising in most Member States, indicating a progressively more open market.

Extra-EC import shares have risen everywhere except Denmark, in some cases, such as Italy, reaching surprisingly high levels. This bears out the evidence from the production data shown in Chapter 13 which highlighted these two countries as the exception to the rule in terms of their output trends. The steady increase in this extra-EC share therefore provides compelling evidence of a favourable impact of the SMP on market access. Although the *prima facie* evidence is that the SMP has been associated with an improvement in the market access of third countries, it could be argued that changing competitive conditions account for this improvement. A means of checking for this is to compare the EC with other, similar importers which have not been subject to the same sort of change as the SMP. For this purpose, the EFTA countries have been selected. These countries have an equivalent level of economic development and economic structures, have been subject to broadly the same macroeconomic influences in the last decade, but unlike the US and Canada with the formation of NAFTA, did not enter into a major new trading arrangement.

The aim of the comparison with EFTA is to show how the EC market shares might have evolved had the SMP changes not been introduced. In other words, the EFTA data could be used to 'normalize'. In the event, the comparison is not very illuminating because in both clothing and footwear the expansion of imports into the EC from third countries was *more* rapid than those into EFTA, in spite of the restrictions imposed on access to the EUR-12 market. Table 15.4 presents these results, revealing that the growth of extra-zone imports into the EC exceeded those into EFTA in each year from 1987 to 1994. Over the full period, the (ECU) value of extra-zone imports of clothing into the EC rose by 146%, and those of footwear by 100%. Over the same period the corresponding figures for the EFTA countries were 29% for clothing and 26% for footwear.

The clear inference to draw from these different exercises in looking at imports in apparent consumption is that access to the EUR-12 market has improved for third-country exporters of both clothing and footwear. Whether this is as a direct result of the SMP or stems from parallel changes in the trade regime cannot, strictly, be resolved purely by analysing apparent consumption. The following sections therefore widen the empirical analysis.

Table 15.4.   Growth in value of extra-zone imports of clothing and footwear

(ECU, % change in period)

	86-87	87-88	88-89	89-90	90-91	91-92	92-93	93-94	86-94
EU - Clothing	21.98	3.47	13.88	14.83	23.73	1.96	9.55	6.72	**99.57**
EFTA - Clothing	12.25	-0.33	7.13	10.09	3.90	-0.34	0.84	2.92	**26.31**
EU - Footwear	21.47	26.17	10.04	10.16	33.35	0.65	9.28	9.54	**145.70**
EFTA - Footwear	5.93	0.65	10.27	5.75	-0.25	-2.68	4.30	8.15	**28.52**

15.3. Trends in quota utilization ratios

QRs only restrict imports to the extent to which they are binding. A prerequisite for any analysis of the effects of QRs on imports of clothing and footwear, including any changes in the degree of restrictiveness, must be an examination of the extent to which quotas have actually constrained imports. The methodology employed in this part of the study has involved the calculation of quota utilization (QU) ratios for EC imports of clothing and footwear and to observe any changes in trend of average utilization ratios. (This method has been used in past studies of the effects of the MFA on clothing and textile imports by others, for example Trela and Whalley (1989) and Erzan, Goto and Holmes (1989)).

15.3.1.   Clothing

For clothing, QU ratios have been calculated for the period 1989–94 (i.e. the duration of MFA 4) for six supplier countries subject to quota restraint in respect of certain products – China, Hong Kong, India, Poland, Indonesia and South Korea – which, in 1993, accounted for, respectively, 12.5%, 11.7%, 5.1%, 4.3%, 3.4%, and 2.3%, or 39% in total of extra-EC imports (GATT, 1995). According to the GATT (1991) MFA-restrained imports account for roughly 46% of all imports of textiles and clothing products, so that the EC was marginally less protectionist than other parts of the world. QU ratios were calculated for each individual Member State and for the Community as a whole. The ratios were calculated using the quota limits for individual MFA categories published in various issues of the *Official Journal of the European Communities* and the volume of imports for these same categories using the customs statistics published by Eurostat. (A concordance was used to aggregate the trade data to fit the MFA categories.)

A key issue addressed concerns what QU ratio percentage constitutes a binding quota. The convention of other empirical work (e.g. Erzan, Goto and Holmes, 1989) has been to take a ratio of 90% or above as binding although the rationale for doing so has never been fully explained. Clearly, the higher the QU ratio, the greater the likelihood that exports will be restrained. However, even a QU ratio of 100% may not be binding if, in the absence of quotas, imports would have amounted to exactly the same amount. A further consideration concerns the flexibility provisions discussed above which may allow exporters to exceed their quota for a particular product in any given year. The Council Regulations setting out 'Common Rules for Imports of Certain Textile Products Originating in Third Countries' include precise details about flexibility provisions along with the actual quotas for different product categories. These make clear that, for all supplier countries, the maximum cumulative increase in the volume of imports for any one year over and above the Community-wide quota was 17% (12% in the case of Hong Kong and South Korea).

However, these provisions should not affect the average QR over products and over time. Advance utilization of a quota for a particular product category or carry-over of amounts not utilized in a previous year will mean that the quota will be under-used in the next or previous year leaving the average rate unchanged over several years (although years at the beginning or end of the time period could be affected). Transfers between product categories are permitted in specific cases. However, for the same reasons, these will simply mean the underuse of other product limits such that the average across product groups (but not within product groups) is unaffected. In some cases, EC regulations prescribe certain sub-limits within MFA quota categories. So, although an exporting country may have underused its quota for the MFA category, nevertheless exports are constrained at a more disaggregated level. Inter-regional transfer of quotas within the Community may affect QU ratios for individual Member States. Thus, an export supplier may exceed its quota in any one Member State if it has under-used its quota in another by less than 80%.

The percentage by which an individual Member State quota could be exceeded for supplies coming from non-dominant suppliers was progressively raised from 2% in 1987, to 4% in 1988, to 8% in 1989, to 12% in 1990 and to 16% in 1991. (However, for Hong Kong, Macao and South Korea, the figures were set at 1% in 1987, 2% in 1988, 4% in 1989, 6% in 1990 and 8% in 1991.)

In view of these flexibility provisions, it is clear that an EC-wide quota may not be truly binding below 117% (112% for Hong Kong and South Korea) and an individual Member State quota below 102% in 1987, 104% in 1988, 108% in 1989, 112% in 1990 and 116% in 1991 (101%, 102%, 104%, 106% and 108% in the case of Hong Kong, Macao and South Korea). On the other hand, if all flexibility provisions have clearly been exhausted and assuming that imports would otherwise have been greater, a QU ratio of 100% may still be binding. We have therefore chosen to stick with the tradition of previous empirical work and to define a binding QU ratio as 90% while recognizing that this may amount to a very lax definition of 'binding' in particular cases and that the movement towards '1992' meant that the QU ratio at which quotas were binding at the individual Member State level was increasing with time.

However, the opposite may also be true: a QU ratio for the Community as a whole of less than 100% could be binding if all flexibility provisions have been exhausted. If, in an important individual Member State market, an external supplier had exhausted its flexibility provisions (116% for non-dominant suppliers in 1991), then the fact that its Community-wide quota was still under 100% (say, 70%) would mean that it was quota-constrained. In other words, account should be taken of whether or not an external supplier was quota-constrained in individual Member State markets and not just at a Community-wide level.

Since, in theory, no Community-wide QU ratio can exceed 117% (112% in the case of Hong Kong and South Korea) and no individual Member State quota can exceed the limits prescribed for the inter-regional transfer of quotas set out above, it is necessary to disregard any QU ratio above these amounts. (Erzan, Goto and Holmes (1989) adopted the same procedure.) This has been done by adjusting the quota upwards to yield a QU ratio of the requisite amount. Data deficiency may be one explanation why in certain cases recorded trade significantly exceeded the maximum quota limit. A further complication arises where recorded imports include both direct and OPT imports. Of the six countries considered, Poland is the only country for which OPT trade has been important. Comparing trade statistics with import licensing figures for product groups in which Poland's imports appeared vastly to exceed quota limits confirmed that QU ratios calculated from trade statistics for these product groups gave a grossly distorted picture. This is not surprising since the figures for OPT trade show that OPT imports account for a high proportion of EC imports from Poland. According to Corado (1994), in 1992, 62% of total MFA imports from Poland were OPT imports. Over the period in question, OPT trade also appears to have been increasing. OPT quotas applied to eight out of the 18 MFA categories for which quota limits applied to Poland's trade. In four of these categories, QU ratios calculated from trade statistics were clearly excessive. In these four cases, QU ratios were recalculated using import licensing statistics drawn from the Textile Surveillance Returns for 1989–92 and SIGL data base in Brussels for 1993–94. These import licensing statistics have the attraction that they distinguish between direct and OPT imports. This means that the OPT element of trade can be excluded, thereby removing this element of inaccuracy.

Although Poland is the only country included in the QU ratio exercise which engaged in OPT trade, import licensing statistics have been used to check QU ratios for other countries where these looked suspiciously high. If the import licensing statistics showed a significantly lower volume of imports for these categories, the QU ratio was recalculated using the import licensing statistics. Finally, imports of a particular product by an individual Member State may exceed quota limit if goods destined for a particular Member State enter the Community through another Member State. Although import licences are only issued when the goods enter into free circulation, customs statistics will show the goods as entering both Member States, first as extra-EC imports and then as intra-EC imports. It follows that the QU ratio will be higher for the country through which the goods are passing and lower for the country for which they are destined. Care should therefore be taken in interpreting the QU ratios for individual Member States.

A further issue concerns the degree to which external suppliers can circumvent quotas even when they are fully utilized and flexibility provisions have been exhausted. Two ways in which external suppliers may get around binding quotas are through altering the product mix (product diversification) and re-routing products through unconstrained countries or countries where quotas have not been fully used (geographical diversification). Where quotas are binding, external suppliers may seek to upgrade the product by moving up-market into higher quality lines within quota categories. In this way, the value of exports may still be increased. In the past, Hong Kong clothing producers appear to have responded to quota constraints by seeking to increase the degree of fashion sophistication of the clothing products exported. Geographical diversification may occur through producers in quota-constrained countries investing in countries where no quotas apply or quotas are not fully utilized. Thus, in recent years, Hong Kong producers have sought to get round quota limits through substantial foreign investment in neighbouring China. A further response of producers in quota-constrained countries may be to falsify the declaration of origin of products exported. Allegations have been rife that Chinese T-shirts have been imported fraudulently under an 'origin of convenience' (Bangladesh or the Emirates). More recently, customs investigations in the United States found that imports of jogging suits made in China were falsely identified as 'made in Turkey' and Chinese-made cotton shorts and trousers were imported with counterfeit certificates of origin from Mongolia (reported *Financial Times*, 11 September 1996).

The EC divides quotas into three groups – IB, IIB and IIIB – according to their 'sensitivity' or level of import penetration. In 1986, there were 5 MFA categories in IB, 21 in IIB and 29 in IIIB, or a total of 55 MFA categories. Group IB contains the most sensitive clothing products, namely, T-shirts (category 4), pullovers (category 5), trousers (category 6), blouses (category 7) and shirts (category 8). Table 15.5 shows the proportion of quota-constrained products within each of the three groups for the six MFA supplier countries considered in this study.

Table 15.5.   Number of products in each MFA category subject to QRs

Country	Group IB	Group IIB	Group IIIB	Total
Hong Kong	5	16	4	25
China	5	17	4	26
South Korea	5	19	4	28
Poland	5	12	1	18
Indonesia	5	-	-	5
India	5	4	-	9

Thus, all six countries were subject to quota restraint for sensitive goods. By contrast, very few categories within the IIIB group were subject to quota restraint. China and South Korea were subject to quota constraint for more than half of all MFA categories, while Indonesia and India were subject to restraint for only a few of the most sensitive product categories.

For each supplier country, QU percentages were calculated for all MFA categories subject to quotas for suppliers both to the Community as a whole and to individual Member States. The detailed calculations may be found in Appendix C. For each year, a weighted average QU ratio has been calculated for each supplier country. The period covered was from 1988–94 covering the second half of MFA4. (The change in trade nomenclature in 1988 meant that it was desirable not to extend the exercise to earlier years.) However, because import licensing figures are not available for 1988 and these are needed where trade statistics are unreliable, it was decided not to include the results obtained for 1988. Table 15.6 sets out the average rates for the six supplier countries examined.

China appears to have faced the greatest degree of restriction, with an average QU ratio in excess of 90% throughout the five-year period. In 1989, it faced binding quotas (90% or more) in only three out of 12 categories. By 1994, this had risen to 10 out of 17, suggesting that the degree of restriction had increased. On average, quotas do not appear to have been binding on Hong Kong for the first four years of this period although the average rate was binding by 1993–94. In 1989, eight out of 23 MFA categories were binding. By 1992, however, only five out of 23 categories were binding. So, although the average QU rate was high by the end of the period, the number of quota-constrained categories had fallen. The average QU ratio was still lower in the case of South Korea and falling from 1991 onwards. At no stage were quotas binding on average. In 1989, only one out of 26 MFA categories were binding. By 1994, none were. This suggests that, for South Korea, the restrictiveness of quotas was diminishing over this period. In the case of India, the average QU rate was a little higher and binding for the years 1991–93. In 1989, in only one of nine restricted categories were quotas binding. By 1994, this had risen to three out of nine. There is therefore some evidence that quotas were becoming more restrictive in the case of India. In the case of Poland, the average is distorted by the decrease in the number of restricted categories over the period. However, the average ratio is noticeably much lower although rising slowly from 1990 onwards. In 1989, only two out of 13 categories were binding. By 1994, out of 10 restricted categories, none were binding. Finally, in the case of Indonesia, the average QU ratio was high, binding after 1991 and rising from 1990 onwards. In 1989, none of the four restricted categories were binding. However, by 1994, four out of the six categories were. Thus, for Indonesia, quotas appear to have exerted an increasingly restrictive effect on its exports to the EC.

Table 15.6.   Average quota utilization rates: clothing

China	1989	1990	1991	1992	1993	1994
Benelux	1.02	1.24	1.16	0.88		
D	1.39	1.14	1.16	1.23		
DK	1.20	1.01	1.06	1.11		
E	1.64	1.46	1.80	2.89		
F	0.80	1.03	0.99	0.76		
GR	0.79	0.31	0.45	0.50		
I	0.60	0.66	0.75	0.89		
IRL	0.91	0.72	0.56	0.80		
P	1.01	1.13	2.12	0.70		
UK	1.18	0.98	0.95	0.97		
EC	1.01	0.99	1.00	1.03	0.96	0.95

Hong Kong	1989	1990	1991	1992	1993	1994
Benelux	0.86	0.78	0.76	1.12		
D	0.86	0.82	0.82	0.89		
DK	0.76	0.77	0.82	0.79		
E	1.52	4.39	3.20	3.84		
F	0.95	0.78	0.78	0.91		
GR	0.70	0.76	0.66	0.60		
I	0.67	0.42	0.51	0.58		
IRL	0.93	0.73	0.53	0.67		
P	0.12	1.92	1.46	0.50		
UK	1.04	0.82	0.81	0.88		
EC	0.89	0.77	0.76	0.86	0.93	0.92

South Korea	1989	1990	1991	1992	1993	1994
Benelux	0.67	0.62	0.76	0.78		
D	0.71	0.77	0.83	0.71		
DK	0.43	0.46	0.58	0.68		
E	1.70	1.89	2.26	2.41		
F	0.74	0.89	0.96	0.60		
GR	0.58	0.52	0.40	0.37		
I	0.61	0.65	0.72	0.49		
IRL	0.83	0.85	0.84	0.62		
P	0.28	0.08	0.09	0.37		
UK	0.80	0.67	0.75	0.60		
EC	0.69	0.68	0.77	0.61	0.57	0.47

Table 15.6.   (continued)

India	1989	1990	1991	1992	1993	1994
Benelux	0.89	0.86	0.90	1.26		
D	0.98	1.13	1.19	1.16		
DK	0.80	0.93	0.96	0.91		
E	0.94	1.94	2.37	2.25		
F	0.77	0.83	0.88	0.82		
GR	0.18	0.25	0.35	0.25		
I	0.30	0.35	0.46	0.51		
IRL	0.73	0.73	0.78	0.70		
P	0.20	0.35	0.74	0.44		
UK	0.91	0.87	0.86	0.96		
EC	0.80	0.87	0.90	0.95	0.91	0.88

Poland	1989	1990	1991	1992	1993	1994
Benelux	0.58	0.46	0.50	0.71		
D	0.67	0.62	0.77	0.84		
DK	0.59	1.12	0.81	2.57		
E	0.02	0.05	0.04	0.02		
F	0.35	0.32	0.42	0.22		
GR	0.00	0.00	0.00	0.00		
I	0.28	0.23	0.38	0.29		
IRL	0.41	0.62	0.16	0.08		
P	0.00	0.00	0.00	0.35		
UK	0.86	0.50	0.34	0.21		
EC	0.39	0.36	0.44	0.45	0.44	0.50

Indonesia	1989	1990	1991	1992	1993	1994
Benelux	0.94	0.95	1.00	1.06		
D	0.92	0.97	1.07	1.04		
DK	1.00	0.85	0.64	1.03		
E	0.86	1.22	0.97	0.69		
F	1.02	0.80	0.89	1.02		
GR	0.22	0.05	0.18	0.13		
I	0.27	0.40	0.48	0.34		
IRL	1.06	0.45	1.20	0.75		
P	0.00	0.00	0.00	0.00		
UK	0.97	1.01	1.22	1.11		
EC	0.81	0.81	0.91	0.95	0.99	0.95

The picture of how binding quotas have been is, therefore, a mixed one. For some countries (Indonesia, China and perhaps India), quotas were fairly restrictive, with some evidence that they were becoming more so over the period in question. In other countries, this clearly was not so. Even where Community quotas were being used more fully, it might have been the case that this reflected the greater flexibility with which goods could be moved from Member States where quotas were underused to Member States where they were already fully used as use of Article 115 was gradually relaxed. It should be noted, however, that QU ratios for individual Member States may be subject to the distortions mentioned above and therefore of reduced value in showing whether or not this was occurring. If such a shift were occurring, one would expect to see QU ratios going up in the markets where quotas were already fully used and going down in the rest.

Changes in market conditions may, in part, offset such a tendency, but when looked at across the board, such a trend should be discernible. We therefore estimated the standard deviations for average QU ratios across Member States for each of the six supplier countries. Significantly, in all six countries, the standard deviation was higher in 1992 than in 1989. (Because regional allocations came to an end in 1993, the effects of abolishing internal borders on QU ratios for individual Member States could not be determined. However, the progressive relaxation of Article 115 in the build-up to 1993 can be expected to have increased flexibility.) This might be taken as evidence that goods were indeed being moved more freely within the EC between 1989–92. It would suggest that third-country suppliers, even if quota-constrained at the EC level, were able to overcome quota-constraint at the individual Member State level by shifting goods from underused quota markets to quota-constrained markets.

Since averages are sometimes deceptive, it is useful to focus attention on specific MFA categories. Clearly, the most interesting are the five Group IB categories as these cover the most sensitive product groups. Table 15.7 sets out the position at the beginning and end of the period for each of these categories.

Table 15.7.   QU rates and numbers of binding quotas: Group IB

MFA category	Measure of restrictiveness	1989	1992
MFA4 (T-shirts)	Average QU rate Number of binding quotas	0.80 1 out of 6	0.81 3 out of 6
MFA5 (Pullovers)	Average QU rate Number of binding quotas	0.85 2 out of 5	0.86 3 out of 6
MFA6 (Trousers)	Average QU rate Number of binding quotas	0.69 2 out of 6	0.70 2 out of 6
MFA7 (Blouses)	Average QU rate Number of binding quotas	0.87 1 out of 5	0.96 4 out of 5
MFA8 (Shirts)	Average QU rate Number of binding quotas	0.84 3 out of 6	0.73 3 out of 6

In all products except shirts, the average QU rate rose and, overall, the number of binding quotas was higher in 1994 than in 1989. This would suggest a trend towards greater restrictiveness in the case of sensitive products. On the other hand, in no case except blouses was the average QU ratio binding. Once again, however, what we need to know is whether countries have been using their Community quotas more efficiently by shifting goods from markets where quotas are underused to those where quotas are already fully used. To test for this, the standard deviation was once again calculated for each supplier country for all five product categories. In most cases (5 out of 5 in Hong Kong and India, 4 out of 5 in China, 3 out of 5 in South Korea, 2 out of 4 in Poland and Indonesia), the standard deviation of QU ratios increased when comparing 1992 with 1989. This suggests that, given the trend towards greater overall restrictiveness, most supplier countries were using the increased flexibility of the SMP to make more efficient use of their quotas in the sensitive product groups.

15.3.2. Footwear

A similar exercise was performed for footwear. As explained above, prior to the completion of the SMP imports of footwear were subject to a wide variety of QRs, some operating at a Community level, others at Member State level. The large number of quotas for different products (usually defined at the eight-digit level) applied by individual Member States and subject to alteration each year means that the calculation of a comprehensive range of QU ratios for footwear imports has not been possible. As with clothing, we have performed a selective exercise. Attention has been focused on the QRs applied to footwear imports from South Korea and Taiwan, the two largest suppliers of footwear to the EC during this period. (In 1988, Taiwan accounted for 18.9% and South Korea for 18.4% of total extra-EC imports.) Thus, the proportion of imports subject to QRs for which this exercise has been performed is about the same as for clothing, although the exercise is more straightforward because of the smaller number of supplier countries considered.

As with clothing, QU percentages were calculated using published quota limits and the official customs statistics. Since quota limits were set in pairs of shoes and customs statistics in tonnes, and since no official conversion rate was provided, a conversion rate derived from trade figures was used. For a number of years, quotas were set for 12-monthly periods commencing half way through the year. In these cases, it was necessary to make a judgement as to how best to allocate imports between the first and last six months for the purpose of calculating a QU percentage. (It was found best to allocate annual imports 60% to the first six months and 40% to the last six months.) Two separate phases in the application of VERs to imports from South Korea and Taiwan can be identified. From 1 July 1988 to 30 June 1990, a bilateral VER operated on imports of footwear to France and Italy only. From 1 July 1990 to 31 December 1992, an EC-wide VER operated on imports to the Community as a whole with no regional allocation.

Table 15.8 sets out the QU ratios for each supplier country for the period 1988 to 1992. Under the bilateral VER applied by France and Italy, the QU ratio fell over the duration of the agreement. Although it appeared to be binding over the first six months of the agreement, this was clearly not the case by the time the agreement had reached its end. In the case of the EC-wide VER which came into play in July 1990, the agreement appears to have been non-binding in the case of imports from Taiwan. However, in the case of South Korea, the ratio has been well in excess of 100%. Moreover, if the data are reliable, it would appear that South Korea failed to restrict exports to the specified limits. (Being a VER, the responsibility for restraining the volume of trade resides with the exporting country. Although the agreement was accompanied by measures for prior import surveillance, this does not imply any actual import restriction.) In other words, the agreement was unsuccessful in achieving the planned levels of quantitative restraint.

Table 15.8.   Quota utilization rates: footwear

Exporting country	Restricting Member State	1988	1989	1990***	1991	1992
South Korea	France	109*	60	48		
	Italy	112**	75	72		
	EC			120	166	127
Taiwan	France	67	70	32		
	Italy	107**	44	33		
	EC			56	68	43

*	In operation from July 1988.
**	In operation from February 1988.
***	National quotas replaced by Community-wide quotas in July 1990.

Clearly, the replacement of a bilateral quota which applied to imports to only two Member States with a Community-wide quota which restricted imports to all Member States could be expected to alter import shares. Specifically, imports to the previously restricted markets (France and Italy) might be expected to expand relative to the unrestricted ones. Table 15.9 shows the share of the restricted markets relative to the non-restricted markets in total imports from the two countries.

Table 15.9.   Share of imports to restricting Member States: footwear

VER Agreement		1988–90	1991–93
South Korea	France	19.82	15.94
	Italy	18.12	20.69
Taiwan	France	12.27	10.59
	Italy	8.39	6.91

In the case of imports from Taiwan, the share of both France and Italy in EC imports from Taiwan fell during the time of the EC-wide agreement when compared with the time of the bilateral agreement. In the case of imports from South Korea, France's share fell while that of Italy rose. Of course, changes in the share of individual Member States in EC markets may reflect a wide variety of influences (changes in the level of economic activity, changes in the pattern of tastes, etc.). However, it is perhaps not surprising that the expected shift towards previously restricted markets did not occur as the evidence suggests that the bilateral VERs were non-binding.

15.3.3.   Conclusions on quota utilization

The analysis in this chapter of the report has made possible an assessment of how binding quotas have been in the period immediately prior to the abolition of internal borders and to determine the extent to which the progressive relaxation of Article 115 has brought about more efficient use of Community quotas by third-country suppliers. Of the six clothing exporters considered, quotas appear to have been binding on average in three countries and the degree of restrictiveness also increased in these cases. In the case of sensitive products, although quotas were on average not generally binding, the number of binding quotas appears to have been increasing and the degree of restrictiveness has increased. There is, however, some evidence that the progressive relaxation of Article 115 has given exporters greater flexibility which they have used to shift products from markets where quotas were underused to those where quotas were more fully used. In the case of footwear, the bilateral VER applied to imports to Italy and France from Taiwan and South Korea appears to have been non-binding. The EC-wide quota applied after 1990 was also relatively ineffective as imports from South Korea consistently exceeded its quota.

16.   A formal model and policy simulations

In this chapter, we construct a simple partial equilibrium model for each of the two sectors and use it to simulate the policy changes relevant to each. The aim of the models is to provide a tool for assessing how the changes brought about by the SMP will affect exports from third countries. The model comprises systems of equations in which supply and demand are balanced for a base year using various simplifying assumptions about prices and the impact of QRs. This process of calibration can be done for any year for which the requisite data are available, although it follows that the relationships so described will reflect the circumstances of that base year. Clearly, if the base year is more remote from the year for which any simulation is to be done, the underlying structure it describes will be less likely to mirror reality, and it is for this reason that the model was calibrated for two years, 1988 and 1994. By departing from this 'base' case, the model can be used to simulate the effects of changes. This is achieved by varying relevant parameters or imposing restrictions.

The next part of this chapter sets out the formal system of equations in the model and describes some of its properties. We then explain how the model was calibrated for the two years. Section 16.3 describes how the simulations were carried out and presents an overview of the findings for the EC. The results of the simulations for individual Member States are then presented, followed by some sensitivity analysis. Concluding remarks complete the chapter.

16.1. The model

The model treats the product of each sector as homogeneous, that is to say it assumes perfect substitutability between domestically-produced and foreign-produced goods. This assumption greatly simplifies calibration of the model and is common in studies of this kind. Although perfect substitutability is a somewhat restrictive assumption, clothing and footwear are two sectors where it is not too unrealistic.

While we treat each good as homogeneous, we distinguish between the various national markets in order to capture the effects of alterations in national restrictions. Although certain Member States have been more active in the use of Article 115 restrictions (see Table A.3 in the appendix), no distinction has been made between restricting and non-restricting Member States. The reasons for this are as follows. In the case of clothing, all Member States were subject to regional allocations. The highly disaggregated analysis of Chapter 15 combined with the problems involved in interpreting quota utilization ratios for individual Member States discussed in Section 15.3.1 meant that it was impossible to say whether or not quotas in aggregate had or had not been binding in different Member States. Furthermore, as Table A.4 illustrates, most Member States appear to have made some use of Article 115 (only Greece and Portugal made no use). In the case of footwear, there is again a complex problem in distinguishing restricting from non-restricting Member States. As is explained in Section 15.3.2, for the period from July 1988 to June 1990, VERs applied to imports from South Korea and Taiwan were restricted only in the French and Italian markets. However, from July 1990 to December 1992, imports to all Member States from these countries were, in theory, quota constrained. The picture is further complicated by the fact that most Member States applied quotas on imports from state trading countries.

Over the period 1980-90, there were 16 Article 115 acceptances covering trade in leather and footwear products for France, five for Ireland, four for Italy, four for Spain and one for the UK

(GATT, 1991). On this basis, a distinction might have been drawn between these countries and the rest in the case of footwear. However, the failure to use Article 115 need not imply unrestricted trade. For these reasons, it was considered more appropriate to treat all the Member States as restricting imports in both sectors.

Trade is broken up into three country groupings: E, extra-EC exporters subject to restrictions; F, extra-EC exporters free of restrictions; and D, domestic (European) suppliers. For each Member State i we construct the following set of equations:

Supply:

$$(1) \quad S_{id} \quad = \quad a_{id} \quad + \quad b_{id}P_{id}$$

$$(2) \quad S_{iE} \quad = \quad a_{iE} \quad + \quad b_{iE}P_{iE}$$

$$(3) \quad S_{iF} \quad = \quad a_{iF} \quad + \quad b_{iF}P_{iF}$$

where S_{id} is domestic supply to the ith Member State, S_{iE} is the export supply from quota-constrained countries to the ith Member State and S_{iF} is export supply from unconstrained countries to the ith Member State.

P_{id}, P_{iE} and P_{iF} are the respective supply prices and b_{id}, b_{iE} and b_{iF} are slope parameters derived using the respective supply elasticities. The elasticity of supply is the rate of change of supply with respect to price and can, therefore, be used to derive the b_i parameters. Thus, if Es is the elasticity of supply, then

$$Es_i = b_i.P_i/S_i$$

Demand:

$$(4) \quad D_i \quad = \quad c_i \quad + \quad d_i P_i$$

where d_i is derived from the price elasticity of demand in a similar manner to that described above for supply. If Ed is the elasticity of demand, then

$$Ed_i = d_i.P_i/D_i$$

Equilibrium condition:

$$(5) \quad D_i \quad = \quad S_{id} \quad + \quad S_{iE} \quad + \quad S_{iF}$$

Prices:

$$(6) \quad P_{id} \quad = \quad (1+t) P_{iF}$$

$$(7) \quad P_{iF} \quad = \quad (1+q_i) P_{iE}$$

where t is the Common External Tariff (CET), and q_i is the import-tariff equivalent of the quota applied by the ith Member State to imports from constrained countries. Thus, while all exporters from the rest of the world sell their goods at the same price in the EC market, namely P_{iF} (the domestic price, P_{id}, less the CET), the price received by the quota-constrained countries contains an element of quota premium given by q_i. Thus, the price at which they would have been prepared to supply the EC market was P_{iE}. By contrast, unconstrained suppliers receive no quota rents, since the price at which they are prepared to supply the quantity in question is P_{iF} which is higher than P_{iE}. The logic behind this is illustrated by Figure B.1 in the appendix. (*Note*: P_{iE} and P_{iF} here correspond to OP_0 in the figure if a zero rate of CET is assumed.)

16.2. Model calibration

Having established the logical structure of the model, the next stage is to assemble data for a base year in order to 'calibrate' so that it can then be used to simulate the effects of a major institutional change such as the SMP. Two different approaches can be adopted. The first is to calibrate the model for an early year as close as possible to the launching of the SMP, thereby capturing the world as it was, and to project forwards the policy changes under consideration. To this end, the model was first calibrated for 1988. However, the drawback of this approach is that it 'freezes' the levels of trade, output, consumption and prices at that time. No account is therefore taken of actual changes in these variables, whether as a direct result of the dynamic consequences of the SMP or consequent upon other influences on markets. The alternative approach is to calibrate the model for as late a year as possible and to run the policy simulations backwards. To resolve this, the model was calibrated to replicate the equilibrium of two separate years – 1988 (to capture the period before the SMP took effect) and 1994 (by which time most of the changes wrought by the SMP were in place). Counterfactual exercises were then performed to simulate the effects of different policy changes.

Eurostat trade statistics were used to obtain the volume of imports from constrained (S_{iE}) and unconstrained countries (S_{iF}) and the unit values of these imports were taken as proxies for the export supply prices (P_{iE} and P_{iF}). Demand in an individual Member State (D_i) was taken to be apparent consumption and was derived from data on domestic production less total exports plus total imports (intra- and extra-EC). Again, this was based on Eurostat data.

Values for the different elasticities needed to calibrate the model were drawn from previous empirical work. To our knowledge, estimates of the elasticity of demand for clothing for the EC as a whole do not exist. However, Deaton (1975) estimated the elasticity of demand for clothing for the UK economy at -1.086 and this was the value used by Greenaway (1985) in his study of the effects of VERs on clothing imports for the UK. This seems the best estimated value to use as other studies either combine clothing with textiles or footwear as a single sector (e.g. Batchelor and Minford, 1977) or relate to the United States (e.g. Houthakker, 1965). For footwear, Deaton (1975) estimated elasticity of demand for the UK economy at -0.25. Winters and Brenton (1991), in a more recent study of the effects of quotas applied to UK footwear imports, derived a value of -0.75. We have chosen to use the estimate in the more recent work of Winters and Brenton. It would seem reasonable to assume that the elasticities for other Member States are not vastly different.

As is well known, supply elasticities are more problematic. The absence of any actual estimates means that most empirical work has had to make assumptions about the value. Thus, Greenaway and Hindley (1985) assumed values of domestic supply elasticity of 1 and 2 for both footwear and clothing. For clothing, Erzan, Goto and Holmes (1989) assumed an elasticity of 1.5 for domestic suppliers and 2.0 for both constrained and unconstrained developing-country suppliers. Winters (1992) uses elasticities of supply of aggregate EC sales ranging from 2 to 5 for domestic suppliers and 2 to 10 for external suppliers, although he regards the lower end of the range as most plausible. Here, the approach adopted by Erzan, Goto and Holmes (1989) is followed, and we assume an elasticity of 1.5 for domestic supply and 2.0 for external supply. (A large importer such as the EU will face an upward sloping world supply curve, but world supply to the EU will be more elastic than domestic supply.) To assess the robustness of the results with respect to changes in the values of the elasticity parameters, sensitivity analysis has been used in both sectors (see Section 16.5, below.)

A key variable in the model is the quota premium, since this reflects the degree of protection that is in place. The concept is, however, an abstract notion, rather than something that is easily measured, and must therefore be inferred. For clothing, the value of the quota premiums were taken from Hamilton (1990b). Hamilton used the market prices for import quotas traded in Hong Kong for clothing imports to derive the import-tariff equivalent (MTE) of the EC's quota restrictions on clothing imports for the period 1980-89. The MTE is given by the quota price divided by the unit value of imports expressed as a percentage. Hamilton calculated the MTE for four Member States, namely, West Germany, France, the UK and Denmark, at 13, 12, 15 and 8% respectively for the year 1988 (see Appendix B, Table B.1). For the other Member States for which similarly calculated MTEs are not available, the difference between the unit value of their imports of clothing from Hong Kong and those of the Member State with the lowest MTE, Denmark, was used to infer an MTE – Denmark also had the lowest unit value of imports from Hong Kong.

One might expect the Member States which were the most prolific users of Article 115 to have the highest quota premiums. This, however, was not always the case. France and Ireland have been the most active users of Article 115 in respect of clothing, but both had relatively low MTEs. However, unit values of imports may reflect quality differences between countries as well as the extent to which imports from third countries are restricted. Moreover, as Hamilton (1990b) has demonstrated and is discussed in Appendix B of Part II, different MTEs may arise where the EC market is still fragmented by the existence of partner, as opposed to third-country, NTBs.

For footwear, it was not possible to determine MTEs in the same way as for clothing from observation of quota prices. Instead, we used estimates of the MTE for footwear imports to the UK as a guide and compared the unit value of UK imports with those of other Member States to obtain an individual quota premium for each Member State. Greenaway (1986) estimated the quota rent for UK imports of footwear from Taiwan in 1982 at 13%. In a later study, Winters and Brenton (1991) estimated that the 'price wedge' for UK imports of footwear from three countries (Poland, Taiwan and Korea) ranged from 16-28% over the period 1978–84. Since the figure for imports from Korea was significantly higher than for imports from Taiwan and seems generally higher for imports from state trading countries, it would seem appropriate to regard Greenaway's estimate as a minimum. We have therefore set the average MTE of QRs for the EC at 15%. Using the difference between the unit value of UK imports from Taiwan and those for other Member States, individual MTEs were obtained. This makes the assumption that the different Member States import broadly the same mix of footwear products, that there are only minimal differences in quality and that transport costs are broadly the same. None of these assumptions are wholly valid. However, it seems likely that whatever differences do exist, these are of not too great a magnitude. Moreover, in the case of footwear, Member State differences in the value of the MTE of quotas are less important than the value of the average EC MTE, because the policy simulation involves the removal of all QRs not quota unification as for clothing.

16.3. Simulations for the EU as a whole

From the perspective of third countries, the critical question is how the SMP affects access to the EC market as a whole. Individual exporters (companies as well as countries) will, no doubt, have stronger contacts with some Member States than with others, and might consequently be concerned about how particular national markets will change. But in order to test the impact of the SMP in aggregate, we start by presenting findings for the EUR-12 as a whole for the two sectors. As noted above, the simulations based on the 1988 calibration 'work forwards' by modelling the effect of introducing the SMP; those derived from the 1994 calibration 'work backwards' by reimposing the restrictions that applied prior to the SMP. In this way, two perspectives on the changes are obtained. The counterfactual exercises consisted of removing or reintroducing quotas, or of moving from/to national to/from Community-wide quotas. The former is of greater interest for the footwear sector, while the latter is of more relevance for clothing. Together, these counterfactuals may be viewed as the two extreme cases. Any reduction in restrictions to trade, or indeed increases in quota utilization ratios which result from market integration, will result in changed conditions of market access somewhere between the two.

16.3.1. Policy simulation results: clothing

The essence of the changes brought in for clothing by the SMP is that separate national quotas are replaced by a single Community-wide quota. The effective removal of Article 115 restrictions means that third-country suppliers are able to shift supplies between Member States so as to equalize the quota rent per unit of imports in all 11 markets. This forms the basis of the first simulation exercise in which it is assumed that the effect of the SMP is that national quotas are replaced with a Community-wide quota exactly equal to their sum. To model this, therefore, all Member States are assumed to have the same quota premium, so that the MTE is equalized in all markets, while the total volume of imports is held constant. A second simulation for clothing sought to approximate the effects of complete elimination of quotas, i.e. full liberalization. This was simulated by assuming that the quota premium disappears, so that there is no longer an MTE. Under this scenario, there are no longer any constrained suppliers to the EC market. Summary results of both simulations for the 1988 calibration are shown in Table 16.1. The detailed workings of the model are included as Appendix D.

The results of the SMP simulation are as one would expect: imports from constrained countries are redistributed within the Community from the less restrictive Member States to the more restrictive ones. At the same time producers in previously more protected markets lose while those in previously more open markets gain. Concurrently, some degree of price convergence takes place, with prices rising in the less restrictive countries and falling in the others. The EC as a whole benefits from this process, although the gains and losses are unevenly distributed both between Member States, and between consumers and producers. Additionally, constrained exporters gain by being able to sell to their preferred markets rather than being constrained by differing national quotas. This freedom to sell at the margin within the Community enables them to equalize their 'quota rents' (i.e. to make the optimal returns), thereby increasing their producer surplus.

The results presented here must, however, be interpreted as a lower bound on the benefits of the SMP. This is because the simulation does not allow for the process of integration to affect quota utilization ratios of constrained countries. As demonstrated in Chapter 15 of this report, there is evidence that the reduction of internal barriers to trade has benefited certain countries by allowing them to transfer unused portions of quotas in some Member States into other, more restrictive states. Quota utilization ratios for the Community as a whole could, therefore, be expected to rise. Although we found evidence of this in half of the restricted countries that we examined, we do not have any estimates for the magnitude of this effect for restricted countries as a whole. To the extent that this process occurs, the market share of imports from these countries can be expected to rise, reinforcing the welfare effects.

Table 16.1.   Policy simulation results: clothing, 1988

		Original calibration	Policy simulation 1 (completion of the single market)	Policy simulation 2 (complete liberalization of trade)
	(1,000 tonnes)			
Imports from constrained countries		501	501	603
Imports from unconstrained countries		316	316	303
Domestic supply to European market		1,702	1,702	1,661
Total demand		2,519	2,519	2,568
Changes in:	*(million ECU)*			
Total consumer surplus			23	1,010
Domestic producer surplus			-2	-590
Net change in welfare	*(million ECU)*		21	420

Evidently, the magnitude of benefits arising from liberalization of trade is much greater. According to our policy simulations, exports from constrained countries would rise by 20%, while domestic supply and imports from unconstrained countries fall. Interestingly, imports from unconstrained countries fall by relatively more than domestic supply. However, the orders of magnitude are small: 4% and 2% respectively.

Calibrating the model for 1994 and running the policy simulations backwards gives changes of much the same relative magnitude. In this case, the counterfactual assumed that the 1988 differences in Member State MTEs were restored, giving the same average MTE rate but with individual differences. The results presented in Table 16.2 show that reverting to national QRs instead of the Community-wide regime would only have a marginal impact on the welfare variables. Full liberalization of trade would, however, result in quite substantial gains in exports for constrained countries.

Table 16.2.   Policy simulation results: clothing, 1994

		Original calibration	Policy simulation 1 (reintroduction of national quotas)	Policy simulation 2 (complete liberalization of trade)
	(1,000 tonnes)			
Imports from constrained countries		1,057	1,057	1,255
Imports from unconstrained countries		546	546	515
Domestic supply to European market		2,081	2,081	2,016
Total demand		3,684	3,684	3,785
Changes in:	*(million ECU)*			
Total consumer surplus			-77	2,020
Domestic producer surplus			1	-901
Net change in welfare	*(million ECU)*		-76	1,120

16.3.2. Policy simulation results: footwear

For footwear, the model calibrated for 1988 is used to simulate the effects of complete quota liberalization. In fact, quotas have not been entirely removed: certain imports of footwear from China are still subject to quota restraint. However, compared to the position prevailing in 1988, there has been a significant movement towards complete quota liberalization. The results of the 1988 calibration and counterfactuals are presented in Table 16.3.

Table 16.3.   Policy simulation results: footwear, 1988

		Original calibration	Policy simulation (complete liberalization of trade)
	(1,000 tonnes)		
Imports from constrained countries		164	205
Imports from unconstrained countries		100	96
Domestic supply to European market		737	715
Total demand		1,000	1,016
Changes in:	*(million ECU)*		
Total consumer surplus			253
Domestic producer surplus			-200
Net change in welfare	*(million ECU)*		54

In this case, the combination of import liberalization and completion of the single market have a much greater impact. Prices fall in all Member States (by an unweighted average of 2.4%), while the volume of imports to the Community rises by 25%. Again, the Community as a whole benefits as a result, although European producers of footwear lose out. Exports from unconstrained countries fall by almost 10%, while European production falls by 3%. Again, there is a redistribution of supply between Member States. However, as discussed in Section 16.1, it is of less significance in this case since data on national MTEs are less accurate. These effects are in any case small relative to the overall changes.

As for clothing, in the 1994 simulation we reintroduced the MTE rates prevailing in 1988. In this case, the group of constrained supplier countries has changed, so the results are not directly comparable. Between 1988 and 1994, restrictions were lifted on all previously restricted countries, but were introduced for China. Therefore, in the 1994 calibration, China is the only restricted country, with the previously constrained countries now falling in the 'unconstrained' category. This means that reintroducing the 1988 MTEs is not the 'mirror image' of the forward simulation from the 1988 calibration. To facilitate comparison, the share of these countries' imports is also calculated.

The reintroduction of restrictions on previously constrained suppliers would benefit both Chinese and European suppliers, while exports from the countries which were subject to restraints in 1988 fall by 23% (Table 16.4). This restoration of pre-SMP quota restrictions would, therefore, have a much smaller impact than the liberalization simulation based on the 1988 calibration. This reflects the fact that although, unlike clothing, aggregate imports into the EC footwear market did not change greatly between 1988 and 1994, there were significant shifts between partner countries, with China, especially, coming to the fore (see Chapter 13 of the report).

Table 16.4.   Policy simulation results: footwear, 1994

	Original calibration	Policy simulation (reintroduction of national quotas)
(1,000 tonnes)		
Imports from constrained countries	143	146
Imports from unconstrained countries	355	329
	of which, previously constrained producers form 63%	of which, previously constrained producers form 47%
Domestic supply to European market	713	726
Total demand	1,211	1,200
Changes in:) *(million ECU)*		
Total consumer surplus		-200
Domestic producer surplus		+130
Net change in welfare *(million ECU)*		-70

16.4. Effects on Member States

The simulations for a shift from national to Community-wide QRs leave the aggregate level of EC imports from third countries unchanged, but result in a redistribution between Member States. It should be noted, however, that these simulations assume that quotas are fully utilized, so that if the switch to a Community-wide restriction alters the degree to which quotas are taken up, there would be a separate effect on total imports. Full liberalization, predictably, increases the level of imports from previously restricted countries in all Member States.

16.4.1. Clothing

The Member States differ in the degree to which they imposed protection through quotas on clothing imports. This is captured in the values for MTEs, with above average levels in the UK and Spain, but below average for Denmark, the Netherlands and Belgium/Luxembourg.

Table 16.5. Effects of move from national to Community-wide QRs for clothing

(% change from 1988 calibration of the model)

	Restricted imports	Unrestricted imports	Domestic production	Domestic demand	Domestic price
France	-1.18	0.08	0.06	-0.05	0.04
Belgium/Lux.	-6.20	0.40	0.30	-0.22	0.20
Netherlands	-4.82	1.83	1.38	-1.00	0.92
Germany	0.41	-0.09	-0.07	0.05	-0.05
Italy	0.46	-0.05	-0.04	0.03	-0.02
UK	3.19	-0.85	-0.64	0.46	-0.43
Ireland	-6.03	0.58	0.44	-0.32	0.29
Denmark	-5.55	2.94	2.21	-1.60	1.47
Greece	2.13	-0.15	-0.11	0.08	-0.08
Portugal	-4.61	0.21	0.16	-0.11	0.10
Spain	2.23	-0.05	-0.04	0.03	-0.03

Table 16.5 summarizes the consequences of moving from separate national QRs to a Community-wide QR, based on the 1988 calibration. Imports from exporting countries subject to restrictions would fall most in Belgium, Ireland, the Netherlands and Denmark, to be redistributed principally to the UK and Spain. The effects on domestic production would be minimal, although some redistribution of supply between national markets would occur, the largest loss of market share taking place in the UK, with gains occurring in the Danish and Dutch markets. On the whole, the effects on unrestricted exporters would also be small, with loss of market in the UK, and gains principally in the Netherlands and Denmark. Price changes would also be small.

Table 16.6. Effects of reverting from a Community-wide QR to pre-SMP national QRs for clothing

(% change from 1994 calibration of the model)

	Restricted imports	Unrestricted imports	Domestic production	Domestic demand	Domestic price
France	1.57	-0.22	-0.16	0.12	-0.11
Belgium/Lux.	6.44	-0.87	-0.65	0.47	-0.43
Netherlands	3.93	-3.29	-2.47	1.79	-1.65
Germany	0.00	0.00	0.00	0.00	0.00
Italy	0.00	0.00	0.00	0.00	0.00
UK	-2.58	0.91	0.69	-0.50	0.46
Ireland	6.31	-0.99	-0.74	0.54	-0.50
Denmark	4.36	-4.68	-3.51	2.54	-2.34
Greece	-1.54	0.22	0.16	-0.12	0.11
Portugal	5.37	-0.08	-0.06	0.05	-0.04
Spain	-1.66	0.09	0.07	-0.05	0.05

Table 16.6 shows the consequences of reverting to national restrictions on clothing imports, based on the 1994 calibration of the model. This means that the 1988 MTEs are restored, but the changes from the base calibration shown in the table reflect the magnitudes of key variables as they were in 1994, rather than 1988. Clothing imports, overall, grew substantially between 1988 and 1994, albeit at different rates for different Member States. For this reason, the size of the changes is not a mirror image of those shown in Table 16.5.

If full liberalization of clothing imports were to occur, previously restricted exporters to the EC market would gain significantly. Table 16.7 summarizes the effect of such a change which would result in price falls and demand increases to varying degrees in all Member States. Sales by restricted exporters would rise by up to a quarter, offset by more modest reductions in both domestic production and sales by unrestricted exporters.

Table 16.7.   Full liberalization of clothing imports

(% change from 1994 calibration of the model)

	Restricted imports	Unrestricted imports	Domestic production	Domestic demand	Domestic price
France	22.49	-3.11	-2.33	1.69	-1.55
Belgium/Lux.	22.57	-3.04	-2.28	1.65	-1.52
Netherlands	13.35	-11.20	-8.40	6.08	-5.60
Germany	18.40	-6.73	-5.05	3.65	-3.36
Italy	21.34	-4.13	-3.10	2.24	-2.06
UK	18.57	-6.58	-4.93	3.57	-3.29
Ireland	22.08	-3.47	-2.60	1.88	-1.73
Denmark	11.75	-12.61	-9.46	6.85	-6.30
Greece	22.43	-3.16	-2.37	1.72	-1.58
Portugal	25.54	-0.40	-0.30	0.22	-0.20
Spain	24.47	-1.36	-1.02	0.74	-0.68

16.4.2. Footwear

Because the footwear MTEs are assumed to be uniform in the model, the variations between Member States are lesser than were found for clothing. Such variations as there are are attributable, instead, to differing structures of supply. As Table 16.8 shows, the elimination of barriers, based on the 1988 calibration, results in substantial increases in market access for restricted countries to all EC Member States. These are offset by smaller reductions in the sales of domestic producers and previously unconstrained exporters to the EC. Consumers gain from price reductions averaging just under 2.0%

In the 1994 calibration for footwear, China is the only country with restricted exports. By reintroducing quota restrictions for other exporters, China benefits, which is the reason that most Member States actually increase their imports from restricted countries in this simulation. EU producers also gain, as can be seen in Table 16.9. By contrast, those exporters which, in 1994, were part of the unconstrained group lose as a result of MTEs being reintroduced.

Table 16.8.   Liberalization of footwear imports

(% change from 1988 calibration of the model)

	Restricted imports	Unrestricted imports	Domestic production	Domestic demand	Domestic price
France	24.40	-4.48	-3.36	1.68	-2.24
Belgium/Lux.	27.79	-5.09	-3.82	1.91	-2.54
Netherlands	23.23	-5.35	-4.01	2.01	-2.67
Germany	27.57	-4.09	-3.07	1.53	-2.04
Italy	19.99	-5.78	-4.34	2.17	-2.89
UK	26.37	-3.16	-2.37	1.18	-1.58
Ireland	30.82	-1.31	-0.98	0.49	-0.65
Denmark	25.13	-5.30	-3.98	1.99	-2.65
Greece	24.18	-3.19	-2.40	1.20	-1.60
Portugal	27.18	-1.68	-1.26	0.63	-0.84
Spain	31.31	-2.03	-1.52	0.76	-1.02

Table 16.9.   Reimposition of quotas for footwear

(% change from 1994 calibration of the model)

	Restricted imports	Unrestricted imports	Domestic production	Domestic demand	Domestic price
France	1.80	-7.16	1.05	-0.53	0.70
Belgium/Lux.	-1.17	-6.52	1.55	-0.77	1.03
Netherlands	4.06	-7.05	2.62	-1.31	1.75
Germany	0.86	-9.84	2.16	-1.08	1.44
Italy	7.42	-7.99	3.22	-1.61	2.15
UK	1.74	-4.38	1.30	-0.65	0.87
Ireland	0.68	-9.82	2.04	-1.02	1.36
Denmark	0.51	-6.14	1.21	-0.60	0.80
Greece	2.33	-5.50	0.31	-0.15	0.20
Portugal	1.20	-3.19	0.31	-0.15	0.21
Spain	-1.09	-7.09	1.57	-0.78	1.05

16.5. Sensitivity analysis

Because estimation of supply and demand elasticities would have been well beyond the scope of the present study, the values for these parameters estimated in previous similar work were used. This could, conceivably, have biased the results. To test for such a bias, sensitivity analysis was carried out to explore the effects of using alternative parameter values. This exercise substituted values of -0.5 (instead of -1.075 for clothing and -0.75 for footwear) for the demand elasticity and of 1 and 0.75 for the supply elasticities (instead of 2.0), and the effects on the change in key variables was then scrutinized. Table 16.10 summarizes these results for clothing, showing the percentage difference in the change from the base calibration of the model.

The base case here is our original calibration of the model. The elasticities used are 1.5 for domestic supply and 2 for foreign supply. The elasticity of domestic demand is assumed to be -1.086 in the case of clothing, and -0.75 in the case of footwear. Case A estimates the effects of changing the supply elasticities to 1 and 0.75 for foreign and domestic suppliers respectively, while leaving the demand elasticity unchanged. Case B is a change in the demand elasticity to a lower level of -0.5, but with the supply elasticities as in the original calibrations.

Here we present the change in imports from constrained supplier countries, as this is the key variable of interest.

These experiments indicate that the results are not, in fact, especially sensitive to the choices of demand elasticities, but that the gains for third-country exporters will tend to be lower, although of the same sign, if supply elasticities are low. Thus, for the direction of change, the findings can be accepted with confidence, but the magnitudes will depend on the supply elasticities. This does not rule out the possibility that implausibly different elasticities would result in bigger differences, but it also has to be borne in mind that the elasticities used are consistent with past research, and this, too, supports the plausibility of the simulation results.

Table 16.10. Sensitivity analysis: clothing, 1988

Imports from constrained countries							
	Policy simulation 1 (quota harmonization)				Policy simulation 2 (complete liberalization of trade)		
Importing country	base case*	case a**	case b***		base case	case a	case b
	(tonnes)	(percentage change from base case)			(tonnes)	(percentage change from base case)	
France	54,069	-0.6	0.0		66,879	8.9	0.4
Belgium/Lux.	9,810	-3.2	0.0		12,217	7.0	0.3
Netherlands	46,703	-2.3	0.0		55,310	5.0	1.2
Germany	194,851	0.2	0.0		23,4187	8.0	1.1
Italy	361,32	0.2	0.0		44,342	9.1	0.6
UK	134,136	1.4	0.0		159,832	8.5	1.5
Ireland	2,227	-3.1	0.0		2,756	6.8	0.4
Denmark	19,611	-2.5	0.0		22,875	3.9	1.3
Greece	445	1.0	0.0		549	10.0	0.5
Portugal	173	-2.4	0.0		215	7.9	0.2
Spain	3,348	1.1	0.0		4,168	10.6	0.2
EC total	501,505	0.0	0.0		603,330	7.9	1.1

*   base case: elasticity of domestic supply = 1.5; elasticity of foreign supply = 2; elasticity of domestic demand = -1.086
**   case a: elasticities of supply changed to 0.75 for domestic suppliers and 1 for foreign suppliers
***   case b: elasticity of demand changed to -0.5

The sensitivity analysis for clothing shows that changing the demand elasticity has virtually no effect. A lower supply elasticity does, however, mean that exporters are less able to meet an increase in demand, with the result that the gains to third countries from full liberalization are less pronounced. Similar results are, unsurprisingly, obtained for footwear, as summarized in Table 16.11. The effect of changing elasticities in the simulation which looks at the effect of switching from national to Community-wide QRs is much more marginal. This is because the magnitude of the policy effect is, itself, pretty modest.

Table 16.11. Sensitivity analysis: footwear, 1988

Imports from constrained countries

Importing country	Policy simulation: Complete liberalization of trade		
	base case*	case a**	case b***
	(tonnes)	(percentage change from base case)	
France	43,841	9.3	0.5
Belgium/Lux.	8,493	10.3	0.5
Netherlands	16,241	8.8	0.6
Germany	50,673	10.4	0.4
Italy	31,287	7.7	0.6
UK	38,988	10.1	0.3
Ireland	1,005	11.6	0.1
Denmark	5,313	9.5	0.5
Greece	3,369	9.4	0.3
Portugal	154	10.5	0.2
Spain	5,627	11.7	0.2
EC total	204,990	9.6	0.5

*   base case:elasticity of domestic supply = 1.5; elasticity of foreign supply = 2; elasticity of domestic demand = -0.75
**   case a: elasticities of supply changed to 0.75 for domestic suppliers and 1 for foreign suppliers
*** case b: elasticity of demand changed to -0.5

17. Conclusions and policy implications

Although the main thrust of the SMP was always to liberalize markets, there were bound to be concerns in third countries that access to the EC market would become more difficult as the single market was consolidated. There are three main routes by which the SMP might have made access more difficult: by diverting demand from third countries to partner countries; by creating a more dynamic EC economy such that European producers gain in competitiveness; and by translating national quantitative restrictions on imports (QRs) into Community barriers that restrain imports more effectively. Part II of this study was concerned exclusively with the third of these and has, therefore, sought to assess whether or not the move away from QRs imposed by Member States has altered market access.

To do so, the study has explored the quantitative impact of the SMP on two sectors in which the SMP has had a direct effect on the trade regime. The first, clothing, has seen a switch from, largely, Member State based QRs to a Community-wide restriction on certain major exporters to the EC. Previously, the Member State constraints on clothing imports had been supported by the use of Article 115 authorizations to prevent single movement of the goods. Now, although Article 115 remains in place (although its new wording appears to give the Commission more power to prevent national measures), it has become virtually unenforceable because implementation of the SMP has all but eliminated internal customs checks. This has seen the number of Article 115 authorizations dwindle to a trickle, itself an indication of the effects of the SMP. In footwear, the second sector examined, the change has been to abolish QRs, except for the imposition of a Community-wide restriction on China, the exporter with the third largest market share in 1990, but which is now the leading supplier. Other exporters now enjoy unfettered access.

The emphatic conclusion of the study is that far from curbing market access, the SMP has led to a steady improvement in the access that third countries enjoy to Community markets. In the process, third-country penetration of the EC market has grown sharply. At the same time, domestic production in both industries has declined, with very substantial falls in some Member States. On its own, this evidence of relative growth in third-country exports to the EC, although a strong pointer, cannot unequivocally be attributed to the SMP, because other influences such as anticipation of the Uruguay Round changes in the commercial policy regime or, indeed, underlying shifts in competitiveness will play a part.

However, the different empirical exercises undertaken in the course of this study all provide complementary evidence that the changes engendered by the SMP have led to an easing of restrictions. Collectively, they enable a convincing case to be made that, at least in the two sectors studied, the SMP has made it easier for third countries to export to the EU. This conclusion does not preclude the possibility that the stimulus that completion of the single market is expected to give to the underlying competitiveness of EC industry may, in time, see indigenous producers regain market share, although in the two industries in question this must be considered unlikely.

Although there are bound to be idiosyncrasies in the circumstances of the two sectors studied, the findings of this study can, with some reservation, be extrapolated to other sectors where similar SMP induced changes take place. Where the SMP leads, as in footwear, to the abolition of national QRs, the expectation must be that this will give a boost to market access for third countries. To the extent that QRs can be seen as symptomatic of a perceived lack of competitiveness of indigenous industry, it would, therefore, be expected that sectors in the EU which lose such protection as a result of the SMP will see indigenous producers experience a fall in market share.

The replacement of national QRs by Community-wide restrictions cannot be so easily predicted. In principle, a simple translation of national QRs into a Community-wide QR redistributes imports from previously unrestricted to previously restricted Member States, raising prices in the former, and lowering them in the latter. But, as the analysis of quota utilization shows, a static comparison of 'before' and 'after' with changed rules may understate the impact of the SMP by neglecting the consequences of changes in the rules. What seems to have happened is that as the '1992' deadlines for single market liberalization approached, some quotas became more fully used, even though few were found to be firmly binding. One explanation for this is that exporters appear to have taken advantage of the increased flexibility provisions as a way of circumventing remaining national restrictions. Thus, a significant increase in the volume of exports was possible without breaching QRs. It can be argued further that anticipation of the single market might induce exporters to maintain high utilization rates because the unwinding of intra-EC border controls would make monitoring less feasible.

Simulations using the partial equilibrium model set out in the preceding chapter indicate how the SMP has affected the supply and price of imports from third countries. As would be expected, unilateral abolition of QRs leads to a jump in extra-EC imports with a fall in price, so that third-country exporters benefit from increased sales while consumers' 'surplus' is increased. When national QRs are replaced by Community-wide measures, the outcome still leaves extra-EC imports slightly higher in some Member States, because the main impact is to redistribute supply from extra-EC exporters.

Although the simulation which looks at the replacement of national QRs by a Community-wide QR does not, on its own, suggest any change in aggregate market access because of the assumption that the new QR is exactly equal to the sum of the national ones, the key question is whether the change allows third country exporters to use their quotas more fully. In this regard, the evidence from the quota utilization exercise that, on the whole, the SMP has coincided with fuller utilization of quotas suggests that market access has improved a little because of the shift away from national QRs. One reason may be the simplification of administrative procedures which means that rather than having to orchestrate indirect access to specific regional markets by various forms of quota-shifting, the exporter has a clear entitlement to the overall EC market.

The modelling exercise is, however, subject to the limitations of the technique; in particular, it does not allow for the fact that as quota utilization rates increase because of more flexible terms for carry forward and other means of 'stretching' quotas, the effectiveness of quotas diminishes. Since this appears to have happened, the model results understate the true gains in market access for third countries. If, however, a Community-wide QR were to be operated more stringently, with strictly enforced rules, it is conceivable that a switch from national QRs to a Community-wide regime might become more restrictive for third countries. However, the weight of evidence is against such an interpretation, and the spirit of the SMP seems, moreover, to have encouraged a generally more liberal trade regime. Given that this will be reinforced by the GATT/WTO agreements that are coming into force, the outlook for third countries' access to the single market should continue to be favourable.

APPENDIX A

The effects of the single market programme

The single market programme has affected market access conditions for third-country suppliers in a variety of ways. The aspect of this process with which this study is primarily concerned is the elimination of quotas applied to third-country imports and which have a specifically national application and/or their conversion into EC-wide measures. Although Articles 110 to 115 of the Treaty of Rome contain clear provisions for a common commercial policy, various (mainly quantitative) restrictions (QRs) on imports from third countries continued to operate at Member State level prior to the elimination of internal borders and despite progress made in other areas. These took the form of both unilaterally imposed quotas and voluntary export restraints (VERs) which Member States had negotiated with third countries. Because of the possibilities which this created for third-country suppliers subject to such restrictions to deflect trade through a Member State where no restrictions applied, Article 115 allowed a Member State at any time to request authorization from the Commission to intervene temporarily at internal frontiers and suspend such products from Community treatment. More precisely, any Member State wishing to impose restrictions on intra-area trade under these provisions was required to make an application to the European Commission setting out the intended duration of such restrictions. The Commission had the task of considering each application on an individual basis and granting the necessary approval before such measures could be enacted.

Although Article 115 still exists, it is clear that its provisions cannot realistically be enforced now that border controls have been removed. The approach of the single market has therefore necessitated that these QRs either be abolished altogether or replaced with EC-wide restrictions. Shortly after the launching of the SMP, the Commission, with the authority of the Council, adopted a programme for the completion of the common commercial policy. This provided for the gradual elimination of all remaining national QRs and/or their replacement with measures applied only at the Community-wide level. In addition, the measures provided for the establishment of a new computerized system for operating at an EC-wide level any QRs that it was deemed desirable to retain. At an internal level, this was to entail a progressively stricter application of Article 115 as the date for the removal of internal borders approached. Thus, between 1987 and 1992, the number of protective measures authorized under Article 115 fell from 157 to 6. At the same time, the number of intra-Community surveillance measures fell from 1,300 to 4. As of 1 July 1992, no textile or clothing products were any longer subject to Article 115 measures. In fact, the only industrial products which remained subject to such measures were cars and motorcycles (CEC, 1992b).

At the external level, for certain products then subject to voluntary export restraint or other similar bilaterally negotiated arrangements, provisions were made for new EC-wide VERs to replace the existing national ones. Thus, in July 1991, a 'consensus' was reached with the Japanese authorities for the regulation of imports of Japanese motor vehicles from 1993 onwards. Under this consensus, all national import restrictions on such imports were to cease with effect from 1 January 1993, and Article 115 measures were no longer to be applied. At the same time, Japan agreed to monitor the growth of its vehicle exports to the EC as a whole and to the five Member States which were at that time applying restrictions for a transitional period lasting up until the end of 1999 when the EC market would become fully liberalized.

In the case of textiles and clothing, existing bilateral quotas were in part governed by the Multifibre Arrangement, the future of which was dependent upon the outcome of the Uruguay Round of multilateral trade negotiations. MFA4 was due to expire in July 1991, but was extended for a further three and a half years to allow time for the Uruguay Round to be concluded. In October 1993, new EC-wide quotas replaced the existing bilateral quotas but with no provisions for regional allocations of quotas as in the past (Council Regulation (EEC) No 3030/93). The new agreement allows the Commission to re-establish regional quotas valid for three years should 'excessive concentration' of exports 'disturb markets' in individual Member States. However, it remains unclear how such quotas could be enforced in the absence of any border controls. In the case of footwear, also, EC-wide measures in part replaced national restrictions. In July 1990, on the authority of the Council, imports of footwear from Taiwan and South Korea, which had previously been subject to restriction in France and Italy only now became subject to an EC-wide self-restraint agreement accompanied by prior import surveillance (Council Regulation (EEC) No 1735/90). The arrangement lasted up until the end of 1992, whereupon it was allowed to expire. It should be pointed out that, under the new Safeguards Agreement reached as part of the Uruguay Round, all WTO Member States are required to phase out all existing 'grey-area measures' such as voluntary export restraints within a period of four years with effect from 1 January 1995, or bring such measures into conformity with the Agreement. However, every Member State was allowed to retain one such measure for a further 12 months to the end of 1999. The EC has named its voluntary export restraint agreement with Japan covering automobiles as the exception.

In respect of products subject to unilaterally imposed national quotas (the so-called 'autonomous measures'), these were either abolished altogether or replaced with EC-wide measures. Some of these measures were eliminated ahead of the removal of internal borders as part of other liberalization measures. For example, many quotas previously applied to the former Communist states of Central and Eastern Europe disappeared following the signing of various trade and co-operation agreements with these countries and then with the enactment of the Europe Agreements providing for these countries to become EC associates. Some quotas were also eliminated in the course of the Uruguay Round as a gesture of unilateral liberalization. Finally, in March 1994 the Council announced the elimination of a further 6,700 national restrictions on a wide variety of different products. On products which still remained subject to restriction (mainly, imports from China), Community quotas replaced national measures. On 6 March 1995, the latter were revised upwards to take account of the accession of new members and to provide for an element of liberalization.

Table 14.1 in the main text sets out a detailed summary of recent changes in EU legislation which have affected market access.

A.1. The import regime for clothing

EC trade with the rest of the world is subject to a wide variety of different kinds of restraints. Firstly, imports from outside the EC are subject to the *Common External Tariff (CET)*. Immediately prior to the conclusion of the Uruguay Round, the simple and weighted average MFN tariffs on imports of textiles and clothing were 10.1 and 7.6% respectively, with a range from 0 to 17%. For clothing, the average was 13% and 13.2% respectively, with a range from 0 to 14% (GATT, 1991). As in most industrial countries, this represented quite a high level of tariffs compared with other sectors. A variety of different groups of countries enjoy tariff-free entry under the EC's preferential regime. Under the Generalized System of Preferences (GSP), all GSP-eligible developing countries enjoy duty-free access within tariff quotas/tariff ceilings. Mediterranean countries with trade or association agreements with the EC enjoy tariff-free preferential treatment generally with no quantitative limits, although in a few cases administrative co-operation exists to avoid disruption of the EC market. Finally, ACP countries also enjoy tariff-free treatment with no limitations.

Table A.1.   Suppliers of textiles and clothing products with bilateral agreements or arrangements with the European Union, 1 January 1995

MFA Agreements	MFA-type Agreements	Preferential Arrangements	Autonomous Arrangements

ASEAN
Indonesia
Malaysia
Philippines
Singapore
Thailand
 	
SOUTH ASIA
India
Pakistan
Sri Lanka
Bangladesh*
 	
FAR EAST
Hong Kong
Republic of Korea
Macao
China
 	
LATIN AMERICA
Argentina
Peru
Brazil
Uruguay*
Columbia*
Guatemala*
Mexico*
	Albania
	Armenia*
	Azerbaijan*
	Belarus
	Georgia*
	Kazakhstan*
	Kyrgyzstan*
	Moldova*
	Russian Federation
	Tajikistan*
	Turkmenistan*
	Uzbekistan
	Ukraine
	Mongolia
	Vietnam
	Estonia*
	Latvia*
	Lithuania*
	Slovenia*
		Mediterranean countries
		Egypt
		Turkey
		Morocco
		Tunisia
		Malta
		
		Europe Agreements
		Czech Republic
		Slovak Republic
		Hungary
		Poland
		Romania
		Bulgaria
			Chinese Taipei
			Bosnia-Herzegovina
			Croatia
			Former Yugoslav Republic
			  of Macedonia
			People's Democratic
			  Republic of Korea

* No restrictions imposed.
Source: GATT, 1995.

Secondly, imports from certain supplier countries are subject to *bilaterally negotiated, quantitative limits under the Multifibre Arrangement (MFA)*. As noted above, the last MFA agreement (MFA4) was scheduled to run from 1 January 1987 to 31 December 1991 but was extended up to the date of the conclusion of the Uruguay Round (i.e. end-1994). (The agreement with China ran from 1 January 1988 because China joined the MFA after the signing of MFA4.) Within the framework of MFA4, the EC negotiated 19 bilateral agreements to restrain imports of textile products (down from 23 under MFA3). The 19 countries were Indonesia, Malaysia, Philippines, Singapore, Thailand (ASEAN); India, Pakistan and Sri Lanka (South Asia); Argentina, Peru and Brazil (Latin America); Czechoslovakia, Hungary, Poland and Romania (Eastern Europe) and Hong Kong, South Korea, Macao, and China (Far East). In addition, there were four further agreements which involved an 'exchange of letters' but did not provide for restraint or the possibility of introducing restraints and two agreements providing for the possibility of restraints in the case of real risk or market disruption. Table A.1 lists the exporting countries subject to MFA Agreements on 1 January 1995.

In each agreement, the restraints on individual products are determined. In addition, three different kinds of flexibility provisions allowed exporters to exceed their quotas for any particular product category in any given year. 'Carry-over' allowed an exporter to use the under-utilized portions of a quota for any one year in the following year. 'Carry-inward' permitted in any one year advance drawing against next year's quota for a particular product. Finally, 'swing' made possible the transfer of free parts of a quota from one product category to another. In most agreements, swing was available for up to 7% of a quota level; in other agreements (with dominant suppliers and East European countries), it was limited to 4%. Carry-over was usually limited to 7% of an individual quota. In the case of dominant suppliers (Korea, Hong Kong and Macao), consultations were to be held when 2% was reached. In the case of carry-forward, the corresponding shares were 5% and 1% respectively. Agreements with the former Czechoslovakia, Hungary, Poland and Romania contained provisions on prices (price clauses). In these cases, consultations could be requested by the EC if a textile product was imported at an abnormally low price. In extreme cases, the EC could temporarily suspend imports of the products concerned until a mutually acceptable solution was reached. However, these provisions do not appear ever to have been applied.

The individual agreements under MFA4 contained undertakings on the part of the EC not to resort to Article 3 of the MFA or Article XIX of the GATT, although the EC may still avail itself of anti-dumping and anti-subsidy measures (see below). Categories which were not restrained were subject to 'basket exit mechanisms' whereby, if imports of a given country reached a specified share of total imports, consultations might be held with a view to introducing mutually agreed limitations. The 'trigger levels' varied across five groups of countries and three product groups. If no agreement was reached, the EC could impose restrictions unilaterally according to a prescribed formula. EC action required the prior assent of Member States to a Commission proposal in the context of the EC Textile Committee. By July 1989, the exit mechanism had been applied 27 times to impose new restrictions. One out of four basket exits was EC-wide, as against one out of 20 under MFA3 (GATT, 1991).

Substantial differences existed among the MFA bilateral agreements as to the number of restrained product categories. In the case of large suppliers, there were up to 40 restrictions. In the case of smaller suppliers, there were only one or two. The EC quantitative limits were allocated among the Member States. There were also cases where individual quantitative limits were applied without an EC-wide limit. Most MFA quotas were set for two or three years, after which they could be modified (European Economy, 1993). On 1 January 1995, the EC's bilateral agreements negotiated under the MFA were superseded by the provisions of the Uruguay Round Agreement on Textiles and Clothing (ATC). (The MFA bilateral agreement with China will continue until it becomes a member of the WTO when the ATC will apply.) Including China, there are now 15 MFA agreements (the original 19 less the 4 East European countries which now have association agreements). As noted above, the new bilateral MFA agreements have no provisions for regional allocation of quotas among Member States which would anyhow be largely unenforceable, but do include provisions which would allow the Commission to re-establish regional quotas valid for three years should excessive concentration of exports disturb markets in individual Member States. On 1 January 1995, MFA quotas were adjusted to take account of the accession of Austria, Finland and Sweden to the EC. Quotas were increased on the basis of either actual 1993 imports into the three new

Member States or, whenever higher, an averaging formula linked to EUR-12 imports of the affected product categories from suppliers restrained in the EC.

In addition to the MFA Agreements, the EC has entered into various kinds of *MFA-type agreements* with certain non-MFA participants. Thus, the EC had an MFA-type agreement with the former Soviet Union which took effect on 1 January 1990 and covered all MFA products. When the USSR broke up, all restrictions contained in the bilateral agreements were attributed on a cumulative basis and by agreement to the new independent states, with the exception of the Baltic states, for whom individual surveillance for each country was introduced. Bulgaria was similarly subject to an MFA-type agreement. In 1993, the EC replaced several unilateral, autonomous regimes (see below) *vis-à-vis* non-GATT contracting parties with bilateral agreements. These included Vietnam, Mongolia. and the former members of the Soviet Union. Table A.1, above, lists the countries subject to MFA-type agreements on 1 January 1995.

Thirdly, imports from certain countries, mainly the former and still existing state-trading countries, have been subject to unilaterally-imposed, *autonomous restrictions*. EC regulations provide for imports from state-trading countries being subject to quantitative restrictions *at Member State level* applied on a yearly basis (Council Regulation (EEC) No 3420/83). In the case of some countries which had concluded MFA or MFA-type agreements with the EC, the autonomous regime applied only to categories not covered by the bilateral agreements and to outward processing traffic (OPT) (see below). Following negotiations with the Central and East European countries (Poland, Hungary, Czech Republic, Slovakia, Bulgaria and Romania), OPT quotas were incorporated into bilateral agreements. Countries subject to autonomous restrictions have included Albania, Mongolia, North Korea, Taiwan and Vietnam. Following the break-up of the former Yugoslavia, the countries concerned also became subject to autonomous arrangements. As noted above, many of these autonomous restrictions have since become subject to MFA-type bilateral agreements. In February 1994, all outstanding measures were either abolished or converted into Community-wide quotas (Council Regulation (EEC) No 517/94). The countries having autonomous arrangements with the EC on 1 January 1995 are listed in Table A.1.

Imports coming from countries which have signed *preferential trading agreements* enjoy privileged access. Producers in the Member States of EFTA have tariff-free entry to the EC market with no quantitative limits. Producers in the Mediterranean countries enjoy tariff preference for a fixed amount of imports (tariff quotas) and, in theory, are not subject to any quantitative restrictions. However, each of the agreements concluded with these countries provides for a system of administrative co-operation whereby exports of certain categories of textiles and apparel to the EC are subject to close monitoring. The aim is to avoid export increases of certain sensitive products causing disruption in the EC market. If this should occur, safeguard measures can be invoked. Administrative arrangements for trade in textiles have existed with Turkey, Egypt, Morocco, Tunisia and Malta, providing for export self-restraint over a two to three year period. On the EC side, a system of import surveillance (see below) is established. In the case of Turkey, which was the second most important supplier of textiles to the EC, self-restraint was agreed with the textiles manufacturer.

The preferential agreements between the EC and the Central and East European countries – the 'Europe Agreements' (EAs) – contained textile protocols. Countries covered were the Czech Republic, Bulgaria, Hungary, Poland, Romania and Slovakia – see Table A.2. In June

1995, EAs were also agreed with the three Baltic states – Estonia, Latvia and Lithuania. Although the full Europe Agreements only came into effect on 1 February 1994 for Hungary and Poland and 1 February 1995 for Bulgaria, the Czech Republic, Romania and the Slovak Republic, Interim Agreements governed the period between the signing of these Agreements and their ratification by national parliaments.

Table A.2.   Europe Agreements

	Interim Agreement	Final Agreement
Hungary	1.3.92 - 31.1.94	1.2.94 -
Poland	1.3.92 - 31.1.94	1.2.94 -
Czech Republic[1]	1.3.92 - 31.1.95	1.2.95 -
Slovak Republic[1]	1.3.92 - 31.1.95	1.2.95 -
Romania	1.5.93 - 31.1.95	1.2.95 -
Bulgaria	31.12.93 - 31.1.95	1.2.95 -

[1] The Interim Agreements with the former Czech and Slovak Federal Republic (CSFR) were subsequently replaced with individual IAs with the Czech Republic and Slovakia.

(Prior to the signing of the Europe Agreements, a number of CEECs had signed trade and commercial and economic agreements with the EC which provided for some liberalization of trade. New protocols in 1990 and 1991 provided for quota increases for Hungary and Poland and for the elimination of residual QRs of Member States. Also, in November 1989, non-MFA textile imports from both these countries were eliminated. OPT quotas for Hungary were suspended for 1990.)

All these countries (except Bulgaria) were MFA signatories and had MFA bilateral agreements with the EC before 1993. (Bulgaria had an MFA-type agreement with the EC.) Under the terms of the textiles protocols contained within the EAs, tariffs on direct imports were to be phased out over six years (in contrast with other products where tariffs were to be either immediately abolished or phased out over a period of one to five years). Tariffs on re-imports of products under the EC's OPT regime (see below) were eliminated immediately on the date of entry into force of the Agreements. With regard to quantitative restraints on textiles and clothing products, the new protocols replaced the previous bilateral agreements and provided for their total elimination within half the period of the Uruguay Round but in no case before 1 January 1998. (Under the Uruguay Round, MFA quotas are to be phased out in three stages within a period of ten years, but the choice as to which products were to be included at each stage, subject to certain limits, is left to individual countries.) Under the accelerated liberalization schedule, tariffs were to be completely eliminated by the end of 1996, while the textile quotas of the CEECs were doubled.

As noted above, before 1993, quotas negotiated under bilateral agreements were generally negotiated for the EC as a whole and allocated to individual Member States according to criteria based on traditional trade patterns. A burden-sharing formula, based on a range of economic indicators, was also applied whereby import growth rates during the term of the agreements were higher in those Member States which, at the beginning, had not been assigned their appropriate share. Special provisions were also set up to facilitate inter-regional transfers of quotas. These were subject to quantitative ceilings which were to be gradually expanded up to 1991 (the expiry date of MFA4). For non-dominant suppliers, quotas of individual Member States could be increased by a maximum of 16% in 1991 compared with

2% in 1987. In September 1988, an important ruling of the European Court of Justice (ECJ) stated that national fixed-scale quotas were contrary to the principle of free competition. However, it recognized that the breakdown of an EC quota by Member States was justifiable on administrative, technical and economic grounds.

Table A.3 sets out the main users of Article 115 for textile and clothing products over the period 1980–90.

Table A.3.   Use of Article 115 by Member State, 1980–90

Member State	Number of cases	Percentage of total
Benelux	85	7.3
Denmark	6	0.5
France	485	41.5
Germany	9	0.8
Greece	0	0
Ireland	402	34.4
Italy	98	8.4
Portugal	0	0
Spain	12	1.0
United Kingdom	72	1.0
Total	**1,169**	**100.0**
Source: GATT, 1991.		

The majority of Article 115 authorizations have concerned textiles and clothing, with France, Ireland, Italy and the UK being the main users. Between 1980–90, there were 1,169 Article 115 authorizations for textiles, of which France accounted for 485, Ireland for 402, Italy for 98, the UK for 72, Benelux for 85, Spain for 12 and Denmark for 6. Hong Kong, China, Taiwan, Korea, India and Pakistan collectively attracted more than 90% of all cases. Following the ECJ ruling, the restrictiveness of these arrangements for dividing quotas among Member States was gradually relaxed. The share of quotas which could be transferred *automatically* to other Member States was increased from 16 to 40% in 1992, with additional transfers available on the approval of the Commission. At the same time, the application of Article 115 to textiles and clothing declined from 48 authorizations in 1990 to 32 in 1991. No further Article 115 authorizations on textiles and clothing were made in 1992. From 1 January 1993, each Member State was entitled to issue import authorizations valid for the entire EC market. All regional quotas and ceilings were eliminated. Community surveillance was to be assured through a computer link between the Commission and the competent national body. However, as noted above, in the event of a regional disturbance, the EC might still seek to negotiate certain supply patterns with third countries, but it can no longer operate internal border controls to ensure compliance. This is permitted under the ATC reached in the Uruguay Round.

Several bilateral agreements (MFA Agreements and preferential trading agreements) contain specific access provisions with respect to outward processing traffic (OPT). This means that, in addition to normal quotas, quotas exist for the amount of imports which have been subject to offshore processing which may be allowed entry to the EC. Offshore processing entails an EC firm supplying a firm in another country with textile fabrics and a design and subcontracting the overseas firm to supply a finished product for sale in the EC market. The main advantage of such an activity for EC firms is to shift the more labour-intensive stages of production to countries where labour costs are relatively low. Providing OPT imports to the EC do not exceed the stipulated quota, they are subject to a tariff only on the value-added abroad, not the final price. In the past, the main users of the OPT provisions have been French and German clothing manufacturers. The main sources of OPT imports have been the former Yugoslavia (36% of all OPTs), the East European countries (38%) and Mediterranean suppliers (16%) (GATT, 1991). In 1992, OPT imports accounted for an estimated 10% of all extra-EC imports, but 62% of imports from the six CEEC countries and 51% for the former Yugoslavia (Corado, 1994). In addition to bilateral agreements, outward processing of MFA and non-MFA clothing in certain countries (Albania, Bulgaria, Romania and the Czech and Slovak Republic) was subject to unilateral import quotas. (The quotas for Hungary and Poland were suspended in 1990.) New arrangements have also been introduced for OPT quotas. Under Council Regulation (EEC) No 3036/94, the conditions of eligibility in the distribution of specific OPT quotas have been harmonized and regional quotas have been replaced by EC-wide OPT quotas. There are no specific origin rules for OPT quotas, only the general origin rules governing EC trade being applied.

Although imports of textiles have been subject to anti-dumping measures, this has not been true of imports of clothing products during the period covered by this study. On 1 September 1990, there were six anti-dumping measures maintained by the EC on textile imports affecting 17 countries. These were acrylic fibres, polyester yarn, polyolefin woven bags, sisal twine and synthetic textile fibre of polyester.

A further source of import restriction may arise from the application of rules of origin. EC rules require that certificates of origin be submitted in respect of all products imported from abroad. Products imported from countries not covered by preferential trade agreements, association agreements or the GSP scheme are subject to the 'last substantial working or processing' rule. That is to say, origin is where a product has been wholly obtained or has undergone its 'last substantial working or processing'. In the case of products covered by trading or association agreements or the GSP scheme, the criterion is one of 'sufficient transformation'. Products are deemed to be sufficiently transformed if the four-digit tariff heading of the final product differs from that of the inputs. With effect from 1 January 1996, however, imports from Turkey do not require a certificate of origin under the customs union agreement reached with that country.

Finally, in addition to quotas, certain categories of imports may be subject to surveillance, which means that importers have to obtain export licences in their applications for import licences so that imports into the EC can be monitored. The aim of surveillance is to provide the EC with immediate information regarding any sudden surge of imports and to check for fraudulent imports, as when the declaration of origin is falsified to get round quota restrictions on imports from the true country of origin. Import surveillance has often been used with regard to imports of clothing products from 'preferential' suppliers such as Morocco and Tunisia. In 1991–92, the EC applied Community surveillance measures on textile and clothing products from the Baltic states (Estonia, Latvia and Lithuania). In theory, surveillance does not imply any restriction of imports. However, in practice, if surveillance is seen to herald a threat of actual quantitative restrictions, exporters may feel constrained.

A.2. The import regime for footwear

Footwear imports have been subject to the same kind of restraints as clothing products. Firstly, the pre-Uruguay Round rate of the Common External Tariff on imports of footwear varied between 4.6 and 20.2% with a simple m.f.n. average of 11.7% and a weighted average of 13.5%. Developing countries eligible for preferential treatment under the GSP face a zero tariff on quotas within the prescribed quota limits. Countries having trade or association agreements with the EC (EFTA states, ACP countries, the East European EA countries and the Mediterranean countries including Turkey) also face zero tariffs.

Quantitative restrictions on imported footwear were rife in the late 1970s and early 1980s. However, by the mid-1980s, many had disappeared. In the past, most were operated at a Member State level, but there have been cases of Community-wide QRs. In August 1977, the United Kingdom unilaterally imposed quotas on imports of non-leather footwear from Taiwan under Article XIX of the GATT following a request from UK manufacturers. The quotas were temporary (for two years) until the end of 1979 and were sanctioned by the EC. One year later, in November 1978, the UK signed an industry-to-industry voluntary export restraint with South Korea covering all footwear. The arrangement was renegotiated in late 1979 and every year thereafter until it expired in December 1987. In 1980, UK manufacturers, with the encouragement of the UK government, began negotiations with their Taiwanese counterparts for a similar arrangement covering imports of leather and non-leather footwear from Taiwan. Temporarily, quotas were re-imposed on non-leather footwear from Taiwan. However, in 1981, agreement was finally reached and a VER came into being covering both products. This last VER arrangement with Taiwan expired in 1984. The effectiveness of both arrangements is in doubt because Taiwanese and Korean exporters appear to have succeeded in redirecting products through Hong Kong. Both received informal backing from the European Commission. Since the mid-1970s, the UK operated industry-to-industry restraints on footwear from the Czech and Slovak Republic and Romania, and with Poland before it was suspended in 1990.

In April 1981, France entered into an industry-to-industry VER with Taiwan limiting exports to France of both leather and rubber footwear. From 1982 onwards, the arrangement had the official sanction of the Commission. However, as imports never exceeded the quota limits agreed, it was not binding. In December 1985, manufacturers in the two countries signed a new VER arrangement covering the period 1986–88. It remained, however, ineffective and was eventually abandoned by the French industry. At the same time, in April 1981, French and Korean manufacturers agreed a VER which lasted until December 1984. France also applied a VER on Chinese exports of slippers and sandals. In addition, in March 1992, France informed the Commission of its decision under the EC safeguard rules to impose quotas on shoe imports from China for one year.

Italy operated a VER applied to non-rubber footwear from South Korea over the period 1979–85, although Korean records show the restriction operating only from 1 June 1981. In June 1981, Italy signed a co-operation agreement with Taiwan but imposed no quota limits. Also, since 1982, national quotas on imports of some types of footwear from Japan have been applied. A long-standing VER on imports of rubber footwear from Poland also operated over the period 1979–85. The Benelux countries applied national quotas on imports of some rubber and leather footwear from Japan commencing in 1982. Denmark applied national import quotas on imports of some types of leather footwear imported from Taiwan from 1982 onwards. Greece had a quota on imports of athletic footwear from Taiwan from January 1983 to January 1984. Ireland applied import quotas on leather and rubber footwear from Taiwan from 1977 which were sanctioned by the Community in 1981. Also, on 1 January 1979, Ireland entered into a VER with South Korea covering both leather and non-leather footwear. This lasted for six years until 1 January 1985. West Germany appears to have been the only Member State during the 1980s not to have used some kind of QR on footwear imports. Since joining the EC, both Spain and Portugal applied global quotas on imports of rubber and plastic footwear.

QRs applied at the EC level have taken the form of both negotiated VERs and unilaterally imposed import quotas. In 1988, the EC negotiated bilateral VERs on imports from South Korea and Taiwan with respect to the French and Italian markets (Council Regulations (EEC) Nos 3283/88 and 1733/88). In July 1990, this arrangement was followed by an EC-wide arrangement accompanied by prior import surveillance (see below). Under this new arrangement, the quotas were applied at an EC level by all the Member States. The arrangement covered footwear excluding slippers and remained in place until the end of 1992 whereupon it was allowed to expire. After 1990, many of the import quotas applied by individual Member States on imports from East and Central European suppliers were liberalized. Quotas on imports from the Soviet Union were removed in August 1991 and the treatment was extended to all former Soviet Union states. Imports from Bulgaria, the Czech and Slovak Republic, Hungary and Poland and Romania were liberalized in 1990 and 1991. From 1 January 1992, selective restrictions on shoe exports from Albania and the Baltic states were lifted and some suspended. In February 1994, all national quota restrictions were abolished except for those applying to imports from China which became subject to a new Community-wide quota (Council Regulation (EEC) No 519/94). The current position is that imports from China are the only imports subject to quantitative restraint. These quotas were expanded in March 1995 to take account of the accession of three new Member States (Council Regulation (EEC) No 538/95). Imports of certain types of sports shoes were liberalized at the same time and the scope for quota exemption was extended for special technology footwear.

Surveillance measures have been widely used with regard to footwear imports. As noted above, surveillance requires the importer to obtain an import licence before the goods can be put into free circulation. Although surveillance does not restrict imports in a formal sense, it is often preceded by measures which do and therefore creates expectations of further protection. Between 1975–78, the EC operated a system of 'retrospective control of imports' which covered leather imports. Briefly, for a period of six months in 1978, this was replaced with a system of 'prior import surveillance' applied only to imports from principal suppliers (namely, Brazil, Hong Kong, Korea, Malaysia, Pakistan, Spain, Taiwan, China, Czechoslovakia, Poland and Romania). Thereafter, a system of 'retrospective control of imports' – so-called 'a posteriori import surveillance' – was operated, covering all types of footwear. In July 1990, the bilateral VER on exports of footwear from South Korea and Taiwan was accompanied by 'prior import surveillance'. Footwear imports from all other sources remained subject to 'retrospective surveillance' (Commission Regulation (EEC) No 74/90). In August 1992, the EC made imports of slippers and other indoors footwear from China subject to prior Community surveillance (Commission Regulation (EEC) No 2327/92).

As with clothing imports, imports of footwear do not appear to have been the subject of any anti-dumping actions during this period. However, in 1981, a voluntary export price restraint was agreed between the EC and Brazil following a complaint by manufacturers that exports had been subject to an export subsidy of 15%. With regard to rules of origins, the same rules apply as for clothing.

APPENDIX B

Relevant trade policy literature

Conceptually, there are two different effects on third-country suppliers arising from the SMP and the completion of the common commercial policy. Firstly, the elimination of national or Community quotas amounts to a relatively straightforward exercise in trade liberalization. Secondly, the replacement of national quotas with Community-wide quotas is more problematic as this will affect individual Member States differently. The simplest case is where a Community-wide quota is introduced which is exactly equivalent to the sum total of the national quotas previously applying. In this appendix, we discuss the various attempts made in previous empirical work to examine and evaluate these different effects.

Substantial amounts of literature now exist on the effects of quantitative restraints (import quotas, voluntary export restraints and other grey-area measures) on trade including empirical work on the effects of such QRs on exporting and importing countries alike. Simple partial-equilibrium models quantify the effects of QRs by converting QRs into import tariff equivalents (MTEs) and then estimating the effects of changes in MTEs on consumption, production and imports in the same manner as is used in studies of the costs of tariffs. In the case of unilaterally imposed import quotas, quota rents accrue entirely to the importing country; in the case of voluntary export restraints, the rent is appropriated by the exporting country. Since the size of quota rents is unknown, MTEs cannot be derived directly. Instead, quota rents must be guessed.

In the case of clothing products, Hamilton (1984b) used the prices of export licences traded in Hong Kong expressed as a percentage of the unit value of imports to calculate the MTE on European clothing imports. Since these licences are often destination-specific, it proved possible to calculate these individually for different EC and EFTA Member States. He found that, because unit import values fluctuate only modestly over time, measured fluctuations in MTEs were largely due to fluctuations in quota prices. However, because quota prices fluctuate quite a lot over time, a long time period is to be preferred over which the average quota price could be measured. Silberston (1984) has argued that the use of quota prices gives a misleading impression because only a small proportion of quotas are actually traded during a given period. On the other hand, as Greenaway (1985) has argued, the same is true of the use of the housing market to estimate the current price of housing. All trading in any market occurs 'at the margin'. Clearly, however, there are problems with the use of quota prices as a proxy for quota rents. For one, imports and domestically-produced goods may not be perfect substitutes. Furthermore, quota prices are likely to fluctuate a great deal during the course of any particular year depending on their relative scarcity at different times of the year. They may also vary over the course of the business cycle as Hamilton (1984b) himself observes. Hamilton (1990b) re-estimated the MTE of EC QRs on clothing imports from Hong Kong for the period 1980–89. Table B.1 shows the results.

An alternative approach is to use differences in the costs of imports as expressed by the unit value of imports to estimate the MTE. This is possible if there exists at least one equivalent market where imports are not subject to quantitative restraint. The unit value of imports in the restricted market can then be compared with the same for the unrestricted market to find the MTE indirectly. For this to be at all accurate, the exercise should be performed for individual supplier countries and account taken of any differences in both transport costs and the composition of imports. A major problem with unit values is that they may reflect quality differences so that comparisons are best made at a disaggregated level and for countries whose import composition is broadly alike. Also, to the extent that QRs encourage exporters to up-grade their product, there will be a tendency for the unit value of imports to restricted markets to increase faster than that of imports to unrestricted ones. With regard to imports of UK footwear from Taiwan, Greenaway (1986) compared the unit value of imports to the UK with the same for imports to Taiwan, an unconstrained country, with an adjustment for transport costs. However, this treats footwear as a single homogeneous good and allows for no differences between types of footwear. The more direct approach preferred by Winters (1991) in his study of UK imports of footwear was to estimate using time-series regressions what he called the 'policy price wedge', i.e. the extent to which exporters actually raised their prices following the introduction of QRs. These were obtained individually for different supplier countries and distinguished between different kinds of footwear (leather, textile, rubber and plastic). Winters (1991) estimated the extent of the policy price wedge at 19% for imports of leather footwear (from Poland), 16% and 27% respectively for imports of textile footwear from Taiwan and Korea and 12% and 285 respectively for imports of rubber and plastic footwear from Taiwan and Korea. (The period covered ranged from 1977 to 1986.)

Table B.1.   Import tariff equivalents of the EC's quantitative restrictions on clothing imports from Hong Kong, 1980–89

	1980	1981	1982	1983	1984	1985	1986	1987	1988	1989	1980-89 average
West Germany	20	18	4	9	13	8	20	16	13	10	14
France	n/a	18	12	7	13	13	27	14	12	15	13
UK	28	17	10	7	13	17	22	15	14	11	15
Denmark	32	13	8	11	13	11	33	17	8	9	15
All above, imp.value weighted	24	17	7	8	13	12	21	16	14	11	14
Standard deviation		2.06	2.96	1.66	0.87	3.27	5.02	1.12	2.28	2.28	
Combined trade barrier[1]	45	37	25	26	32	31	42	36	33	30	33
Italy	n/a	n/a	n/a	n/a	n/a	12	16	19	55	36	
Rents to Hong Kong 1989 price $ million	n/a	213	82	91	136	108	237	231	220	166	165

[1] The import tariff equivalent multiplied by the EC ad valorem tariff of 17%.
Source: Hamilton, 1990b.

An interesting finding of Brenton and Winters (1991) was that a large element of product rationing was apparent in the case of UK footwear imports such that actual prices failed to reflect the true scarcity value of footwear which could exceed actual prices by as much as three times.

A further difficulty with measuring the effects of QRs is the possibility that quotas may not be binding. To determine whether or not a particular quota is binding, it is necessary to calculate quota utilization percentages, defined as the ratio of actual imports to quota-restrained imports. Erzan, Goto and Holmes (1989) of the World Bank conducted such an exercise for textiles and clothing imports to the EC, the US, Canada and Sweden covered by the Multifibre

Arrangement. They defined a binding quota as one where imports amounted to more than 90% of the quota limit. They found that the percentage of total imports subject to quotas was fairly stable within the narrow range of 46–50% which, given that new suppliers were drawn into the MFA and additional products were put under quotas, implied a disproportionate expansion of non-restricted imports. In other words, imports subject to quotas experienced a relative slowdown in their volume growth. The percentage of imports subject to binding quotas increased from 28 to 35% over the period covered. The percentage of restricted imports subject to binding quotas increased from 61 to 71%. Finally, quota utilization ratios increased in all four markets from an average of 69% to 82%, providing some evidence that the MFA was becoming more restrictive over the period in question. These figures were combined with measures of the percentage of trade covered by quotas in two-dimensional scatter diagrams to determine the trend in the degree of restrictiveness of the MFA. Quota utilization rates, however, can only provide partial evidence that a particular quota has been binding or not. The various flexibility provisions under the MFA allow countries to exceed quotas. In the case of the EC, as we have seen, quotas are subject to regional allocation. A supplier country may have underused its Community-wide quota, yet used up its quota in a particular Member State and be unable to shift supplies from other Member States to meet the higher demand in the market where the quota has become binding. Even where quotas have become fully used, exporters may be able to circumvent the quota by redirecting supplies through some third country with unused quotas or no restrictions and falsifying the declarations of origin. If the latter is not possible, production may, given time, be shifted to unrestricted countries (so-called 'quota hopping') (see Trela and Whalley (1989) for a discussion of these issues in relation to the MFA).

One aspect of the analysis of reducing or removing QRs as distinct from tariffs is that QRs are generally source-specific in their application. This means that QRs cause an element of trade diversion away from restricted to unrestricted supplier countries. Any attempt to quantify the effects of such QRs must of necessity take into account this aspect of welfare loss for the importing country. Figure B.1 illustrates the effects of a VER in a situation where imports from certain 'preferred' suppliers are not restrained.

$D_D D_D$ is the domestic demand curve for the product and $S_D S_D$ is the domestic supply curve. $S_W S_W$ is the supply curve for constrained suppliers (which is assumed to be perfectly elastic) and $S_{DN} S_{DN}$ is the combined supply curve for domestic and unconstrained (i.e. preferred) suppliers. (The situation is analogous to the formation of a customs union where tariffs are eliminated on trade between the home and partner countries but not on trade with the rest of the world.) Under free trade and in the absence of transport costs, the domestic price is equal to the world price, i.e. OP_0. Demand equals OQ_4, domestic production OQ_1 and imports $Q_1 Q_4$. If a VER is negotiated with certain suppliers which is designed to increase domestic production to OQ_2, imports fall to $BE = Q_2 Q_4$, the domestic price will rise to OP_1 and consumption fall to OQ_3. However, imports from unconstrained suppliers increase from AF to BD, while imports from constrained suppliers fall from FG to DE. Thus, trade has been diverted from constrained to unconstrained suppliers. By shifting $S_D S_D$ parallel to the right so that it crosses point E, the extent of trade diverted, namely CD, can be measured. The static welfare loss to the importing country from the VER is measured in the conventional way as the loss of consumer surplus (equal to area $P_0 P_1 EG$) less the gain in producers' surplus (equal to area $P_0 P_1 BA$).

Figure B.1.   The effects of a voluntary export restraint on the pattern of trade

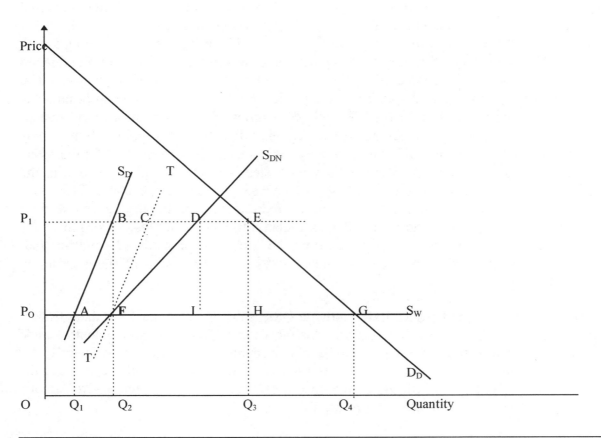

Source: Hamilton, 1984c.

However, to this must be added the additional cost from trade diversion. The units of the goods now obtained from unconstrained suppliers are obtained at an increased cost of P_0P_1 amounting to an additional welfare loss of FDI. Constrained suppliers gain increased rent income equal to the area DFIH, while preferred suppliers enjoy increased producers' surplus equal to ABDF.

The greatest difficulty facing economists in measuring the effects of QRs concerns how to treat the products in question. Theoretical models which assume a homogeneous product are relatively straightforward to handle, but are oversimplistic. Assumptions of product homogeneity have been made in the study of trade liberalization in both of the sectors covered by this study. For example, Hamilton (1981) studied the effects of Sweden relaxing its VER on foreign country exports of textile and clothing products subject to the MFA assuming perfect substitutability as between foreign and domestic supplies. Hamilton estimated the effects on foreign and domestic prices of a 50% relaxation of the Swedish VER, distinguishing between constrained and unconstrained third countries and using 26 five-digit product groups.

Estimates of the elasticity of the rest-of-the-world price with respect to changes in Sweden's VER were obtained mathematically from available information regarding the export supply elasticity of the rest of the world and world import demand elasticity. Assuming perfect substitution between domestic and foreign supplies but imperfect substitution between export markets, the results showed that a 50% relaxation of the Swedish VER would reduce Swedish clothing prices by a modest 6.8% on average. The effects on consumer welfare were found to be a gain of roughly $102 million matched by a loss of employment equivalent to 2,938 man-years or about 8% of total employment in the sector. Both the price and welfare effects were therefore quite small.

Greenaway and Hindley (1985) sought to estimate the effects of UK VERs as applied to both clothing and footwear, treating the two products as separate homogeneous goods. Estimating the MTE for clothing using the prices of clothing quotas traded in Hong Kong, Greenaway (1985) estimated the combined effect of tariffs and QRs as sufficient to raise UK prices by 34% giving a total cost to the UK economy of £68.4 million a year. For imports of non-leather footwear, the cost was some £43.4 million, or between £7,500 and £15,000 per job saved. Where, however, products are assumed to be heterogeneous, it becomes necessary to include parameters representing the elasticities of substitution. Such an approach has been adopted by Winters (1992) in relation to footwear. Estimates of the coefficients of variation of the unit values of imports into six EC markets from 17 sources implied something less than perfect substitutability both between suppliers and markets. The results suggested that products may be heterogeneous and/or that markets are segmented within the EC (see below for a discussion of the results of this empirical study). Empirical work in the clothing sector has more frequently assumed product homogeneity. Erzan, Goto and Holmes (1989), however, constructed a relatively simple partial equilibrium model covering six broad categories of clothing imports. Distinguishing between constrained and unconstrained foreign suppliers, they found that unconstrained developing country suppliers enjoyed a small gain from the existence of the MFA of $194.9 million or 14.1% of the 1986 shipments but that the main beneficiaries were domestic producers in the United States whose output was higher to the tune of $1.6 million or roughly 10%. A quantity effect was estimated using changes in the value of shipments of the six items under MFA quotas valued at the non-quota price. This revealed that the volume of imports from constrained developing country suppliers fell by 19% due to the MFA. However, this decline was largely offset by higher prices due to the quotas, such that the revenue losses amounted to only 4%. The assumption of product homogeneity more obviously breaks down in other sectors of manufacturing. Thus, studies of the impact of VERs applied to exports of Japanese cars (e.g. de Melo and Messerlin, 1988) have used more complex models which incorporate producer differentiation.

The transformation of national into Community-wide quotas (quota unification) involves a rather different set of considerations. Winters (1988) demonstrated that the replacement of individual Member State quotas with a Community-wide quota on imports which is exactly equal to the sum of the members' individual quotas will raise total union welfare. However, it would affect consumers differently in the various Member State markets. Clearly, consumers would gain in Member States where the restrictions bit deepest, which would be those where Article 115 restrictions had been most vigorously used, as prices would fall following quota unification. Prices, however, would rise in other Member States reducing their welfare. However, total union welfare would still increase because the same quantity of imports would be allocated more efficiently. Every unit shifted from less restricted to more restricted Member States would generate a net increase in welfare because consumers in the more restricted

Member States value an additional unit more than consumers in less restricted Member States. As an illustration, Winters simulated the effects of quota unification for imports of jeans from Hong Kong on the assumption that, in the absence of Article 115, quota rents are equalized and that each Member State faced linear demand curves having equal elasticities. Consumer prices rose by 3% and 12% in France and Germany respectively but fell by 19% in the UK, entailing a net welfare gain of between ECU 3 and 8 million overall.

An important aspect of the process of adjustment following quota unification is that, where quotas are bilateral, the price of imports rises after unification because foreign exporters are able to act in concert to appropriate higher scarcity rents for themselves. This effect was demonstrated by Gros (1992) and the model applied to the European automobile industry. The logic underlying the argument is that the opening up of previously restricted Member State markets (e.g. Germany in the case of cars) increases the size of the market in which foreign exporters (e.g. Japan) can now sell. Since the amount which foreign suppliers can sell is the same where Community and national quotas are assumed to be equally restrictive, it follows that the average price of imports must increase. In the case of automobiles, a differentiated goods model predicted that Japanese producers' prices would rise by between 8 and 18% on average. This implied a total transfer to Japanese producers of between ECU 0.5 and 1.3 billion per year. As in Winters' model, consumers in less restricted markets (e.g. Germany) lose, while those in more restricted markets (e.g. France) gain. The net aggregate effect on consumer welfare depends on the elasticities of demand. However, Gros found that, even on favourable assumptions, the gain to consumers amounted to only between one-third and one-tenth of the transfer to foreign producers.

Global economic welfare, however, is higher because imports are redistributed from markets where consumers' marginal utility is relatively low to those where it is relatively high. (This is reflected in the fact that foreign producers could potentially compensate consumers in the Community and still be better off.) From this, it follows that the replacement of national quotas with an exactly equivalent Community-wide quota will lower Community welfare even though consumers are likely to gain in aggregate. For the Community to gain, the degree of restriction should either be lowered following unification or the VER abolished altogether.

Hamilton (1990b) expected abolition of Article 115 to have little effect on price levels for clothing within the EC because of the existence of market segmentation. Where intra-EC trade is restricted by 'third-country non-tariff barriers' such as Article 115, import tariff equivalents should be lower in the more restrictive Member States (e.g. France) than the less restrictive ones (e.g. Germany). This is easily demonstrated. Since the EC applies a common external tariff and costs of transport are identical for imports of clothing from, say, Hong Kong and since clothing may be regarded as approximating a homogeneous product, the price levels for clothing in France and Germany, P_d and P_f, may be expressed as follows:

$$P_d = P_x (1 + U_{xd}) (1 + S_{xd})$$

$$P_f = P_x (1 + U_{xf}) (1 + S_{xf})$$

where P_x is the Hong Kong supply price, U_x the *ad valorem* MTE of the VER and S_x the MTE of the third-country NTB imposed by each country. (Third-country NTBs are assumed to be binding.) If France applies Article 115 but Germany does not, $S_{xd} = 0 < S_{xf}$. Since in a customs union $P_d = P_f$, a binding French third-country NTB must be reflected in $U_{xf} < U_{xd}$. Using estimates of MTEs based on quota prices in Hong Kong, Hamilton found no evidence for significant differences in MTEs between individual EC Member States. It follows that the application of Article 115 by France must have failed in the attempt to restrict imports. One way of seeing this is that producers in the less restrictive Member States (Germany) increased their supplies to the more restrictive Member States (France) while third countries supplied more to Germany and less to France. The free circulation of intra-union-produced perfect substitutes thus offset any restrictive tendency of Article 115. If, however, market segmentation exists, P_{xd} does not equal P_{xf}. The effectiveness, then, of third-country NTBs will depend on the existence of 'partner non-tariff barriers' giving rise to market segmentation. It follows that the abolition of these impediments to internal trade will be more important than abolition of Article 115 in equalizing prices in different Member States.

Relatively little empirical work has been carried out of the effects of the SMP on external trade. Winters (1988) carried out a policy simulation for footwear imports using a partial equilibrium model which allowed for product heterogeneity and imperfect substitution between markets. Using a model calibrated for 1987 which identified four different markets, six different groups of suppliers and six different types of footwear, he simulated the effects of translating the national VERs applied to imports from Taiwan and South Korea into Community-wide quotas. Since the national VERs applied only to imports into France and Italy, quota unification had strong distributional effects. French and Italian consumers gained at the expense of consumers in the rest of the Community. Aggregate consumer welfare, however, fell. Domestic producers in France and Italy lose, but this is more than offset by the gain to producers in the rest of the Community. Total welfare costs were found to rise from ECU 38 to 46 million. Korean and Taiwanese exporters also benefited from higher quota rents (although these fall in per unit terms, they applied to a wider range of trade).

Winters also estimated for the effects of Spanish and Portuguese accession to the EC and for the effects of tariffs and QRs being abolished on imports from Eastern Europe. With regard to the former, Spain and Portugal were found to have both benefited substantially but, as a result of trade diversion, the rest of the EC were marginal losers. Quota rents for non-EC suppliers also fell. The effects of abolishing tariffs and QRs on imports from Eastern Europe as under the Europe Agreements was found to have a potentially significant welfare-enhancing effect, although at the expense of EC footwear producers in Italy and Spain.

An alternative to simulating the effects of quota unification using a theoretical model calibrated for an earlier year is to examine actual trends in extra-area trade resulting from the process of bringing about a single market. This is problematic since internal borders were only abolished on 1 January 1993, leaving only a short time period over which to analyse any effects on trade patterns. On the other hand, the SMP involved a progressive reduction in the use of Article 115 in the years leading up to 1993. Sapir (1989) examined the external impact of completing the European Internal Market using three measures – the share of apparent consumption accounted for by both intra- and extra-EC imports as opposed to domestic production, the ratio of intra-EC to total imports and an index of revealed comparative advantage (defined as net trade divided by total trade). Using the work of Buigues and Ilzkovitz (1988), he identified three-digit manufacturing sectors most affected by NTBs and assessed the relative competitiveness of EC producers in each. Industries were then grouped as either ones where domestic suppliers were practically unrivalled, those where domestic producers were principal suppliers of local markets but faced strong competition from EC or third-country firms, and those where domestic suppliers accounted for no more than 40% of domestic sales and the main source of supply was foreign. He found that, for goods in the first and third categories, the completion of the single market would have relatively little external impact because EC suppliers had either a very strong or a very weak position. Most of the impact would be in the second category. High technology sectors with scale economies might be revitalized by integration at the expense of foreign producers. In those sectors with low to medium R&D intensity where EC comparative advantage was declining, foreign producers would generally benefit from the single market; however, in some of those sectors, EC producers had succeeded in obtaining various forms of protection. Sapir (1995) updated and extended his analysis of the external impact of the SMP.

Different aspects of the SMP are likely to have different effects on extra-area trade. Where NTBs may prevent the exploitation of economies of scale (e.g. discriminatory public procurement), the completion of the SM could be expected to boost the intra-area share and lower the extra-area share. However, for certain other types of NTBs such as national quotas imposed on extra-imports, the extra-area share should increase relative to the intra-area and domestic production share. For a third group of NTBs, the effect of their removal would be to raise both the intra- and extra-area share at the expense of domestic production. At the aggregate level, Sapir found evidence for both internal and external trade creation as reflected by a steady decline in the share of domestic production in apparent consumption and a constant ratio of imports to consumption. Using an earlier classification of manufacturing sectors by NTB intensity (Buigues and Ilzkovitz, 1988), Sapir found that both internal and external trade creation occurred in all three sectors. Internal trade creation was least in sectors with low NTB intensity and greatest in sectors with medium NTB intensity (including footwear and clothing). External trade creation was greatest in sectors with medium NTB intensity and weakest in those with high NTB intensity. (Clothing and footwear both show only external trade creation.)

Empirical studies of the effects of protectionism on particular sectors have generally used a partial equilibrium framework which seeks to compare the equilibrium situations of the market first with and then without protection. The effects on domestic production, consumption and the volume of imports can be determined if either the elasticities of demand and supply are known or (more likely) can be assumed. Costs to consumers, producers and the economy as a whole can then be readily measured. In the case of quantitative restrictions such as import quotas or VERs, the procedure discussed above and illustrated by Figure B.1 must be employed. This treats the imported product as a homogeneous good for which perfect substitution between domestic and foreign supplies is assumed. Thus, there is one single price for the product regardless of whether it is foreign or domestically produced. The QR is then assumed to raise the market price by the import tariff equivalent (MTE) in a manner similar to that of a tariff. The effects on producers, consumers and imports can then be estimated in the same way as with a tariff if reasonable assumptions can be made about the value of elasticities. However, since QRs are generally source-specific, it is necessary to distinguish between constrained and unconstrained suppliers. Trade diversion caused by discrimination must then be treated as an additional source of welfare loss over and above the dead-weight loss from the fall in the volume of imports. Moreover, in the case of a VER, the welfare loss exceeds that of a tariff because the revenue which accrues to the importing authorities in the case of a tariff instead is appropriated as a quota rent in the case of a VER.

The effects of the SMP on third-country suppliers are more complex than the simple case of quota liberalization. In particular, there is a need to distinguish between the different Member

State markets as, prior to the abolition of Article 115, each applied separate national quotas. The equilibrium in each of these markets is therefore likely to differ. Quota unification, however, will enable foreign suppliers to move products between different markets within the EC and indeed they can be expected to do so until quota rents per unit are equal across Member States. There is therefore a need to have separate supply and demand equations for each Member State. The equilibrium after quota unification must then be compared with that before in order to measure the effects on production, consumption and imports in each case. Having done so, the effects on consumers, producers, foreign suppliers and total welfare can be measured in the usual manner. As in the simpler case of trade liberalization, assumptions must of necessity be made regarding elasticity values. There is also the need to measure the size of the quota premium for each Member State market in order to measure the import tariff equivalent.

Table B.2.   Empirical studies of the effects of quantitative restrictions on imports of clothing and footwear and the external impact of the EC's SMP

Study	Subject matter	Methodology	Results
		Footwear	
Greenaway (1986)	Effects of tariffs and VERs on footwear.	Estimated MTE of VER using difference in unit values of imports from constrained v. unconstrained suppliers. Elasticity values taken from Deaton (1975).	Net welfare loss to UK of £43.4 million per annum.
Hamilton (1988a)	Effects of the New Protectionism on footwear trade.	Estimated shares of imports in apparent consumption to analyse trends in comparative advantage in non-rubber footwear.	No quantitative estimates.
Winters (1991)	Effect of VERs on the prices of UK footwear imports.	Use of time-series regressions to estimate policy price wedges for UK imports from Eastern Europe and welfare costs of VERs.	Extent of price wedge: leather (from Poland) 19% textile (Taiwan) 16% (Korea) 27% rubber & plastic (Taiwan) 12% (Korea) 28% Total loss to the UK: leather £7.5 million textile £13.7 million rubber & plastic £3.3 million
Winters (1992)	Effects of EC SMP on European footwear trade. Simulations of: 1. Effects of Spanish and Portuguese accession to the EC, 2. Effects of abolishing Article 115, 3. Effects of abolishing barriers on imports from Eastern Europe.	Complex model distinguishing between 4 markets, 6 groups of suppliers and 6 product groups. Calibrated for 1987. Used to run various policy simulations.	Effect of 1992: Consumer welfare costs rise by ECU 8.8 million per annum. Total welfare costs rise by ECU 7.3 million. Strong distributional effects.

Table B.2.   (continued)

Clothing

Hamilton (1981)	Effects of a 50% relaxation of the Swedish VER on foreign country exports and domestic employment.	Model assumed both perfect substitution between foreign and domestic supplies but allowed for imperfect substitution between export markets. Distinguished 26 5-digit product groups.	Average price fall 6.8%. Consumer gain: $102.341m. Jobs lost: 2,938 man-years.
Hamilton (1983)	Measured the trade-diverting effects of source-specific QRs for clothing, textiles and footwear.	Estimated changes in the shares of apparent consumption between 1970-79 for different groups of suppliers. Normalized changes using 'other manufacturers' as a control group.	Evidence for strong trade diversion towards other developed countries.
Hamilton (1984b)	Measurement of MTEs of VERs.	Used prices of quotas traded in Hong Kong to estimate MTEs.	
Greenaway (1985)	Effects of MFA quotas on UK clothing imports.	Used quota premia from prices of traded quotas to determine the MTE of quotas. Used Deaton (1975) for demand elasticities.	Total loss to UK = £68.4 million per annum, or £8,500 per job saved.
Trela & Whalley (1989)	Measurement of the degree of restrictiveness of the MFA.	Used quota utilization ratios for US and EC, distinguishing between supplier countries.	Evidence that MFA slowed growth of imports over time but many quotas may not be binding.
Erzan, Goto & Holmes (1989)	Measured the effects of the MFA over the period 1981-87 for the US, the EC, Canada and Sweden.	Measured the proportion of imports covered by binding quotas, and the QU ratios. Constructed a relatively simple six-product model calibrated for 1986 and simulated the effects of removing quotas.	Results confirm tendency for MFA to become more restrictive. Also evidence of trade diversion in favour of unconstrained countries. Main beneficiaries of the MFA are US producers. The volume loss of constrained countries is offset by price gains.

Other

Winters (1988)	Analysis of the likely effects of a completed SM on EC external trade.	Measurement of the welfare effects of abolishing Article 115 on imports of jeans from Hong Kong, using Hamilton's estimates of quota rents.	Overall welfare gain of ECU 3-8 million, but some countries gain (e.g. UK) while others lose (e.g. France and Germany).
Gros (1992)	Analysis of effects of replacing national with EC-wide VERs.	Measurements of effect for Japanese automobiles using a differentiated goods model.	Gain to EC consumers of between ECU 50-430 million, but more than offset by gain to Japanese producers of between ECU 500-1,300 million.

Table B.2.   (continued)

Sapir (1989)	Analysis of likely effect of completing the SM.	Used Buigues-Ilzkovitz sectoral classification of NTB intensity and various measures of competitiveness of different sectors: share of imports in apparent consumption, ratio of intra-area to extra-area imports and revealed comparative advantage.	Found that external impact greatest in sectors where domestic suppliers face strong competition.
Sapir (1995)	Ex-post analysis of the effects of the SM on external trade.	Used changes in shares of intra- and extra-area imports and domestic production in apparent consumption and ratio of intra- to extra-area trade.	Found evidence for both internal and external trade creation with sectoral differences determined.

APPENDIX C

Quota utilization rates

Table C.1. Quota utilization rates for China, 1989–94

1989	4	5	6	7	8	12	13	16	18	21	24	26	27	29	31	68	73	76	78	83	10
BNL	1.69	0.86	0.46	2.12	0.68	1.57	0.25		0.72	0.73	0.98	0.57			0.64		1.25	0.53			0.84
D	0.78	1.22	0.90	1.09	0.75	0.85	0.61		0.62	1.77	1.40	0.97					1.29	1.09		0.47	0.54
DK	0.56	0.86	0.75	0.62	1.11	2.24			0.55	1.61		0.48					1.37	0.41			0.40
E	8.39	0.97	0.72	1.06	0.49	0.62			1.66	0.93		0.07					0.09	0.42			0.72
F	1.16	0.82	0.56	0.66	0.45	0.77	0.50	0.01	0.53	0.88	0.77	0.56		0.01	0.64	0.94	0.89	0.79	0.32	0.13	0.54
GR	0.00	0.24	0.00	0.00	0.42	1.16			2.00	0.10		0.00					0.00	0.17			2.48
I	0.26	0.40	0.41	0.21	0.58	0.44		0.02	1.08	0.50	0.46	0.52		0.17			0.08	0.50	0.38		0.93
IRL	1.29	1.14	0.84	0.33	0.84	0.69	0.56		0.60	0.43		0.00					0.52	1.25			1.07
P	0.00	0.00	0.00	0.00	0.00	0.00			0.00	0.00		0.00					0.00	0.00			1.28
UK	1.71	2.28	0.88	1.30	1.60	0.55	0.55	0.15	0.89	1.01	0.91	0.41	0.79		1.01	1.10	0.75	0.72			0.88
EC	0.99	1.17	0.69	0.87	0.82	0.83			0.76	1.17		0.63					0.89	0.84			0.75

1990	4	5	6	7	8	12	13	16	18	21	24	26	27	29	31	68	73	76	78	83	10
BNL	0.91	1.00	0.94	0.29	0.99	2.63	0.64		0.77	1.66	2.22	0.66			0.95		0.57	0.79			0.49
D	1.00	1.08	0.85	0.90	0.86	1.23	1.03		0.65	1.24	1.83	0.72					1.23	1.13		0.83	0.43
DK	0.93	0.77	0.45	1.18	1.47	1.73			0.50	1.12		0.56					1.20	0.65			0.40
E	2.69	1.48	0.74	1.49	0.90	0.50			1.33	1.61		0.06					0.35	0.94			0.44
F	1.72	0.83	1.04	0.49	0.76	1.11	0.84	0.02	0.79	1.11	1.06	0.46		0.06	0.65	1.13	0.62	0.74	0.62	0.14	0.54
GR	0.00	0.10	0.08	0.00	0.29	0.62			0.45	0.28		0.00					0.00	0.10			1.65
I	0.72	0.69	0.49	0.30	0.64	0.23		0.05	1.02	0.60	0.86	0.56		0.00			0.20	0.73	0.54		0.69
IRL	0.49	0.53	0.75	0.48	0.80	0.32	0.17		0.67	0.83		0.00					0.00	1.14			0.55
P	1.68	0.04	0.00	0.00	0.00	0.00			0.00	0.00		0.00					0.00	0.00			0.00
UK	1.11	1.16	0.63	0.47	1.17	0.91	0.50	0.05	0.96	1.24	1.04	0.68	0.57		0.88	0.91	0.47	0.47			0.87
EC	1.01	0.96	0.79	0.52	0.89	1.15			0.83	1.17		0.59					0.73	0.87			0.53

1991	4	5	6	7	8	12	13	16	18	21	24	26	27	29	31	68	73	76	78	83	10
BNL	0.65	1.23	0.70	0.56	0.81	2.04	0.60		1.08	1.46	2.28	1.00			0.93		1.21	0.76			0.40
D	0.88	0.86	0.72	1.67	0.80	0.97	1.09		0.98	1.27	1.84	1.06					1.99	1.39		1.38	0.74
DK	0.93	1.14	0.91	0.66	0.85	2.33			1.09	1.16		0.82					1.38	0.67			0.34
E	3.13	0.93	0.94	1.95	0.67	0.91			1.70	2.11		0.25					0.38	0.75			0.89
F	1.14	0.83	1.04	0.96	0.79	1.39	0.59	0.03	0.87	1.04	1.24	0.62		0.05	0.91	1.12	0.96	0.71	1.01	0.41	0.91
GR	1.60	0.34	0.11	0.21	0.10	0.00			0.93	0.24		0.00					0.05	0.20			1.73
I	0.47	0.70	0.72	0.42	0.60	0.79		0.03	0.91	0.90	0.72	0.39		0.01			0.09	0.78	0.80		0.59
IRL	0.51	0.56	0.92	0.00	0.53	0.00	0.32		0.00	0.49		0.00					1.23	0.60			0.31
P	6.23	0.54	0.13	0.00	0.00	0.00			0.00	0.30		0.00					0.00	0.00			4.17
UK	0.95	1.12	0.53	0.63	1.18	1.96	0.64	0.12	1.12	0.96	0.43	0.63	0.40		1.02	1.17	0.73	0.72			0.81
EC	0.79	0.91	0.75	0.85	0.81	1.37			1.00	1.17		0.75					1.19	1.06			0.60

Table C.1.   (continued)

1992	4	5	6	7	8	12	13	16	18	21	24	26	27	29	31	68	73	76	78	83	10
BNL	0.80	1.24	0.53	0.50	0.53	1.73	0.42		0.77	0.78	1.70	0.51		0.79			1.03	0.60			0.89
D	1.37	1.03	0.81	1.14	0.79	1.28	1.01		1.13	1.33	1.71	1.43					1.62	1.34		1.01	
DK	1.26	0.80	0.64	0.26	0.88	1.95			0.72	1.35		0.69					0.97	0.75			
E	10.20	2.02	1.98	4.18	2.18	0.68			2.50	2.28		0.38					1.01	2.66			
F	1.03	0.69	0.47	0.56	0.61	0.89	0.73	0.38	0.87	0.86	1.05	0.76		0.33	0.68	0.62	1.05	0.69	0.50	0.57	0.52
GR	0.22	0.43	0.13	0.10	0.08	0.61			0.81	0.52		0.00					0.88	0.19			
I	0.83	0.86	0.56	0.52	0.50	0.43		0.25	0.87	1.23	1.53	0.35		0.76			0.26	0.46	0.71		0.57
IRL	0.45	0.66	0.79	0.00	1.11	0.00	0.09		0.67	0.98		0.00					0.32	0.71			
P	0.53	0.38	0.43	0.00	0.23	0.33			2.94	0.47		0.00					0.00	0.00			
UK	1.09	1.06	0.62	0.68	1.68	1.78	0.47	0.12	1.14	1.01	0.68	0.46	0.22		0.94	0.74	0.88	0.51			
EC	1.07	0.95	0.68	0.70	0.87	1.17			1.02	1.17		0.80					1.07	0.93			

	4	5	6	7	8	12	13	16	18	21	24	26	27	29	31	68	73	76	78	83	10
1993	1.05	1.10	1.08	1.14	1.08	1.18	0.53	0.23	1.10	1.17	1.15	0.68			0.92		1.01	0.74	0.81	0.56	0.72
1994	0.94	1.00	1.16	1.17	0.92	1.18	0.61	0.23	1.04	1.17	0.99	0.83			0.90		1.44	0.82	0.90	0.51	

Table C.2.   Quota utilization rates for Hong Kong, 1989–94

1989	4	5	6	7	8	12	13	16	18	21	24	26	27	28	29	31	68	73	77	78	83	10	72	74	86
BNL	0.85	1.01	0.88	1.03	1.07	1.57	0.73	0.02	0.47	0.93	0.88	0.46	0.50		0.06	0.71	0.90	0.96	0.22	0.43	0.55	0.60	0.86	0.49	
D	0.97	1.03	0.76	0.96	0.95	0.71	0.98	0.08	0.22	0.93	1.31	0.44	0.45		0.08	0.77	0.77	1.04	0.38	0.33	0.67	0.42	0.75	0.29	
DK	0.72	0.82	0.73	1.30	0.94	0.65	0.64	0.06	0.30	0.46	0.91	0.24	0.53		0.00	0.68	0.84	1.97	0.21	0.24	0.23	0.78	0.83	0.39	
E	4.75	1.10	1.82	2.06	1.19	0.17	0.23	0.00	0.47	1.23	0.77	0.52	0.39		0.11	0.58	0.07	0.92	2.33	0.49	0.00	0.87	0.12	0.23	
F	1.62	1.05	0.68	0.86	1.04	0.20	1.38	0.01	0.46	1.22	1.03	0.67	0.55		0.03	0.60	0.91	0.59	0.23	0.56	0.58	1.14	0.49	0.33	
GR	0.58	0.92	0.33	1.22	0.62	0.00	0.00	0.00	0.00	0.44	0.20	0.24	0.41		0.00	0.41	0.04	1.19	0.00	0.00	0.34	1.43	0.00	0.19	
I	0.69	0.76	0.24	0.21	0.60	0.00	0.08	0.00	0.39	0.97	0.55	0.09	0.08		0.00	0.75	0.35	1.37	0.18	0.09	3.17	0.51	0.05	0.32	
IRL	0.61	0.97	0.71	1.04	1.01	0.00	2.06	0.00	1.00	1.19	0.62	0.00	0.41		0.00	0.33	0.90	0.97	1.00	0.34	1.36	1.26	0.54	0.00	
P	0.00	0.00	0.00	0.00	0.00	0.00	0.00	0.00	0.00	0.00	0.00	0.00	0.00		0.00	0.00	0.00	0.33	0.00	0.00	0.00	0.00	0.00	0.00	
UK	1.31	0.93	1.11	1.18	1.02	7.56	0.96	0.10	0.83	1.05	1.03	0.97	1.04	0.67	0.17	0.84	1.25	1.04	0.20	0.65	0.69	0.96	0.76	0.68	0.46
EC	1.12	0.97	0.90	1.01	0.98	0.99	0.86	0.07	0.44	0.96	1.02	0.60	0.59		0.09	0.74	0.91	1.04	0.29	0.43	0.79	0.79	0.68	0.45	

1990	4	5	6	7	8	12	13	16	18	21	24	26	27	28	29	31	68	73	77	78	83	10	72	74	86
BNL	0.92	1.16	0.97	0.91	1.16	2.16	0.75	0.03	0.46		0.77	0.42	0.55		0.02	0.75	0.82	0.22	0.12	0.38	1.50	0.43	0.90	0.30	
D	1.02	1.17	0.78	1.07	1.15	0.52	0.89	0.04	0.19	**	1.22	0.47	0.52		0.06	0.68	0.84	0.93	0.32	0.34	0.72	0.47	0.80	0.26	
DK	0.63	0.90	0.90	1.15	1.04	0.49	0.56	0.05	0.29		1.00	0.16	0.37		0.00	0.31	0.92	0.80	0.07	0.21	5.68	0.74	0.90	0.37	
E	12.6	1.91	6.74	2.65	5.13	0.45	0.25	0.04	0.38		2.00	0.46	0.34		0.32	0.60	0.12	0.63	0.75	0.80	0.74	0.30	0.51	0.27	
F	1.45	0.96	0.64	0.97	1.04	0.06	1.47	0.01	0.44		1.08	0.84	0.54		0.02	0.67	1.03	0.73	0.21	0.81	0.84	0.95	0.60	0.35	
GR	0.69	0.92	0.25	1.84	0.48	0.00	0.17	0.00	0.03		0.09	0.33	0.33		0.00	0.19	0.03	1.34	0.00	0.00	0.00	1.10	0.00	0.09	
I	0.60	0.66	0.16	0.13	0.76	0.00	0.07	0.00	0.26		0.40	0.08	0.04		0.12	0.47	0.16	0.26	0.08	0.10	0.10	0.51	0.01	0.14	
IRL	0.58	0.71	0.40	1.45	0.91	0.00	1.84	0.00	0.94		0.58	0.10	0.59		0.34	0.61	0.56	1.11	0.33	0.33	0.00	1.31	0.59	0.00	
P	0.00	0.44	0.00	0.00	0.00	0.00	0.00	0.00	0.00		0.00	0.00	0.00		0.00	0.00	0.00	0.00	0.00	0.00	0.00	3.47	0.00	0.00	
UK	1.26	0.97	0.91	0.97	0.78	2.39	0.95	0.05	0.71		0.96	0.67	0.79	0.99	0.08	1.22	1.11	0.79	0.13	0.74	0.76	0.84	0.73	0.27	0.29
EC	1.12	1.05	0.84	1.01	0.98	0.49	0.83	0.04	0.39		0.96	0.52	0.55		0.06	0.76	0.87	0.75	0.21	0.47	0.86	0.71	0.71	0.26	

Table C.2. (continued)

Year	4	5	6	7	8	12	13	16	18	21	24	26	27	28	29	31	68	73	78	83	10	72	74	86
1991																								
BNL	1.13	1.22	0.96	0.96	0.94	0.59	0.84	0.02	0.36		0.70	0.58	0.60		0.03	0.72	0.56	0.33	0.06	0.36	1.21	0.31	0.88	0.50
D	0.84	1.15	0.77	1.04	1.24	0.58	1.12	0.02	0.23	**	1.36	0.97	0.55		0.05	0.72	0.87	1.04	0.29	0.33	1.16	0.40	0.95	0.43
DK	0.81	1.26	0.93	1.29	1.05	0.75	0.85	0.00	0.28		1.00	0.64	0.60		0.00	0.41	0.72	1.28	0.14	0.19	1.51	0.71	0.85	0.54
E	11.2	2.81	6.20	2.04	4.29	0.05	1.10	0.07	0.61		0.41	0.48	0.56		0.12	0.54	0.31	1.98	1.20	1.61	0.50	0.59	0.46	0.18
F	1.46	1.03	0.56	0.69	1.24	0.08	1.89	0.00	0.25		1.01	0.76	0.46		0.07	0.62	0.90	0.44	0.43	0.83	0.78	0.81	0.55	0.20
GR	0.77	0.93	0.14	1.40	0.50	0.00	0.09	0.00	0.10		0.09	0.21	0.41		0.00	0.17	0.09	0.00	0.33	0.08	0.38	0.87	0.00	0.36
I	0.79	0.63	0.19	0.29	1.12	0.00	0.04	0.03	0.25		0.33	0.11	0.04		0.06	0.48	0.12	0.48	0.38	0.15	0.06	0.25	0.03	0.03
IRL	0.26	0.80	0.65	0.64	0.87	0.00	0.50	0.00	0.49		0.40	0.10	0.19		0.00	0.55	0.66	1.25	0.00	0.24	0.00	1.11	0.92	0.00
P	0.90	0.40	0.13	0.00	0.00	0.00	0.23	0.00	0.08		0.00	0.00	0.00		0.00	0.00	0.00	0.00	0.00	0.06	0.00	3.79	0.00	0.00
UK	1.40	0.90	0.86	0.98	0.76	0.19	1.19	0.22	0.81		0.82	0.77	0.78	0.65	0.11	0.77	1.13	0.59	0.16	0.59	0.73	0.83	0.64	0.34
EC	1.12	1.04	0.82	0.99	1.01	0.42	1.03	0.06	0.40		0.92	0.79	0.57		0.07	0.68	0.83	0.77	0.25	0.43	0.84	0.65	0.73	0.35
1992																								
BNL	1.27	1.47	1.47	1.11	0.90	0.62	0.64	0.37	0.25	1.42	0.51	0.88	0.61		0.84	0.84	0.50	0.43	0.03	0.34	1.30	0.30	0.73	1.97
D	0.94	1.16	0.78	0.76	1.13	0.44	1.02	0.05	0.22	0.89	0.98	0.99	0.43		0.12	0.54	0.53	0.54	0.38	0.18	0.77	0.56	0.81	0.24
DK	1.04	1.10	0.81	1.25	0.83	0.55	0.67	0.40	0.29	0.43	0.99	0.82	0.46		0.86	0.23	0.55	0.55	0.75	0.12	1.01	0.64	0.47	0.66
E	6.02	3.54	7.57	3.60	4.14	0.05	0.96	0.70	1.90	3.06	0.43	1.10	0.35		0.69	0.87	0.21	1.00	1.00	0.64	1.06	0.68	0.92	0.41
F	1.08	1.12	0.44	0.75	0.87	0.12	2.03	0.17	0.24	1.36	0.73	0.86	0.29		0.42	0.69	0.70	0.54	0.69	0.51	0.69	0.95	0.36	0.00
GR	0.71	0.79	0.14	0.79	0.24	0.00	0.11	0.20	0.00	0.83	0.08	0.29	0.14		0.00	0.16	0.00	0.10	0.00	0.01	0.00	1.08	0.00	0.43
I	0.70	0.70	0.23	0.32	0.75	0.00	0.03	0.01	0.18	0.95	0.45	0.14	0.07		0.43	0.39	0.20	0.58	0.40	0.14	0.18	0.19	0.03	0.01
IRL	0.50	0.95	0.46	0.48	0.91	0.00	0.86	0.00	0.81	0.61	0.63	0.10	0.06		0.00	1.01	0.30	1.54	0.00	0.22	0.67	1.72	0.51	0.00
P	0.28	0.77	0.42	0.17	0.09	0.00	0.00	0.00	0.00	0.00	0.00	0.00	0.00		0.17	0.00	0.00	0.00	0.00	0.38	0.00	1.13	0.00	0.00
UK	1.24	0.80	0.92	1.05	0.80	0.81	1.40	0.16	0.85	0.86	0.52	0.76	0.66	0.70	0.27	1.00	1.01	0.56	0.13	0.42	0.73	0.79	0.65	0.26
EC	1.12	1.02	0.88	0.87	0.95	0.41	0.97	0.14	0.41	0.95	0.67	0.85	0.47		0.29	0.68	0.65	0.55	0.32	0.29	0.76	0.67	0.62	0.41
1993	0.90	1.05	1.12	1.01	1.06	0.40	1.05	0.14	0.34	0.99	0.84	0.66	0.40		0.20	0.47	0.49	0.18	0.17	0.47	0.93	0.54	0.19	0.07
1994	0.84	1.05	1.02	1.01	1.12	0.25	0.81	0.08	0.25	1.01	0.53	0.64	0.37		0.27	0.83	0.55	0.55	0.16	0.42	0.88	0.58	0.53	0.19

** denotes data deficiency

Table C.3.   Quota utilization rates for India, 1989–94

Year	MFA Category								
1989	**4**	**5**	**6**	**7**	**8**	**15**	**26**	**27**	**29**
BNL	0.90	0.98	0.19	0.84	1.11	0.12	0.47	0.40	0.01
D	1.10	0.85	0.19	0.97	1.19	0.21	0.26	0.57	0.04
DK	0.83	0.53	0.12	0.99	0.91	0.23	0.31	0.67	0.01
E	1.13	0.22	0.31	1.27	0.99	0.15	0.55	0.57	0.00
F	0.89	0.74	0.10	0.82	0.91	0.16	0.80	0.48	0.00
GR	0.16	0.16	0.05	0.37	0.13	0.07	0.13	0.07	0.07
I	0.38	0.37	0.11	0.34	0.25	0.04	0.33	0.16	0.00
IRL	0.57	0.19	0.04	0.67	0.96	0.00	0.37	0.32	0.14
P	0.00	0.00	0.00	0.25	0.00	0.00	0.00	0.03	0.00
UK	1.13	0.53	0.13	0.80	1.13	0.07	0.80	0.74	0.10
EC	0.86	0.67	0.15	0.84	1.00	0.13	0.53	0.52	0.04
1990	**4**	**5**	**6**	**7**	**8**	**15**	**26**	**27**	**29**
BNL	0.95	0.53	0.23	1.08	0.90	0.09	0.57	0.51	0.00
D	1.02	0.62	0.17	1.35	1.26	0.15	0.37	0.56	0.03
DK	0.90	0.34	0.05	1.25	0.95	0.11	0.41	0.50	0.00
E	1.58	0.38	0.54	2.97	2.34	0.21	0.98	0.77	0.08
F	0.86	0.37	0.12	1.01	0.88	0.22	0.85	0.65	0.00
GR	0.00	0.06	0.12	0.43	0.27	0.09	0.08	0.12	0.03
I	0.44	0.20	0.12	0.42	0.36	0.01	0.18	0.16	0.00
IRL	0.66	0.00	0.07	0.98	0.71	0.04	0.73	0.39	0.13
P	0.45	0.19	0.00	0.43	0.26	0.00	0.00	0.03	0.00
UK	1.05	0.52	0.09	0.93	0.88	0.05	0.92	0.81	0.06
EC	0.85	0.49	0.15	1.09	0.94	0.11	0.60	0.57	0.03
1991	**4**	**5**	**6**	**7**	**8**	**15**	**26**	**27**	**29**
BNL	1.12	1.05	0.21	1.02	0.86	0.10	0.65	0.48	0.01
D	1.30	1.24	0.15	1.24	1.38	0.17	0.55	0.43	0.01
DK	1.06	0.68	0.05	1.16	1.00	0.21	0.70	0.71	0.00
E	2.29	0.76	0.33	3.12	2.99	0.18	1.05	0.93	0.01
F	1.17	0.75	0.10	0.84	0.97	0.15	0.93	0.74	0.00
GR	0.04	0.12	0.14	0.56	0.17	0.08	0.34	0.33	0.00
I	0.43	0.40	0.14	0.49	0.60	0.02	0.23	0.14	0.00
IRL	0.95	0.00	0.00	0.91	0.82	0.11	0.83	0.36	0.03
P	1.12	0.37	0.00	0.78	0.04	0.03	0.70	0.10	0.00
UK	1.08	1.03	0.04	0.81	0.67	0.06	1.02	0.93	0.04
EC	1.00	0.99	0.13	0.99	0.97	0.12	0.71	0.57	0.01
1992	**4**	**5**	**6**	**7**	**8**	**15**	**26**	**27**	**29**
BNL	1.35	0.89	0.76	1.59	1.17	0.15	1.41	0.48	0.22
D	1.41	1.28	0.40	1.23	1.26	0.15	0.77	0.26	0.15
DK	1.02	0.99	0.29	1.29	0.80	0.14	0.61	0.29	0.21
E	1.85	0.59	0.42	3.56	2.46	0.14	1.34	0.73	0.42
F	0.81	0.78	0.31	0.92	0.97	0.11	0.99	0.56	0.25
GR	0.46	0.00	0.02	0.32	0.28	0.02	0.15	0.12	0.04
I	0.39	0.35	0.36	0.62	0.66	0.01	0.38	0.08	0.05
IRL	0.87	1.03	0.00	0.65	0.66	0.00	0.53	0.16	0.03
P	0.59	0.08	0.00	0.58	0.15	0.00	0.33	0.00	0.05
UK	1.16	1.16	0.57	1.05	0.70	0.08	1.18	0.82	0.35
EC	1.00	0.97	0.42	1.15	0.97	0.11	0.92	0.45	0.21
	4	**5**	**6**	**7**	**8**	**15**	**26**	**27**	**29**
1993	1.01	1.01	0.41	1.17	0.69	0.10	1.01	0.60	0.21
1994	0.99	0.79	0.53	1.17	0.55	0.14	1.01	1.03	0.27

Table C.4. Quota utilization rates for Indonesia, 1989–94

Year	MFA category					
1989	**4**	**5**	**6**	**7**	**8**	**21**
BNL	0.59		1.15	0.99	1.30	
D	0.72		1.03	1.19	0.87	
DK	0.70		1.25	0.67	1.20	
E	0.59		0.11	0.49	1.40	
F	1.12		0.93	0.45	1.07	
GR	0.24		0.00	0.00	0.00	
I	0.35		0.06	0.19	0.18	
IRL	0.00		0.08	0.25	1.31	
P	0.00		0.00	0.00	0.00	
UK	1.03		0.89	0.97	0.96	
EC	0.75		0.85	0.82	0.87	
1990	**4**	**5**	**6**	**7**	**8**	
BNL	0.49		1.14	1.09	1.31	
D	0.66		1.00	1.25	1.08	
DK	0.31		1.17	0.48	0.87	
E	1.41		0.38	1.32	1.01	
F	0.56		0.98	0.57	0.95	
GR	0.00		0.00	0.00	0.10	
I	0.36		0.08	0.36	0.52	
IRL	0.00		0.52	0.12	0.22	
P	0.00		0.00	0.00	0.00	
UK	1.07		0.85	1.09	1.02	
EC	0.65		0.84	0.91	0.96	
1991	**4**	**5**	**6**	**7**	**8**	
BNL	0.88		1.08	1.14	1.09	
D	0.99		0.69	1.37	1.22	
DK	0.45		0.68	0.57	1.00	
E	0.98		0.49	1.30	0.84	
F	0.71		0.76	0.56	1.30	
GR	0.08		0.25	0.00	0.09	
I	0.46		0.22	0.82	0.43	
IRL	0.78		0.21	1.33	1.53	
P	0.00		0.00	0.00	0.00	
UK	1.52		0.77	0.78	0.97	
EC	0.93		0.69	0.96	1.02	
1992	**4**	**5**	**6**	**7**	**8**	**21**
BNL	1.05	1.03	1.05	0.91	1.42	
D	0.97	1.03	0.74	1.42	1.16	
DK	0.75	1.14	0.69	0.20	1.41	
E	0.67	0.38	0.45	1.04	0.87	
F	0.65	1.20	0.71	0.55	1.27	
GR	0.26	0.05	0.03	0.16	0.08	
I	0.20	0.36	0.41	0.43	0.36	
IRL	0.84	0.43	0.60	0.21	0.97	
P	0.00	0.00	0.00	0.00	0.00	
UK	1.29	1.12	0.65	0.80	1.20	
EC	0.87	1.03	0.70	0.85	1.06	
	4	**5**	**6**	**7**	**8**	**21**
1993	0.98	1.12	0.74	1.01	1.17	0.93
1994	1.04	1.06	0.82	1.10	1.17	0.85

Table C.5. Quota utilization rates for Poland, 1989–94

Year	MFA category																	
1989	4	5	6	7	8	12	13	14	15	16	17	18	24	26	28	73	83	69
BNL	0.43	0.94	0.67		1.78	0.00	0.13	0.36	0.37	2.64		0.27	0.73	0.18		0.00	0.05	
D	0.43	1.26	2.42		0.78	1.09	0.88	1.24	0.46	1.07		0.67	1.31	0.77		0.35		
DK	0.55	1.06	4.24		0.00	0.70	2.40	0.34	0.27	0.55		0.74	0.10	0.69		0.19		
E	0.00	0.00	0.00		0.00	0.00	0.00	0.05	0.00	0.00		0.00	0.00	0.00		0.00		
F	0.13	0.81	0.58		0.05	1.10	0.25	0.31	0.14	0.08		0.49	0.77	0.27	0.14	0.05	0.06	0.91
GR	0.00	0.00	0.00		0.00	0.00	0.00	0.00	0.00	0.00		0.00	0.00	0.00		0.00		
I	0.01	0.00	0.31		0.20	0.03	0.00	0.30	0.00	0.99		0.33	0.03	0.00		0.39		
IRL	0.00	0.17	0.00	0.23	0.00	0.00	0.00	0.00	0.19	1.60	0.31	1.00	0.00	0.00		0.00		
P	0.00	0.00	0.00		0.00	0.00	0.00	0.00	0.00	0.00		0.00	0.00	0.00		0.00		
UK	0.34	0.17	0.24		0.01	0.45	0.21	1.58	0.05	1.16	0.97	0.14	0.86	0.10		0.37		
EC	0.30	0.68	1.17		0.50	0.79	0.67	0.79	0.23	0.94		0.46	0.79	0.41		0.19		
1990	4	5	6	7	8	12	13	14	15	16	17	18	24	26	28	73	83	69
BNL	0.58	0.90	0.61		0.42	1.02	0.37	0.71	0.47	1.56		0.00	0.42	0.17		0.08	0.03	
D	0.52	1.26	1.55		0.85	1.86	1.03	1.16	0.53	0.76		0.53	0.72	0.85		0.14		
DK	1.51	3.78	2.91		0.06	0.67	3.87	0.53	0.48	0.40		0.65	0.02	1.21		1.38		
E	0.00	0.03	0.01		0.02	0.00	0.00	0.10	0.01	0.00		0.11	0.00	0.00		0.05		
F	0.17	0.40	0.32		0.04	1.48	0.24	0.23	0.12	0.20		0.20	0.86	0.09	0.18	0.06	0.18	0.69
GR	0.00	0.00	0.00		0.00	0.00	0.00	0.00	0.00	0.00		0.00	0.00	0.00		0.00		
I	0.05	0.33	0.31		0.04	0.00	0.11	0.11	0.06	0.63		0.02	0.00	0.00		0.92		
IRL	0.00	0.00	0.00	0.00	0.00	0.00	0.00	0.00	0.00	1.07	0.11	0.00	0.12	0.00		0.00		
P	0.00	0.00	0.00		0.00	0.00	0.00	0.00	0.00	0.00		0.00	0.00	0.00		0.00		
UK	0.29	0.18	0.04		0.03	0.03	0.11	0.92	0.03	0.55	0.80	0.08	0.65	0.32		0.05		
EC	0.37	0.71	0.82		0.43	1.12	0.78	0.72	0.28	0.60		0.28	0.56	0.44		0.19		
1991	4	5	6	7	8	12	13	14	15	16	17	18	24	26	28	73	83	69
BNL	0.50	0.96	0.66		0.29	1.90	0.79	0.90	0.82	1.25		0.05	0.13	0.39		0.02	0.08	
D	0.84	1.52	1.32		0.53	2.07	1.39	1.73	1.04	0.76		0.39	0.60	1.23		0.10		
DK	1.29	2.80	1.86		0.14	0.65	3.10	0.43	0.79	1.68		0.24	0.07	2.88		3.06		
E	0.05	0.02	0.00		0.00	0.00	0.00	0.12	0.03	0.00		0.06	0.00	0.03		0.00		
F	0.07	0.66	0.12		0.11	0.92	1.48	0.41	0.29	0.57		0.05	0.54	0.13	0.14	0.11	0.16	0.29
GR	0.00	0.00	0.00		0.00	0.00	0.00	0.00	0.00	0.00		0.00	0.00	0.00		0.00		
I	0.08	0.27	0.30		0.04	0.02	0.39	0.33	0.07	0.54		0.00	0.07	0.04		3.34		
IRL	0.00	0.00	0.00	0.00	0.00	0.00	0.00	0.24	0.16	0.00	0.14	0.00	0.00	0.00		0.00		
P	0.00	0.00	0.00		0.00	0.00	0.00	0.00	0.00	0.00		0.00	0.00	0.00		0.00		
UK	0.23	0.19	0.10		0.01	0.27	0.06	0.85	0.11	0.50	0.50	0.09	0.22	0.13		0.00		
EC	0.45	0.82	0.72		0.28	1.17	1.17	1.01	0.56	0.66		0.18	0.36	0.64		0.43		
1992	4	5	6	7	8	12	13	14	15	16	17	18	24	26	28	73	83	69
BNL	0.40	1.01	0.66		0.26	1.13		0.55	0.81	0.83			0.06	0.71				
D	0.59	1.35	1.34		0.57	0.87		1.57	0.49	0.38			0.19	1.05				
DK	3.77	3.64	3.78		0.20	0.39		0.36	0.81	0.91			0.10	1.76				
E	0.00	0.01	0.01		0.00	0.00		0.06	0.02	0.00			0.00	0.00				
F	0.05	0.42	0.13		0.03	0.24		0.31	0.17	0.25			0.19	0.09				
GR	0.00	0.00	0.00		0.00	0.00		0.00	0.00	0.00			0.00	0.00				
I	0.08	0.38	0.07		0.00	0.06		0.53	0.05	0.44			0.18	0.02				
IRL	0.00	0.00	0.08		0.00	0.00		0.00	0.08	0.00			0.00	0.00				
P	0.00	0.35	0.00		0.00	0.00		0.00	0.00	0.00			0.00	0.00				
UK	0.04	0.12	0.09		0.01	0.20		0.52	0.04	0.23			0.15	0.05				
EC	0.35	0.71	0.55		0.25	0.49		0.83	0.35	0.36			0.16	0.50				
	4	5	6	7	8	12	13	14	15	16	17	18	24	26	28	73	83	69
1993	0.51	0.63	0.51		0.24	0.51		0.76	0.31	0.30			0.20	0.62				
1994	0.51	0.61	0.56		0.18	0.50		0.89	0.44	0.36			0.14	0.73				

Table C.6.   Quota utilization rates for South Korea, 1989–94

Year	4	5	6	7	8	12	13	14	15	16	17	18	21	24	26	27	28	29	31	68	73	77	78	83	10	69	70	86
1989																												
BNL	0.85	0.66	0.27	0.65	0.80	0.83	1.09	0.16	0.40	0.04	0.37	0.10	0.73	0.75	0.20	0.65	0.34	0.00	0.25	0.67	0.95	0.17	0.61	0.60	0.20		0.56	0.44
D	0.66	0.66	0.35	1.04	0.92	0.82	0.70	0.20	0.53	0.18	0.30	0.08	0.81	0.55	0.35	0.67	0.38	0.43	0.26	0.82	0.67	0.34	0.28	0.14	0.10		0.27	0.45
DK	0.52	0.68	0.22	0.53	0.88	0.63	0.11	0.11	0.15	0.09	0.29	0.08	0.40	0.14	0.10	0.29	0.13	0.00	0.57	0.63	0.90	0.24	0.44	0.00	0.21			0.26
E	7.56	2.31	1.31	2.90	1.47	0.80	0.09	0.82	0.20	0.00	0.72	0.10	1.04	0.00	0.10	0.09	0.44	0.00	0.22	0.20	1.43	0.50	0.44	0.40	0.29			0.40
F	0.88	0.85	0.52	1.03	1.22	1.05	0.78	0.38	0.41	0.05	0.50	0.81	0.66	0.83	0.58	0.39	0.58	0.13	0.57	0.56	1.12	0.41	0.66	0.75	0.17			0.17
GR	0.00	0.00	0.00	0.00	0.10	0.00	0.00	0.23	0.23	0.00	0.00	0.00	0.71	0.00	0.00	0.00	0.00	0.00	0.00	0.00	0.00	0.00	0.70	0.00	0.35	0.25		
I	1.02	0.13	0.06	0.26	0.66	0.16	0.00	0.17	0.03	0.04	0.22	0.01	0.81	0.00	0.22	0.03	0.27	0.00	0.06	0.11	0.03	0.89	0.13	0.08	0.63			
IRL	0.82	0.98	1.37	0.56	1.12	0.80	0.46	0.41	0.12	0.00	0.08	0.00	0.74	0.00	0.00	0.00	0.00	0.00	0.00	0.14	0.00	0.00	0.26	0.00	0.15		0.09	0.08
P	0.00	0.00	0.00	0.00	0.00	0.00	0.00	0.00	0.00	0.00	0.00	0.00	0.05	0.00	0.00	0.00	0.00	0.00	0.00	0.00	0.00	0.00	0.00	0.00	0.61			
UK	1.04	0.88	0.60	0.76	1.12	1.05	0.14	0.43	0.58	0.12	0.21	0.07	0.88	0.08	0.60	0.75	0.77	0.45	0.45	0.83	1.40	0.44	0.61	0.38	0.61		0.40	0.24
EC	0.88	0.75	0.40	0.81	0.91	0.78	0.52	0.25	0.45	0.11	0.27	0.15	0.78	0.51	0.38	0.56	0.48	0.29	0.34	0.65	0.88	0.36	0.51	0.31	0.28			0.32
1990																												
BNL	0.71	0.65	0.32	0.42	0.84	0.84	0.98	0.07	0.07	0.01	0.23	0.10	0.58	0.28	0.21	0.33	0.82	0.00	0.19	0.48	0.52	0.18	0.29	1.67	0.11		0.29	0.34
D	0.79	1.11	0.26	0.97	0.87	0.84	0.61	0.09	0.35	0.17	0.11	0.13	0.85	0.58	0.19	0.72	0.58	0.07	0.12	0.77	0.60	0.10	0.20	0.15	0.11		0.05	0.23
DK	0.36	0.93	0.22	0.33	0.37	0.61	0.00	0.00	0.08	0.00	0.16	0.04	0.25	0.00	0.02	0.32	0.50	0.00	0.00	0.44	1.31	0.17	0.15	0.00	0.20			
E	6.71	1.85	0.85	2.06	1.13	0.89	0.00	1.63	0.21	0.00	0.91	0.04	1.97	0.07	0.18	0.26	0.67	0.00	0.20	0.21	1.06	0.56	1.00	0.45	0.30			0.23
F	1.03	1.26	0.52	1.24	1.06	0.99	0.91	0.31	0.32	0.00	0.30	0.57	0.94	0.61	0.28	0.80	0.85	0.00	0.68	0.65	0.45	0.20	0.19	0.78	0.15			0.24
GR	0.00	0.37	0.00	0.00	0.00	0.00	0.00	0.14	0.15	0.00	0.00	0.00	0.72	0.00	0.00	0.00	0.00	0.00	0.00	0.00	0.21	0.00	0.25	0.00	0.16	0.25		
I	0.39	0.10	0.07	0.24	0.75	0.20	0.03	0.12	0.03	0.15	0.12	0.19	1.03	0.00	0.09	0.03	0.14	0.00	0.53	0.07	1.24	0.29	0.14	0.14	0.41			
IRL	1.02	0.87	1.18	0.53	1.02	0.70	0.46	0.46	0.00	0.00	0.04	0.00	0.78	0.00	0.16	0.00	0.40	0.00	0.00	0.00	0.00	0.00	0.05	0.00	0.23		0.15	
P	0.00	0.00	0.00	0.00	0.00	0.00	0.00	0.00	0.00	0.00	0.00	0.00	0.05	0.00	0.00	0.00	0.00	0.00	0.00	0.00	0.00	0.00	0.11	0.00	0.18			
UK	1.19	0.69	0.50	0.49	0.92	0.77	0.16	0.30	0.22	0.02	0.16	0.05	0.80	0.00	0.18	0.50	0.77	0.09	0.25	0.30	1.32	0.19	0.18	0.19	0.45			0.17
EC	0.92	0.78	0.35	0.65	0.86	0.76	0.50	0.16	0.23	0.06	0.16	0.16	0.80	0.37	0.19	0.49	0.65	0.05	0.28	0.50	0.82	0.15	0.21	0.23	0.21			0.22

MFA category

Table C.6.   **(continued)**

Year	MFA category																											
1991	4	5	6	7	8	12	13	14	15	16	17	18	21	24	26	27	28	29	31	68	73	77	78	83	10	69	70	86
BNL	0.66	0.79	0.58	0.35	0.94	0.84	0.97	0.15	0.08	0.01	0.20	0.09	0.89	0.27	0.34	0.38	0.82	0.00	0.22	0.46	0.50	0.18	0.29	1.43	0.11		0.26	0.44
D	0.71	1.33	0.59	1.09	0.96	0.84	0.56	0.08	0.22	0.14	0.13	0.18	0.81	0.51	0.11	0.57	0.53	0.16	0.18	0.72	0.53	0.07	0.19	0.12	0.09		0.04	0.24
DK	0.33	1.12	0.33	0.43	0.13	0.58	0.00	0.03	0.06	0.00	0.02	0.00	0.26	0.00	0.02	0.38	0.46	0.00	0.25	0.45	1.22	0.07	0.07	0.00	0.19			0.21
E	5.02	1.79	0.62	2.69	1.52	0.72	0.00	1.37	0.24	0.00	2.37	0.08	3.00	0.06	0.95	0.33	0.62	0.00	0.00	0.09	1.02	0.17	1.22	0.42	0.27			0.13
F	0.95	1.49	0.50	1.10	1.09	0.94	0.89	0.34	0.29	0.08	0.22	0.35	1.16	0.61	0.22	0.87	0.79	0.00	0.45	0.49	0.43	0.14	0.15	0.70	0.15	0.24		0.36
GR	0.00	0.42	0.17	0.00	0.00	0.00	0.00	0.06	0.12	0.00	0.00	0.54	0.53	0.00	0.00	0.00	0.00	0.00	0.00	0.00	0.21	0.00	0.23	0.00	0.14			
I	0.35	0.12	0.20	0.66	0.91	0.19	0.03	0.19	0.06	0.43	0.00	0.30	1.20	0.00	0.07	0.05	0.13	0.00	0.16	0.05	1.20	0.33	0.23	0.13	0.38			0.24
IRL	0.93	1.05	0.11	0.76	0.98	0.65	0.46	0.45	0.00	0.00	0.00	0.00	0.93	0.00	0.00	0.00	0.40	0.00	0.00	0.14	0.00	0.00	0.22	0.00	0.22			
P	0.00	0.00	0.00	0.00	0.00	0.00	0.00	0.00	0.00	0.00	0.00	0.00	0.13	0.00	0.00	0.00	0.00	0.00	0.00	0.00	0.00	0.00	0.08	0.00	0.17			
UK	1.09	0.84	0.38	0.59	1.01	0.73	0.16	0.26	0.23	0.00	0.02	0.04	0.93	0.00	0.13	0.56	0.75	0.05	0.07	0.30	1.29	0.06	0.35	0.19	0.42			0.04
EC	0.84	0.94	0.47	0.73	0.96	0.74	0.48	0.17	0.19	0.07	0.10	0.16	0.92	0.35	0.16	0.48	0.61	0.06	0.21	0.44	0.77	0.10	0.27	0.22	0.19			0.24
1992	4	5	6	7	8	12	13	14	15	16	17	18	21	24	26	27	28	29	31	68	73	77	78	83	10	69	70	86
BNL	0.53	1.07	0.27	0.21	0.79	0.82	0.18	0.15	0.03	0.00	0.10	0.06	0.60	0.15	0.06	0.39	0.67	0.14	0.21	0.48	0.16	0.11	0.15	0.38	0.11		2.20	
D	0.53	1.20	0.35	0.74	0.59	1.06	1.56	0.05	0.10	0.22	0.09	0.11	0.49	0.23	0.20	0.41	0.49	0.35	0.03	0.79	0.66	0.07	0.21	1.12	0.14		0.30	
DK	0.42	0.76	0.06	0.19	0.18	1.11	0.00	0.01	0.00	0.00	0.00	0.00	0.06	0.12	0.00	0.25	0.11	0.17	0.00	1.00	0.00	0.00	0.03	1.00	0.06		0.00	
E	2.43	4.73	0.60	3.96	1.78	0.76	0.00	1.10	0.43	0.00	0.51	0.18	2.86	0.00	0.65	0.54	0.69	0.59	0.00	0.12	1.67	0.27	0.70	0.23	0.18		0.05	
F	0.55	0.92	0.28	0.55	0.68	0.88	1.47	0.18	0.17	0.02	0.05	0.27	0.60	0.24	0.19	0.77	0.33	0.23	0.20	0.37	0.16	0.12	0.11	0.45	0.33		0.83	
GR	0.00	0.23	0.00	0.00	0.00	0.00	0.00	0.09	0.12	0.00	0.00	0.71	0.39	0.00	0.00	0.00	0.00	0.00	0.00	0.25	0.00	0.00	0.17	0.20	0.38		0.00	
I	0.38	0.15	0.03	0.27	0.67	0.25	0.00	0.08	0.03	0.00	0.05	0.07	0.73	0.00	0.05	0.00	0.06	0.34	0.00	0.05	0.77	0.10	0.09	0.31	0.52		0.69	
IRL	1.05	0.43	0.11	0.00	1.00	0.22	0.00	0.12	0.00	0.00	0.04	0.00	0.26	0.00	0.00	0.00	0.00	0.00	0.00	0.00	0.00	0.00	0.00		0.00		0.00	
P	1.50	0.09	0.00	0.00	0.00	0.12	0.00	0.00	0.00	0.00	1.43	0.00	0.13	0.00	0.00	0.00	0.00	0.00	0.00	0.43	0.00	0.00	0.00	0.00	0.15		0.00	
UK	0.83	0.66	0.30	0.28	0.37	1.07	13.8	0.19	0.08	0.00	0.00	0.02	0.45	0.02	0.24	0.32	0.77	0.04	0.02	0.30	0.11	0.02	0.14	0.20	0.66		0.13	
EC	0.59	0.87	0.27	0.43	0.63	0.89	0.38	0.12	0.09	0.06	0.05	0.10	0.54	0.15	0.17	0.38	0.50	0.19	0.08	0.45	0.45	0.07	0.16	0.48	0.29		0.46	
	4	5	6	7	8	12	13	14	15	16	17	18	21	24	26	27	28	29	31	68	73	77	78	83	10	69	70	86
1993	0.54	0.80	0.27	0.48	0.62	0.81	0.47	0.11	0.08	0.06	0.04	0.10	0.37	0.18	0.13	0.42	0.51	0.19	0.08	0.41	0.49	0.07	0.15	0.26	0.27		0.13	
1994	0.53	0.62	0.12	0.35	0.41	0.78	0.36	0.04	0.02	0.02	0.01	0.04	0.31	0.18	0.08	0.26	0.42	0.16	0.01	0.35	0.06	0.01	0.10	0.48	0.22		0.02	

APPENDIX D

Detailed model calibration

Table D.1.   Clothing 1988 – Model calibration

Price equations

	Unit value (unrest'd) (Pif)	CET	Domestic price (Pir)	Quota premium	Unit value (restricted) (Pie)
France	17,249	1.13	19,492	1.12	15,401
Belgium/Luxembourg	17,367	1.13	19,625	1.09	15,933
Netherlands	18,658	1.13	21,083	1.09	17,117
Germany	23,403	1.13	26,446	1.13	20,711
Italy	23,399	1.13	26,441	1.13	20,707
United Kingdom	23,057	1.13	26,055	1.15	20,050
Ireland	21,905	1.13	24,753	1.09	20,096
Denmark	19,710	1.13	22,273	1.08	18,250
Greece	22,912	1.13	25,891	1.14	20,098
Portugal	24,533	1.13	27,723	1.10	22,303
Spain	28,246	1.13	31,918	1.14	24,778

Supply equations

I. Constrained suppliers

	Supply elasticity	Price (Pie)	Volume of imports (Sie)	Slope (Bie)	Intercept (Aie)
France	2	15,401	54,717	7.11	-54,717
Belgium/Luxembourg	2	15,933	10,459	1.31	-10,459
Netherlands	2	17,117	49,067	5.73	-49,067
Germany	2	20,711	194,051	18.74	-194,051
Italy	2	20,707	35,967	3.47	-35,967
United Kingdom	2	20,050	129,993	12.97	-129,993
Ireland	2	20,096	2,370	0.24	-2,370
Denmark	2	18,250	20,763	2.28	-20,763
Greece	2	20,098	436	0.04	-436
Portugal	2	22,303	181	0.02	-181
Spain	2	24,778	3,275	0.26	-3,275

II. Unconstrained suppliers

	Supply elasticity	Price (Pif)	Volume of imports (Sif)	Slope (Bif)	Intercept (Aif)
France	2	17,249	69,922	8.11	-69,922
Belgium/Luxembourg	2	17,367	15,155	1.75	-15,155
Netherlands	2	18,658	24,165	2.59	-24,165
Germany	2	23,403	143,431	12.26	-143,431
Italy	2	23,399	13,051	1.12	-13,051
United Kingdom	2	23,057	39,669	3.44	-39,669
Ireland	2	21,905	927	0.08	-927
Denmark	2	19,710	6,998	0.71	-6,998
Greece	2	22,912	375	0.03	-375
Portugal	2	24,533	555	0.05	-555
Spain	2	28,246	1,538	0.11	-1,538

Table D.1.   (continued)

III. Domestic supply

	Supply elasticity	Price (Pir)	Volume of production (Sir)	Slope (Bir)	Intercept (Air)
France	1.5	19,492	487,504	37.52	-243,752
Belgium/Luxembourg	1.5	19,625	101,745	7.78	-50,873
Netherlands	1.5	21,083	50,296	3.58	-25,148
Germany	1.5	26,446	407,056	23.09	-203,528
Italy	1.5	26,441	238,988	13.56	-119,494
United Kingdom	1.5	26,055	274,713	15.82	-137,356
Ireland	1.5	24,753	16,899	1.02	-8,449
Denmark	1.5	22,273	13,203	0.89	-6,601
Greece	1.5	25,891	4,090	0.24	-2,045
Portugal	1.5	27,723	2,355	0.13	-1,178
Spain	1.5	31,918	105,315	4.95	-52,657

Equilibrium conditions

	Volume of restricted imports (Sie)	Volume of unrestr'd imports (Sif)	Volume of domestic production (Sir)	Volume of domestic demand (Dir)
France	54,717	69,922	487,504	612,143
Belgium/Luxembourg	10,459	15,155	101,745	127,359
Netherlands	49,067	24,165	50,296	123,528
Germany	194,051	143,431	407,056	744,538
Italy	35,967	13,051	238,988	288,006
United Kingdom	129,993	39,669	274,713	444,375
Ireland	2,370	927	16,899	20,196
Denmark	20,763	6,998	13,203	40,964
Greece	436	375	4,090	4,901
Portugal	181	555	2,355	3,091
Spain	3,275	1,538	105,315	110,128

Demand equations

	Demand elasticity	Price (Pir)	Volume of domestic demand (Dir)	Slope (dir)	Intercept (cir)
France	-1.086	19,492	612,143	-34.11	1,276,931
Belgium/Luxembourg	-1.086	19,625	127,359	-7.05	265,672
Netherlands	-1.086	21,083	123,528	-6.36	257,680
Germany	-1.086	26,446	744,538	-30.57	1,553,106
Italy	-1.086	26,441	288,006	-11.83	600,781
United Kingdom	-1.086	26,055	444,375	-18.52	926,966
Ireland	-1.086	24,753	20,196	-0.89	42,128
Denmark	-1.086	22,273	40,964	-2.00	85,450
Greece	-1.086	25,891	4,901	-0.21	10,224
Portugal	-1.086	27,723	3,091	-0.12	6,448
Spain	-1.086	31,918	110,128	-3.75	229,726

Table D.2. Clothing 1988 – Counterfactual I: Replacement of national quotas with Community-wide restrictions

Price equations

	Unit value (unrestr'd) (Pif)	CET	Domestic price (Pir)	Quota premium	Unit value (restricted) (Pie)
France	17,256	1.13	19,500	1.13	15,310
Belgium/Luxembourg	17,402	1.13	19,664	1.13	15,439
Netherlands	18,829	1.13	21,277	1.13	16,705
Germany	23,392	1.13	26,434	1.13	20,754
Italy	23,393	1.13	26,434	1.13	20,754
United Kingdom	22,959	1.13	25,944	1.13	20,369
Ireland	21,969	1.13	24,825	1.13	19,491
Denmark	20,000	1.13	22,600	1.13	17,744
Greece	22,895	1.13	25,871	1.13	20,312
Portugal	24,559	1.13	27,752	1.13	21,789
Spain	28,239	1.13	31,910	1.13	25,054

Supply equations

I. Constrained suppliers

	Supply elasticity	Price (Pie)	Volume of imports (Sie)	Slope (Bie)	Intercept (Aie)
France	2	15,310	54,069	7.11	-54,717
Belgium/Luxembourg	2	15,439	9,810	1.31	-10,459
Netherlands	2	16,705	46,703	5.73	-49,067
Germany	2	20,754	194,851	18.74	-194,051
Italy	2	20,754	36,132	3.47	-35,967
United Kingdom	2	20,369	134,136	12.97	-129,993
Ireland	2	19,491	2,227	0.24	-2,370
Denmark	2	17,744	19,611	2.28	-20,763
Greece	2	20,312	445	0.04	-436
Portugal	2	21,789	173	0.02	-181
Spain	2	25,054	3,348	0.26	-3,275

II. Unconstrained suppliers

	Supply elasticity	Price (Pif)	Volume of imports (Sif)	Slope (Bif)	Intercept (Aif)
France	2	17,256	69,981	8.11	-69,922
Belgium/Luxembourg	2	17,402	15,216	1.75	-15,155
Netherlands	2	18,829	24,608	2.59	-24,165
Germany	2	23,392	143,297	12.26	-143,431
Italy	2	23,393	13,045	1.12	-13,051
United Kingdom	2	22,959	39,332	3.44	-39,669
Ireland	2	21,969	932	0.08	-927
Denmark	2	20,000	7,204	0.71	-6,998
Greece	2	22,895	374	0.03	-375
Portugal	2	24,559	556	0.05	-555
Spain	2	28,239	1,537	0.11	-1,538

Table D.2.   (continued)

III. Domestic supply

	Supply elasticity	Price (Pir)	Volume of production (Sir)	Slope (Bir)	Intercept (Air)
France	1.5	19,500	487,813	37.52	-243,752
Belgium/Luxembourg	1.5	19,664	102,054	7.78	-50,873
Netherlands	1.5	21,277	50,988	3.58	-25,148
Germany	1.5	26,434	406,770	23.09	-203,528
Italy	1.5	26,434	238,903	13.56	-119,494
United Kingdom	1.5	25,944	272,960	15.82	-137,356
Ireland	1.5	24,825	16,972	1.02	-8,449
Denmark	1.5	22,600	13,494	0.89	-6,601
Greece	1.5	25,871	4,085	0.24	-2,045
Portugal	1.5	27,752	2,359	0.13	-1,178
Spain	1.5	31,910	105,274	4.95	-52,657

Equilibrium conditions

	Volume of restricted imports (Sie)	Volume of unrestr'd imports (Sif)	Volume of domestic production (Sir)	Volume of domestic demand (Dir)
France	54,069	69,981	487,813	611,863
Belgium/Luxembourg	9,810	15,216	102,054	127,080
Netherlands	46,703	24,608	50,988	122,298
Germany	194,851	143,297	406,770	744,917
Italy	36,132	13,045	238,903	288,080
United Kingdom	134,136	39,332	272,960	446,427
Ireland	2,227	932	16,972	20,132
Denmark	19,611	7,204	13,494	40,309
Greece	445	374	4,085	4,905
Portugal	173	556	2,359	3,088
Spain	3,348	1,537	105,274	110,159

Demand equations

	Demand elasticity	Price (Pir)	Volume of domestic demand (Dir)	Slope (dir)	Intercept (cir)
France	-1.086	19,500	611,863	-34.11	1,276,931
Belgium/Luxembourg	-1.086	19,664	127,080	-7.05	265,672
Netherlands	-1.086	21,277	122,298	-6.36	257,680
Germany	-1.086	26,434	744,917	-30.57	1,553,106
Italy	-1.086	26,434	288,080	-11.83	600,781
United Kingdom	-1.086	25,944	446,427	-18.52	926,966
Ireland	-1.086	24,825	20,132	-0.89	42,128
Denmark	-1.086	22,600	40,309	-2.00	85,450
Greece	-1.086	25,871	4,905	-0.21	10,224
Portugal	-1.086	27,752	3,088	-0.12	6,448
Spain	-1.086	31,910	110,159	-3.75	229,726

Table D.3.   Clothing 1988 – Counterfactual II: Removal of all restrictions to trade

Price equations

	Unit value (unrestr'd) (Pif)	CET	Domestic price (Pir)	Quota premium	Unit value (restricted) (Pie)
France	17,113	1.13	19,337	1.00	17,113
Belgium/Luxembourg	17,272	1.13	19,517	1.00	17,272
Netherlands	18,206	1.13	20,573	1.00	18,206
Germany	22,853	1.13	25,824	1.00	22,853
Italy	23,118	1.13	26,123	1.00	23,118
United Kingdom	22,351	1.13	25,257	1.00	22,351
Ireland	21,733	1.13	24,558	1.00	21,733
Denmark	19,179	1.13	21,672	1.00	19,179
Greece	22,700	1.13	25,651	1.00	22,700
Portugal	24,428	1.13	27,603	1.00	24,428
Spain	28,157	1.13	31,817	1.00	28,157

Supply equations

I. Constrained suppliers

	Supply elasticity	Price (Pie)	Volume of imports (Sie)	Slope (Bie)	Intercept (Aie)
France	2	17,113	66,879	7.11	-54,717
Belgium/Luxembourg	2	17,272	12,217	1.31	-10,459
Netherlands	2	18,206	55,310	5.73	-49,067
Germany	2	22,853	234,187	18.74	-194,051
Italy	2	23,118	44,342	3.47	-35,967
United Kingdom	2	22,351	159,832	12.97	-129,993
Ireland	2	21,733	2,756	0.24	-2,370
Denmark	2	19,179	22,875	2.28	-20,763
Greece	2	22,700	549	0.04	-436
Portugal	2	24,428	215	0.02	-181
Spain	2	28,157	4,168	0.26	-3,275

II. Unconstrained suppliers

	Supply elasticity	Price (Pif)	Volume of imports (Sif)	Slope (Bif)	Intercept (Aif)
France	2	17,113	68,815	8.11	-69,922
Belgium/Luxembourg	2	17,272	14,989	1.75	-15,155
Netherlands	2	18,206	22,995	2.59	-24,165
Germany	2	22,853	136,682	12.26	-143,431
Italy	2	23,118	12,738	1.12	-13,051
United Kingdom	2	22,351	37,238	3.44	-39,669
Ireland	2	21,733	912	0.08	-927
Denmark	2	19,179	6,620	0.71	-6,998
Greece	2	22,700	368	0.03	-375
Portugal	2	24,428	550	0.05	-555
Spain	2	28,157	1,528	0.11	-1,538

Table D.3.   (continued)

III. Domestic supply

	Supply elasticity	Price (Pir)	Volume of production (Sir)	Slope (Bir)	Intercept (Air)
France	1.5	19,337	481,714	37.52	-243,752
Belgium/Luxembourg	1.5	19,517	100,910	7.78	-50,873
Netherlands	1.5	20,573	48,470	3.58	-25,148
Germany	1.5	25,824	392,691	23.09	-203,528
Italy	1.5	26,123	234,683	13.56	-119,494
United Kingdom	1.5	25,257	262,089	15.82	-137,356
Ireland	1.5	24,558	16,700	1.02	-8,449
Denmark	1.5	21,672	12,668	0.89	-6,601
Greece	1.5	25,651	4,033	0.24	-2,045
Portugal	1.5	27,603	2,340	0.13	-1,178
Spain	1.5	31,817	104,812	4.95	-52,657

Equilibrium conditions

	Volume of restricted imports (Sie)	Volume of unrestr'd imports (Sif)	Volume of domestic production (Sir)	Volume of domestic demand (Dir)
France	66,879	68,815	481,714	617,407
Belgium/Luxembourg	12,217	14,989	100,910	128,116
Netherlands	55,310	22,995	48,470	126,775
Germany	234,187	136,682	392,691	763,560
Italy	44,342	12,738	234,683	291,762
United Kingdom	159,832	37,238	262,089	459,159
Ireland	2,756	912	16,700	20,368
Denmark	22,875	6,620	12,668	42,164
Greece	549	368	4,033	4,950
Portugal	215	550	2,340	3,106
Spain	4,168	1,528	104,812	110,508

Demand equations

	Demand elasticity	Price (Pir)	Volume of domestic demand (Dir)	Slope (dir)	Intercept (cir)
France	-1.086	19,337	617,407	-34.11	1,276,931
Belgium/Luxembourg	-1.086	19,517	128,116	-7.05	265,672
Netherlands	-1.086	20,573	126,775	-6.36	257,680
Germany	-1.086	25,824	763,560	-30.57	1,553,106
Italy	-1.086	26,123	291,762	-11.83	600,781
United Kingdom	-1.086	25,257	459,159	-18.52	926,966
Ireland	-1.086	24,558	20,368	-0.89	42,128
Denmark	-1.086	21,672	42,164	-2.00	85,450
Greece	-1.086	25,651	4,950	-0.21	10,224
Portugal	-1.086	27,603	3,106	-0.12	6,448
Spain	-1.086	31,817	110,508	-3.75	229,726

Table D.4.   Clothing 1994 – Model calibration

Price equations

	Unit value (unrestr'd) (Pif)	CET	Domestic price (Pir)	Quota premium	Unit value (restricted) (Pie)
France	17,382	1.13	19,642	1.13	15,383
Belgium/Luxembourg	13,922	1.13	15,732	1.13	12,320
Netherlands	18,337	1.13	20,721	1.13	16,227
Germany	23,056	1.13	26,053	1.13	20,404
Italy	18,960	1.13	21,425	1.13	16,779
United Kingdom	16,420	1.13	18,555	1.13	14,531
Ireland	19,328	1.13	21,840	1.13	17,104
Denmark	23,673	1.13	26,751	1.13	20,950
Greece	16,456	1.13	18,595	1.13	14,563
Portugal	18,731	1.13	21,166	1.13	16,576
Spain	13,006	1.13	14,697	1.13	11,510

Supply equations

I. Constrained suppliers

	Supply elasticity	Price (Pie)	Volume of imports (Sie)	Slope (Bie)	Intercept (Aie)
France	2	15,383	119,654	15.56	-119,654
Belgium/Luxembourg	2	12,320	40,730	6.61	-40,730
Netherlands	2	16,227	109,183	13.46	-109,183
Germany	2	20,404	391,041	38.33	-391,041
Italy	2	16,779	88,622	10.56	-88,622
United Kingdom	2	14,531	229,728	31.62	-229,728
Ireland	2	17,104	3,943	0.46	-3,943
Denmark	2	20,950	44,081	4.21	-44,081
Greece	2	14,563	3,864	0.53	-3,864
Portugal	2	16,576	1,491	0.18	-1,491
Spain	2	11,510	24,675	4.29	-24,675

II. Unconstrained suppliers

	Supply elasticity	Price (Pif)	Volume of imports (Sif)	Slope (Bif)	Intercept (Aif)
France	2	17,382	130,183	14.98	-130,183
Belgium/Luxembourg	2	13,922	35,936	5.16	-35,936
Netherlands	2	18,337	43,203	4.71	-43,203
Germany	2	23,056	201,745	17.50	-201,745
Italy	2	18,960	40,058	4.23	-40,058
United Kingdom	2	16,420	69,582	8.48	-69,582
Ireland	2	19,328	1,563	0.16	-1,563
Denmark	2	23,673	7,245	0.61	-7,245
Greece	2	16,456	1,456	0.18	-1,456
Portugal	2	18,731	1,593	0.17	-1,593
Spain	2	13,006	13,800	2.12	-13,800

Table D.4.   (continued)

III. Domestic supply

	Supply elasticity	Price (Pir)	Volume of production (Sir)	Slope (Bir)	Intercept (Air)
France	1.5	19,642	464,105	35.44	-232,053
Belgium/Luxembourg	1.5	15,732	174,240	16.61	-87,120
Netherlands	1.5	20,721	3,250	0.24	-1,625
Germany	1.5	26,053	421,729	24.28	-210,865
Italy	1.5	21,425	269,307	18.85	-134,654
United Kingdom	1.5	18,555	322,061	26.04	-161,030
Ireland	1.5	21,840	15,891	1.09	-7,946
Denmark	1.5	26,751	4,617	0.26	-2,308
Greece	1.5	18,595	17,851	1.44	-8,925
Portugal	1.5	21,166	70,600	5.00	-35,300
Spain	1.5	14,697	317,159	32.37	-158,580

Equilibrium conditions

	Volume of restricted imports (Sie)	Volume of unrestr'd imports (Sif)	Volume of domestic production (Sir)	Volume of domestic demand (Dir)
France	119,654	130,183	464,105	713,942
Belgium/Luxembourg	40,730	35,936	174,240	250,906
Netherlands	109,183	43,203	3,250	155,636
Germany	391,041	201,745	421,729	1,014,515
Italy	88,622	40,058	269,307	397,987
United Kingdom	229,728	69,582	322,061	621,371
Ireland	3,943	1,563	15,891	21,397
Denmark	44,081	7,245	4,617	55,943
Greece	3,864	1,456	17,851	23,171
Portugal	1,491	1,593	70,600	73,684
Spain	24,675	13,800	317,159	355,634

Demand equations

	Demand elasticity	Price (Pir)	Volume of domestic demand (Dir)	Slope (dir)	Intercept (cir)
France	-1.086	19,642	713,942	-39.47	1,489,284
Belgium/Luxembourg	-1.086	15,732	250,906	-17.32	523,390
Netherlands	-1.086	20,721	155,636	-8.16	324,656
Germany	-1.086	26,053	1,014,515	-42.29	2,116,279
Italy	-1.086	21,425	397,987	-20.17	830,202
United Kingdom	-1.086	18,555	621,371	-36.37	1,296,180
Ireland	-1.086	21,840	21,397	-1.06	44634
Denmark	-1.086	26,751	55,943	-2.27	116,697
Greece	-1.086	18,595	23,171	-1.35	48,334
Portugal	-1.086	21,166	73,684	-3.78	153,705
Spain	-1.086	14,697	355,634	-26.28	741,853

Table D.5.   Clothing 1994 – Counterfactual I: Replacement of Community-wide restrictions with national quotas

Price equations

	Unit value (unrestr'd) (Pif)	CET	Domestic price (Pir)	Quota premium	Unit value (restricted) (Pie)
France	17,364	1.13	19,621	1.12	15,503
Belgium/Luxembourg	13,862	1.13	15,664	1.09	12,717
Netherlands	18,035	1.13	20,379	1.09	16,546
Germany	23,056	1.13	26,053	1.13	20,404
Italy	18,960	1.13	21,425	1.13	16,779
United Kingdom	16,495	1.13	18,640	1.15	14,344
Ireland	19,232	1.13	21,732	1.09	17,644
Denmark	23,119	1.13	26,124	1.08	21,407
Greece	16,474	1.13	18,615	1.14	14,451
Portugal	18,723	1.13	21,157	1.10	17,021
Spain	13,012	1.13	14,704	1.14	11,414

Supply equations

I. Constrained suppliers

	Supply elasticity	Price (Pie)	Volume of imports (Sie)	Slope (Bie)	Intercept (Aie)
France	2	15,503	121,529	15.56	-119,654
Belgium/Luxembourg	2	12,717	43,354	6.61	-40,730
Netherlands	2	16,546	113,469	13.46	-109,183
Germany	2	20,404	391,041	38.33	-391,041
Italy	2	16,779	88,622	10.56	-88,622
United Kingdom	2	14,344	223,801	31.62	-229,728
Ireland	2	17,644	4,192	0.46	-3,943
Denmark	2	21,407	46,004	4.21	-44,081
Greece	2	14,451	3,805	0.53	-3,864
Portugal	2	17,021	1,571	0.18	-1,491
Spain	2	11,414	24,265	4.29	-24,675

II. Unconstrained suppliers

	Supply elasticity	Price (Pif)	Volume of imports (Sif)	Slope (Bif)	Intercept (Aif)
France	2	17,364	129,901	14.98	-130,183
Belgium/Luxembourg	2	13,862	35,625	5.16	-35,936
Netherlands	2	18,035	41,780	4.71	-43,203
Germany	2	23,056	201,745	17.50	-201,745
Italy	2	18,960	40,058	4.23	-40,058
United Kingdom	2	16,495	70,218	8.48	-69,582
Ireland	2	19,232	1,548	0.16	-1,563
Denmark	2	23,119	6,906	0.61	-7,245
Greece	2	16,474	1,459	0.18	-1,456
Portugal	2	18,723	1592	0.17	-1,593
Spain	2	13,012	13,813	2.12	-13,800

Table D.5.   (continued)

III. Domestic supply

	Supply elasticity	Price (Pir)	Volume of production (Sir)	Slope (Bir)	Intercept (Air)
France	1.5	19,621	463,352	35.44	-232,053
Belgium/Luxembourg	1.5	15,664	173,108	16.61	-871,20
Netherlands	1.5	20,379	3,169	0.24	-1,625
Germany	1.5	26,053	421,729	24.28	-210,865
Italy	1.5	21,425	269,307	18.85	-134,654
United Kingdom	1.5	18,640	324,269	26.04	-161,030
Ireland	1.5	21,732	15,773	1.09	-7,946
Denmark	1.5	26,124	4,455	0.26	-2,308
Greece	1.5	18,615	17,880	1.44	-8,925
Portugal	1.5	21,157	70,555	5.00	-35,300
Spain	1.5	14,704	317,379	32.37	-158,580

Equilibrium conditions

	Volume of restricted imports (Sie)	Volume of unrestr'd imports (Sif)	Volume of domestic production (Sir)	Volume of domestic demand (Dir)
France	121,529	129,901	463,352	714,782
Belgium/Luxembourg	43,354	35,625	173,108	252,086
Netherlands	113,469	41,780	3,169	158,419
Germany	391,041	201,745	421,729	1,014,515
Italy	88,622	40,058	269,307	397,987
United Kingdom	223,801	70,218	324,269	618,287
Ireland	4,192	1,548	15,773	21,512
Denmark	46,004	6,906	4,455	573,64
Greece	3,805	1,459	17,880	23,143
Portugal	1,571	1,592	70,555	73,718
Spain	24,265	13,813	317,379	355,456

Demand equations

	Demand elasticity	Price (Pir)	Volume of domestic demand (Dir)	Slope (dir)	Intercept (cir)
France	-1.086	19,621	714,782	-39.47	1,489,284
Belgium/Luxembourg	-1.086	15,664	252,086	-17.32	523,390
Netherlands	-1.086	20,379	158,419	-8.16	324,656
Germany	-1.086	26,053	1,014,515	-42.29	2,116,279
Italy	-1.086	21,425	397,987	-20.17	830,202
United Kingdom	-1.086	18,640	618,287	-36.37	1,296,180
Ireland	-1.086	21,732	21,512	-1.06	44,634
Denmark	-1.086	26,124	57,364	-2.27	116,697
Greece	-1.086	18,615	23,143	-1.35	48,334
Portugal	-1.086	21,157	73,718	-3.78	153,705
Spain	-1.086	14,704	355,456	-26.28	741,853

Table D.6.   Clothing 1994 – Counterfactual II: Removal of all restrictions to trade

Price equations

	Unit value (unrestr'd) (Pif)	CET	Domestic price (Pir)	Quota premium	Unit value (restricted) (Pie)
France	17,112	1.13	19,337	1.00	17,112
Belgium/Luxembourg	13,711	1.13	15,493	1.00	13,711
Netherlands	17,310	1.13	19,561	1.00	17,310
Germany	22,280	1.13	25,177	1.00	22,280
Italy	18,569	1.13	20,983	1.00	18,569
United Kingdom	15,880	1.13	17,945	1.00	15,880
Ireland	18,992	1.13	21,461	1.00	18,992
Denmark	22,181	1.13	25,064	1.00	22,181
Greece	16,196	1.13	18,302	1.00	16,196
Portugal	18,693	1.13	21,123	1.00	18,693
Spain	12,918	1.13	14,597	1.00	12,918

Supply equations

I. Constrained suppliers

	Supply elasticity	Price (Pie)	Volume of imports (Sie)	Slope (Bie)	Intercept (Aie)
France	2	17,112	146,562	15.56	-119,654
Belgium/Luxembourg	2	13,711	49,923	6.61	-40,730
Netherlands	2	17,310	123,756	13.46	-109,183
Germany	2	22,280	462,975	38.33	-391,041
Italy	2	18,569	107,531	10.56	-88,622
United Kingdom	2	15,880	272,383	31.62	-229,728
Ireland	2	18,992	4,814	0.46	-3,943
Denmark	2	22,181	49,261	4.21	-44,081
Greece	2	16,196	4,731	0.53	-3,864
Portugal	2	18,693	1,872	0.18	-1,491
Spain	2	12,918	30,712	4.29	-24,675

II. Unconstrained suppliers

	Supply elasticity	Price (Pif)	Volume of imports (Sif)	Slope (Bif)	Intercept (Aif)
France	2	17,112	126,138	14.98	-130,183
Belgium/Luxembourg	2	13,711	34,845	5.16	-35,936
Netherlands	2	17,310	38,366	4.71	-43,203
Germany	2	22,280	188,168	17.50	-201,745
Italy	2	18,569	38,405	4.23	-40,058
United Kingdom	2	15,880	65,005	8.48	-69,582
Ireland	2	18,992	1,509	0.16	-1563
Denmark	2	22,181	6,331	0.61	-7,245
Greece	2	16,196	1,410	0.18	-1,456
Portugal	2	18,693	1,587	0.17	-1,593
Spain	2	12,918	13,613	2.12	-13,800

Table D.6.   (continued)

III. Domestic supply

	Supply elasticity	Price (Pir)	Volume of production (Sir)	Slope (Bir)	Intercept (Air)
France	1.5	19,337	453,289	35.44	-232,053
Belgium/Luxembourg	1.5	15,493	170,273	16.61	-87,120
Netherlands	1.5	19,561	2,977	0.24	-1,625
Germany	1.5	25,177	400,444	24.28	-210,865
Italy	1.5	20,983	260,971	18.85	-134,654
United Kingdom	1.5	17,945	306,174	26.04	-161,030
Ireland	1.5	21,461	15,478	1.09	-7,946
Denmark	1.5	25,064	4,180	0.26	-2,308
Greece	1.5	18,302	17,427	1.44	-8,925
Portugal	1.5	21,123	70,387	5.00	-35,300
Spain	1.5	14,597	313,931	32.37	-158,580

Equilibrium conditions

	Volume of restricted imports (Sie)	Volume of unrestr'd imports (Sif)	Volume of domestic production (Sir)	Volume of domestic demand (Dir)
France	146,562	126,138	453,289	725,989
Belgium/Luxembourg	49,923	34,845	170,273	255,041
Netherlands	123,756	38,366	2,977	165,098
Germany	462,975	188,168	400,444	1,051,588
Italy	107,531	38,405	260,971	406,907
United Kingdom	272,383	65,005	306,174	643,563
Ireland	4,814	1,509	15,478	21,800
Denmark	49,261	6,331	4,180	59,773
Greece	4,731	1,410	17,427	23,568
Portugal	1,872	1,587	70,387	73,845
Spain	30,712	13,613	313,931	358,255

Demand equations

	Demand elasticity	Price (Pir)	Volume of domestic demand (Dir)	Slope (dir)	Intercept (cir)
France	-1.086	19,337	725,989	-39.47	1,489,284
Belgium/Luxembourg	-1.086	15,493	255,041	-17.32	523,390
Netherlands	-1.086	19,561	165,098	-8.16	324,656
Germany	-1.086	25,177	1,051,588	-42.29	2,116,279
Italy	-1.086	20,983	406,907	-20.17	830,202
United Kingdom	-1.086	17,945	643,563	-36.37	1,296,180
Ireland	-1.086	21,461	21,800	-1.06	44,634
Denmark	-1.086	25,064	59,773	-2.27	116,697
Greece	-1.086	18,302	23,568	-1.35	48,334
Portugal	-1.086	21,123	73,845	-3.78	153,705
Spain	-1.086	14,597	358,255	-26.28	741,853

Table D.7. Footwear 1988 – Model calibration

Price equations

	Unit value (unrestr'd) (Pif)	CET	Domestic price (Pir)	Quota premium	Unit value (restricted) (Pie)
France	14,254	1.13	16,107	1.15	12,420
Belgium/Luxembourg	12,214	1.13	13,802	1.17	10,451
Netherlands	11,763	1.13	13,292	1.15	10,257
Germany	19,424	1.13	21,949	1.16	16,722
Italy	10,887	1.13	12,302	1.13	9611
United Kingdom	9,359	1.13	10,576	1.15	8,139
Ireland	7927	1.13	8,958	1.16	6,824
Denmark	15,222	1.13	17,200	1.16	13,164
Greece	11,483	1.13	12,975	1.14	10,080
Portugal	14,313	1.13	16,174	1.15	12,495
Spain	11,065	1.13	12,504	1.17	9,470

Supply equations

I. Constrained suppliers

	Supply elasticity	Price (Pie)	Volume of imports (Sie)	Slope (Bie)	Intercept (Aie)
France	2	12,420	35,242	5.68	-35,242
Belgium/Luxembourg	2	10,451	6,646	1.27	-6,646
Netherlands	2	10,257	13,180	2.57	-13,180
Germany	2	16,722	39,721	4.75	-39,721
Italy	2	9,611	26,074	5.43	-26,074
United Kingdom	2	8,139	30,853	7.58	-30,853
Ireland	2	6,824	768	0.23	-768
Denmark	2	13,164	4,246	0.65	-4,246
Greece	2	10,080	2,713	0.54	-2,713
Portugal	2	12,495	121	0.02	-121
Spain	2	9,470	4,285	0.90	-4,285

II. Unconstrained suppliers

	Supply elasticity	Price (Pif)	Volume of imports (Sif)	Slope (Bif)	Intercept (Aif)
France	2	14,254	14,535	2.04	-14,535
Belgium/Luxembourg	2	12,214	2,916	0.48	-2,916
Netherlands	2	11,763	6,897	1.17	-6,897
Germany	2	19,424	30,810	3.17	-30,810
Italy	2	10,887	11,639	2.14	-11,639
United Kingdom	2	9,359	27,078	5.79	-27,078
Ireland	2	7,927	1,032	0.26	-1,032
Denmark	2	15,222	3,484	0.46	-3,484
Greece	2	11,483	458	0.08	-458
Portugal	2	14,313	147	0.02	-147
Spain	2	11,065	796	0.14	-796

Table D.7.   (continued)

III. Domestic supply

	Supply elasticity	Price (Pir)	Volume of production (Sir)	Slope (Bir)	Intercept (Air)
France	1.5	16,107	141,208	13.15	-70,604
Belgium/Luxembourg	1.5	13,802	26,490	2.88	-13,245
Netherlands	1.5	13,292	38,052	4.29	-19,026
Germany	1.5	21,949	187,222	12.79	-93,611
Italy	1.5	12,302	57,226	6.98	-28,613
United Kingdom	1.5	10,576	185,501	26.31	-92,750
Ireland	1.5	8,958	14,566	2.44	-7,283
Denmark	1.5	17,200	12,210	1.06	-6,105
Greece	1.5	12,975	16,788	1.94	-8,394
Portugal	1.5	16,174	1,521	0.14	-760
Spain	1.5	12,504	56,325	6.76	-28,163

Equilibrium conditions

	Volume of restricted imports (Sie)	Volume of unrestr'd imports (Sif)	Volume of domestic production (Sir)	Volume of domestic demand (Dir)
France	35,242	14,535	141,208	190,985
Belgium/Luxembourg	6,646	2,916	26,490	36,052
Netherlands	13,180	6,897	38,052	58,129
Germany	39,721	30,810	187,222	257,753
Italy	26,074	11,639	57,226	94,939
United Kingdom	30,853	27,078	185,501	243,432
Ireland	768	1,032	14,566	16,366
Denmark	4,246	3,484	12,210	19,940
Greece	2,713	458	16,788	19,959
Portugal	121	147	1,521	1,789
Spain	4,285	796	56,325	61,406

Demand equations

	Demand elasticity	Price (Pir)	Volume of domestic demand (Dir)	Slope (dir)	Intercept (cir)
France	-0.75	16,107	190,985	-8.89	334,223
Belgium/Luxembourg	-0.75	13,802	36,052	-1.96	63,091
Netherlands	-0.75	13,292	58,129	-3.28	101,726
Germany	-0.75	21,949	257,753	-8.81	451,068
Italy	-0.75	12,302	94,939	-5.79	166,144
United Kingdom	-0.75	10,576	243,432	-17.26	426,005
Ireland	-0.75	8,958	16,366	-1.37	28,641
Denmark	-0.75	17,200	19,940	-0.87	34,894
Greece	-0.75	12,975	19,959	-1.15	34,929
Portugal	-0.75	16,174	1,789	-0.08	3,130
Spain	-0.75	12,504	61,406	-3.68	107,461

Table D.8.   Footwear 1988 – Counterfactual: Removal of all restrictions to trade

Price equations

	Unit value (unrestr'd) (Pif)	CET	Domestic price (Pir)	Quota premium	Unit value (restricted) (Pie)
France	13,935	1.13	15,746	1.00	13,935
Belgium/Luxembourg	11,904	1.13	13,451	1.00	11,904
Netherlands	11,448	1.13	12,937	1.00	11,448
Germany	19,027	1.13	21,500	1.00	19,027
Italy	10,572	1.13	11,947	1.00	10,572
United Kingdom	9,212	1.13	10,409	1.00	9,212
Ireland	7,875	1.13	8,899	1.00	7,875
Denmark	14,818	1.13	16,744	1.00	14,818
Greece	11,299	1.13	12,768	1.00	11,299
Portugal	14,193	1.13	16,038	1.00	14,193
Spain	10,953	1.13	12,377	1.00	10,953

Supply equations

I. Constrained suppliers

	Supply elasticity	Price (Pie)	Volume of imports (Sie)	Slope (Bie)	Intercept (Aie)
France	2	13,935	43,841	5.68	-35,242
Belgium/Luxembourg	2	11,904	8,493	1.27	-6,646
Netherlands	2	11,448	16,241	2.57	-13,180
Germany	2	19,027	50,673	4.75	-39,721
Italy	2	10,572	31,287	5.43	-26,074
United Kingdom	2	9,212	38,988	7.58	-30,853
Ireland	2	7,875	1,005	0.23	-768
Denmark	2	14,818	5,313	0.65	-4,246
Greece	2	11,299	3,369	0.54	-2,713
Portugal	2	14,193	154	0.02	-121
Spain	2	10,953	5,627	0.90	-4,285

II. Unconstrained suppliers

	Supply elasticity	Price (Pif)	Volume of imports (Sif)	Slope (Bif)	Intercept (Aif)
France	2	13,935	13,884	2.04	-14,535
Belgium/Luxembourg	2	11,904	2,768	0.48	-2,916
Netherlands	2	11,448	6,528	1.17	-6,897
Germany	2	19,027	29,550	3.17	-30,810
Italy	2	10,572	10,966	2.14	-11,639
United Kingdom	2	9,212	26,223	5.79	-27,078
Ireland	2	7,875	1,018	0.26	-1,032
Denmark	2	14,818	3,299	0.46	-3,484
Greece	2	11,299	443	0.08	-458
Portugal	2	14,193	145	0.02	-147
Spain	2	10,953	780	0.14	-796

Table D.8.   (continued)

III. Domestic supply

	Supply elasticity	Price (Pir)	Volume of production (Sir)	Slope (Bir)	Intercept (Air)
France	1.5	15,746	136,465.60	13.15	-70,604
Belgium/Luxembourg	1.5	13,451	25,479.02	2.88	-13,245
Netherlands	1.5	12,937	36,525.99	4.29	-19,026
Germany	1.5	21,500	181,481.40	12.79	-93,611
Italy	1.5	11,947	54,744.88	6.98	-28,613
United Kingdom	1.5	10,409	181,105.20	26.31	-92,750
Ireland	1.5	8,899	14,423.14	2.44	-7,283
Denmark	1.5	16,744	11,723.95	1.06	-6,105
Greece	1.5	12,768	16,386.03	1.94	-8,394
Portugal	1.5	16,038	1,501.65	0.14	-760
Spain	1.5	12,377	55,467.55	6.76	-28,163

Equilibrium conditions

	Volume of restricted imports (Sie)	Volume of unrestr'd imports (Sif)	Volume of domestic production (Sir)	Volume of domestic demand (Dir)
France	43,841	13,884	136,466	194,191
Belgium/Luxembourg	8,493	2,768	25,479	36,740
Netherlands	16,241	6,528	36,526	59,295
Germany	50,673	29,550	181,481	261,704
Italy	31,287	10,966	54,745	96,998
United Kingdom	38,988	26,223	181,105	246,316
Ireland	1,005	1,018	14,423	16,446
Denmark	5,313	3,299	11,724	20,336
Greece	3,369	443	16,386	20,198
Portugal	154	145	1,502	1,800
Spain	5,627	780	55,468	61,874

Demand equations

	Demand elasticity	Price (Pir)	Volume of domestic demand (Dir)	Slope (dir)	Intercept (cir)
France	-0.75	15,746	194,191	-8.89	334,223
Belgium/Luxembourg	-0.75	13,451	36,740	-1.96	63,091
Netherlands	-0.75	12,937	59,295	-3.28	101,726
Germany	-0.75	21,500	261,704	-8.81	451,068
Italy	-0.75	11,947	96,998	-5.79	166,144
United Kingdom	-0.75	10,409	246,316	-17.26	426,005
Ireland	-0.75	8,899	16,446	-1.37	28,641
Denmark	-0.75	16,744	20,336	-0.87	34,894
Greece	-0.75	12,768	20,198	-1.15	34,929
Portugal	-0.75	16,038	1,800	-0.08	3,130
Spain	-0.75	12,377	61,874	-3.68	107,461

Table D.9.   Footwear 1994 – Model calibration

Price equations

	Unit value (unrestr'd) (Pif)	CET	Domestic price (Pir)	Quota premium	Unit value (restricted) (Pie)
France	12,254	1.13	13,847	1.15	10,655
Belgium/Luxembourg	11,709	1.13	13,232	1.15	10,182
Netherlands	9,800	1.13	11,074	1.15	8,522
Germany	16,047	1.13	18,133	1.15	13,954
Italy	11,558	1.13	13,061	1.15	10,051
United Kingdom	10,679	1.13	12,068	1.15	9,286
Ireland	9,645	1.13	10,899	1.15	8,387
Denmark	14,613	1.13	16,513	1.15	12,707
Greece	11,096	1.13	12,539	1.15	9,649
Portugal	26,342	1.13	29,767	1.15	22,906
Spain	12,924	1.13	14,604	1.15	11,238

Supply equations

I. Constrained suppliers

	Supply elasticity	Price (Pie)	Volume of imports (Sie)	Slope (Bie)	Intercept (Aie)
France	2	10,655	25,434	4.77	-25,434
Belgium/Luxembourg	2	10,182	14,344	2.82	-14,344
Netherlands	2	8,522	21,366	5.01	-21,366
Germany	2	13,954	44,389	6.36	-44,389
Italy	2	10,051	10,057	2.00	-10,057
United Kingdom	2	9,286	9,016	1.94	-9,016
Ireland	2	8,387	7,251	1.73	-7,251
Denmark	2	12,707	2,613	0.41	-2,613
Greece	2	9,649	2,964	0.61	-2,964
Portugal	2	22,906	889	0.08	-889
Spain	2	11,238	5,056	0.90	-5,056

II. Unconstrained suppliers

	Supply elasticity	Price (Pif)	Volume of imports (Sif)	Slope (Bif)	Intercept (Aif)
France	2	12,254	44,560	7.27	-44,560
Belgium/Luxembourg	2	11,709	7,734	1.32	-7,734
Netherlands	2	9,800	39,557	8.07	-39,557
Germany	2	16,047	93,644	11.67	-93,644
Italy	2	11,558	76,521	13.24	-76,521
United Kingdom	2	10,679	68,821	12.89	-68,821
Ireland	2	9,645	3,771	0.78	-3,771
Denmark	2	14,613	6,087	0.83	-6,087
Greece	2	11,096	3,594	0.65	-3,594
Portugal	2	26,342	1,796	0.14	-1,796
Spain	2	12,924	9,121	1.41	-9,121

Table D.9.   (continued)

III. Domestic supply

	Supply elasticity	Price (Pir)	Volume of production (Sir)	Slope (Bir)	Intercept (Air)
France	1.5	13,847	149,981	16.25	-74,991
Belgium/Luxembourg	1.5	13,232	21,666	2.46	-10,833
Netherlands	1.5	11,074	28,614	3.88	-14,307
Germany	1.5	18,133	226,486	18.74	-113243
Italy	1.5	13,061	82,090	9.43	-41,045
United Kingdom	1.5	12,068	120,195	14.94	-60,098
Ireland	1.5	10,899	6,829	0.94	-3,414
Denmark	1.5	16,513	17,034	1.55	-8,517
Greece	1.5	12,539	25,870	3.09	-12,935
Portugal	1.5	29,767	9,156	0.46	-4,578
Spain	1.5	14,604	25,065	2.57	-12,532

Equilibrium conditions

	Volume of restricted imports (Sie)	Volume of unrestr'd imports (Sif)	Volume of domestic production (Sir)	Volume of domestic demand (Dir)
France	25,434	44,560	149,981	219,975
Belgium/Luxembourg	14,344	7,734	21,666	43,744
Netherlands	21,366	39,557	28,614	89,537
Germany	44,389	93,644	226,486	364,519
Italy	10,057	76,521	82,090	168,668
United Kingdom	9,016	68,821	120,195	198,032
Ireland	7,251	3,771	6,829	17,851
Denmark	2,613	6,087	17,034	25,734
Greece	2,964	3,594	25,870	32,428
Portugal	889	1,796	9,156	11,841
Spain	5,056	9,121	25,065	39,242

Demand equations

	Demand elasticity	Price (Pir)	Volume of domestic demand (Dir)	Slope (dir)	Intercept (cir)
France	-0.75	13,847	219,975	-11.91	384,957
Belgium/Luxembourg	-0.75	13,232	43,744	-2.48	76,551
Netherlands	-0.75	11,074	89,537	-6.06	156,689
Germany	-0.75	18,133	364,519	-15.08	637,908
Italy	-0.75	13,061	168,668	-9.69	295,169
United Kingdom	-0.75	12,068	198,032	-12.31	346,557
Ireland	-0.75	10,899	17,851	-1.23	31,239
Denmark	-0.75	16,513	25,734	-1.17	45,035
Greece	-0.75	12,539	32,428	-1.94	56,750
Portugal	-0.75	29,767	11,841	-0.30	20,722
Spain	-0.75	14,604	39,242	-2.02	68,673

Table D.10.   Footwear 1994 – Counterfactual: Reintroduction of national quotas on imports from countries previously restricted

Price equations

	Unit value (unrestr'd) (Pif)	CET	Domestic price (Pir)	Quota premium	Unit value (restricted) (Pie)
France	12,340	1.13	13,944	1.15	10,752
Belgium/Luxembourg	11,830	1.13	13,368	1.17	10,122
Netherlands	9,971	1.13	11,267	1.15	8,695
Germany	16,278	1.13	18,394	1.16	14,013
Italy	11,807	1.13	13,341	1.13	10,423
United Kingdom	10,772	1.13	12,172	1.15	9,367
Ireland	9,776	1.13	11,047	1.16	8,415
Denmark	14,730	1.13	16,645	1.16	12,739
Greece	11,119	1.13	12,564	1.14	9,761
Portugal	26,397	1.13	29,828	1.15	23,044
Spain	13,059	1.13	14,757	1.17	11,177

Supply equations

I. Constrained suppliers

	Supply elasticity	Price (Pie)	Volume of imports (Sie)	Slope (Bie)	Intercept (Aie)
France	2	10,752	25,893	4.77	-25,434
Belgium/Luxembourg	2	10,122	14,176	2.82	-14,344
Netherlands	2	8,695	22,233	5.01	-21,366
Germany	2	14,013	44,769	6.36	-44,389
Italy	2	10,423	10,803	2.00	-10,057
United Kingdom	2	9,367	9,173	1.94	-9,016
Ireland	2	8,415	7,300	1.73	-7,251
Denmark	2	12,739	2,626	0.41	-2,613
Greece	2	9,761	3,033	0.61	-2,964
Portugal	2	23,044	900	0.08	-889
Spain	2	11,177	5,001	0.90	-5,056

II. Previously unconstrained suppliers

	Supply elasticity	Price (Pif)	Volume of imports (Sif)	Slope (Bif)	Intercept (Aif)
France	2	12,340	41,371	7.27	-44,560
Belgium/Luxembourg	2	11,830	7,229	1.32	-7,734
Netherlands	2	9,971	36,769	8.07	-39,557
Germany	2	16,278	84,431	11.67	-93,644
Italy	2	11,807	70,408	13.24	-76,521
United Kingdom	2	10,772	65,809	12.89	-68,821
Ireland	2	9,776	3,401	0.78	-3,771
Denmark	2	14,730	5,713	0.83	-6,087
Greece	2	11,119	3,396	0.65	-3,594
Portugal	2	26,397	1,739	0.14	-1,796
Spain	2	13,059	8,475	1.41	-9,121

Table D.10.   (continued)

III. Domestic supply

	Supply elasticity	Price (Pir)	Volume of production (Sir)	Slope (Bir)	Intercept (Air)
France	1.5	13,944	151,556	16.25	-74,991
Belgium/Luxembourg	1.5	13,368	22,000.47	2.46	-10,833
Netherlands	1.5	11,267	29,362.65	3.88	-14,307
Germany	1.5	18,394	231,380.60	18.74	-113,243
Italy	1.5	13,341	84,736.91	9.43	-41,045
United Kingdom	1.5	12,172	121,761	14.94	-60,098
Ireland	1.5	11,047	6,967.992	0.94	-3,414
Denmark	1.5	16,645	17,239.58	1.55	-8,517
Greece	1.5	12,564	25,949.42	3.09	-12,935
Portugal	1.5	29,828	9,184.425	0.46	-4,578
Spain	1.5	14,757	25,458.06	2.57	-12,532

Equilibrium conditions

	Volume of restricted imports (Sie)	Volume of unrestr'd imports (Sif)	Volume of domestic production (Sir)	Volume of domestic demand (Dir)
France	25,893	41,371	151,556	218,820
Belgium/Luxembourg	14,176	7,229	22,000	43,406
Netherlands	22,233	36,769	29,363	88,364
Germany	44,769	84,431	231,381	360,580
Italy	10,803	70,408	84,737	165,948
United Kingdom	9,173	65,809	121,761	196,743
Ireland	7,300	3,401	6,968	17,669
Denmark	2,626	5,713	17,240	25,579
Greece	3,033	3,396	25,949	32,379
Portugal	900	1,739	9,184	11,823
Spain	5,001	8,475	25,458	38,934

Demand equations

	Demand elasticity	Price (Pir)	Volume of domestic demand (Dir)	Slope (dir)	Intercept (cir)
France	-0.75	13,944	218,820	-11.91	384,957
Belgium/Luxembourg	-0.75	13,368	43,406	-2.48	76,551
Netherlands	-0.75	11,267	88,364	-6.06	156,689
Germany	-0.75	18,394	360,580	-15.08	637,908
Italy	-0.75	13,341	165,948	-9.69	295,169
United Kingdom	-0.75	12,172	196,743	-12.31	346,557
Ireland	-0.75	11,047	17,669	-1.23	31,239
Denmark	-0.75	16,645	25,579	-1.17	45,035
Greece	-0.75	12,564	32,379	-1.94	56,750
Portugal	-0.75	29,828	11,823	-0.30	20,722
Spain	-0.75	14,757	38,934	-2.02	68,673

Bibliography

Ahern, R.J. [1992], 'US Access to the EC-92 Market: Opportunities, Concerns and Policy Challenges', study paper submitted to the Subcommittee on International Economic Policy and Trade and the Subcommittee on Europe and the Middle East of the Committee on Foreign Affairs (US House of Representatives, June 1992).

Atkins International Limited [1996], 'Review of the Internal Market 1996: Technical Barriers to Trade', Draft Final Report, Version 1 (Epsom, W.S. Atkins International Limited, 8 July 1996).

Batchelor, R. and Minford, P. [1977], 'Import Controls and Devaluation Policies as Medium-Term Policies', in Corbet, Corden, Hindley, Batchelor and Minford (eds), *On how to cope with Britain's Trade Position* (London, Trade Policy Research Centre, 1977).

Brenton, P.A. and Winters, L.A. [1991], 'Non-tariff Barriers and Rationing: UK Footwear Imports', Discussion Paper No. 365 (London, Centre for Economic Policy Research, 1991).

Buigues, P. and Ilzkovitz, F. [1988], 'The Sectoral Impact of the Internal Market', mimeo (Brussels, European Commission, 1988).

Buigues, P., Ilzkovitz, F. and Lebrun, J.-F. [1990], 'The impact of the internal market by industrial sector; the challenge for the Member States', *European Economy/Social Europe* (Luxembourg, Office for Official Publications of the EC, 1990).

CEC [1985], 'Completing the internal market' (White Paper from the Commission to the European Council), COM(85) 310 final (Luxembourg, Office for Official Publications of the EC, 1985).

CEC [1988], *Seventeenth Report on Competition Policy* (Luxembourg, Office for Official Publications of the EC, 1988).

CEC [1989], 'Communication from the Commission to the Council: A global approach to certification and testing: Quality measures for industrial products', COM(89) 209 final, (Luxembourg, Office for Official Publications of the EC, 24 July 1989).

CEC [1990], 'Commission Communication on the development of European standardization', COM(90) 456 final (Luxembourg, Office for Official Publications of the EC, 8 October 1990).

CEC [1991], *Consumer Policy in the Single Market* (Luxembourg, Office for Official Publications of the EC, 1991).

CEC [1992a], 'Lés dispositions qui créent le marché interieur avec volet externe: Tableau de Bord', mimeo (Brussels, European Commission, 1 January 1992).

CEC [1992b], *Completion of the Common Commercial Policy in the Context of the Internal Market and Other External Aspects of the Internal Market* (Brussels, European Commission, 1992).

CEC [1993a], *Twenty-Second Report on Competition Policy* (Luxembourg, Office for Official Publications of the EC, 1993).

CEC [1993b], 'The European Community as a world trade partner', *European Economy*, No 52, Luxembourg, Office for Official Publications of the EC.

CEC [1994a], *Internal Market: Current status 1 July 1994. The Elimination of Frontier Controls* (Luxembourg, Office for Official Publications of the EC, 1994).

CEC [1994b], 'The Community internal market: 1993 report', COM(94) 55 final (Luxembourg, Office for Official Publications of the EC, 1994).

CEC [1994c], *Internal Market: Current status 1 July 1994. A Common Market for Services.* (Luxembourg, Office for Official Publications of the EC, 1994).

CEC [1994d], *Twenty-Third Report on Competition Policy* (Luxembourg, Office for Official Publications for the EC, 1994).

CEC [1995a] 'Report on Application of Directive 89/552/EEC', COM(95) 86 final (Luxembourg, Office for Official Publications of the EC, 1995).

CEC [1995b], *The Single Market in 1994: Report* COM(95) 238 final (Luxembourg, Office for Official Publications of the EC, 1995).

CEC [1996a] 'The Single Market in 1995: Report from the Commission to the Council and the European Parliament', COM(96) 51 final (Luxembourg, Office for Official Publications of the EC, 1996).

CEC [1996b], *Panorama of EU Industry 1995/96* (Luxembourg, Office for Official Publications of the EC, 1996).

Committee of Enquiry [1994], *Road Freight Transport in the Single European Market* (Brussels, Commission of the European Communities, DG VII, 1994).

Corado, C. [1994], ' Textiles and Clothing Trade With Central and Eastern Europe: Impact on Members of the EC', *Discussion Paper No. 1004* (London, Centre for Economic Policy Research, 1994).

Davenport, M. [1990], 'The external policy of the Community and its effects upon the manufactured exports of the developing countries', *Journal of Common Market Studies*, Vol. XXIX(2), December 1990, pp. 181-200.

Davenport, M. and Page, S. [1991], *Europe: 1992 and the Developing World* (London, Overseas Development Institute, 1991).

Deaton, A. [1975], *Models and Projections of Demand in Post War Britain* (London, Chapman and Hall, 1975).

DG I [1995a], 'A Guide to European Community Negotiations with Third Countries Concerning the Mutual Recognition of Conformity Assessment' (Brussels, European Commission, DG I, 1995).

DG I [1995b], 'Mutual Recognition Agreements in the Regulated Sector: An Explanatory Note', OECD Committee on Consumer Policy Conference on Consumer Product Safety Standards and Conformity Assessment: Their Effect on International Trade (Paris, 7-8 December 1995).

DG I [1996], 'Japan's Request Regarding EU Regulations and Access to EU Markets', GM9383, ECJISG/40.96 (Brussels, European Commission, DG I, 23 April 1996).

DRI [1995], 'Survey of the Trade Associations' Perception of the Effects of the Single Market', Volume 1, Draft Final Report for the Commission of the European Communities, (Brussels, DRI, November 1995).

EAG [1996], 'The Development of Foreign Direct Investment Flows inside the EU due to the Internal Market Programme: Final Report' (London, Economists Advisory Group Limited, June 1996).

EFTA Secretariat [1992], 'Effects of '1992' on the Manufacturing Industries of the EFTA Countries', *EFTA Economic Affairs Department Occasional Paper No. 38* (Geneva, April 1992).

Emerson, M., Aujean, M., Catinat, M., Goybet, P. and Jacquemin, A. [1988], *The Economics of 1992* (Oxford, Oxford University Press, 1988).

Erzan, R., Goto, J. and Holmes, P. [1989], 'Effects of the MFA on Developing Countries' Trade', Seminar Paper No. 449, Stockholm, Institute for International Economic Studies, 1989.

Eurostat [1995], *Intra- and extra-EU trade (annual data - Combined Nomenclature)*, Supplement 2/1995 (CD-ROM) (Luxembourg, Office for Official Publications of the EC, 1995).

Eurostat. [1997], *Single Market Review – Results of the Business Survey* (Luxembourg, Office for Official Publications of the EC and London, Kogan Page/Earthscan, 1997).

Faini, R., de Melo, J. and Takacs, W. [1992], 'The effects of EC-92 on the Multifibre Arrangement', *European Economic Review*, Vol. 36(2-3), 1992, pp. 527-38.

Gardener, E.P.M. and Teppett, J.L. [1992], 'The Impact of 1992 on the Financial Services Sectors of EFTA Countries', *EFTA Economic Affairs Department Occasional Paper No. 33* (Geneva, 1992).

GATT [1991], *Trade Policy Review: The European Communities 1991* (Geneva, General Agreement on Tariffs and Trade, 1991).

GATT [1993], *Trade Policy Review: The European Communities 1993* (Geneva, General Agreement on Tariffs and Trade, 1993).

Greenaway, D. [1985], 'Clothing Imports from Hong Kong and Other Developing Countries', in Greenaway, D. and Hindley, B.V. , *What Britain Pays for Voluntary Export Restraints*, Thames Essay 43 (London, Trade Policy Research Centre, 1985).

Greenaway, D. [1986], 'Estimating the Welfare Effects of Voluntary Export Restraints and Tariffs: An Application to Non-leather Footwear in the UK', *Applied Economics*, Vol. 18, 1986, pp. 1065-83.

Greenaway, D. and Hindley, B.V. [1985], *What Britain Pays for Voluntary Export Restraints*, Thames Essay 43 (London, Trade Policy Research Centre, 1985).

Gros, D. [1992], 'A Note on Trade Policy After 1992: The Effects of Replacing Existing National Import Quotas by Community Quotas that are "Equally Restrictive"', *Weltwirtschaftliches Archiv*, Vol. 39, 1992, pp. 125-35.

Hamilton, C.B. [1981], 'A New Approach to Estimation of the Effects of Non-tariff Barriers to Trade on Prices, Employment and Imports: An Application to the Swedish Textile and Clothing Industry', Seminar Paper No. 168 (Stockholm, Institute for International Economic Studies, 1981).

Hamilton, C.B. [1983], 'Voluntary Export Restraints, Trade Diversion and Retaliation', Seminar Paper No. 253 (Stockholm, Institute for International Economic Studies, 1983).

Hamilton, C.B. [1984a], 'Voluntary Export Restraints: ASEAN Systems for Allocation of Export Licences', Seminar Paper No. 275 (Stockholm, Institute for International Economic Studies, 1984).

Hamilton, C.B. [1984b], 'Voluntary Export Restraints on Asia: Tariff Equivalents, Rents and Trade Barrier Formation', Seminar Paper No. 276 (Stockholm, Institute for International Economic Studies, 1984).

Hamilton, C.B. [1984c], 'Economic Aspects of Voluntary Export Restraints', Seminar Paper No. 290 (Stockholm, Institute for International Economic Studies, 1984).

Hamilton, C.B. [1984d], 'The Upgrading Effect of Voluntary Export Restraints', Seminar Paper No. 291 (Stockholm, Institute for International Economic Studies, 1984).

Hamilton, C.B. [1987], 'An Assessment of Voluntary Restraints on Hong Kong Exports to Europe and the USA', *Econometrica*, Vol. 53, 1987, pp. 339-50.

Hamilton, C.B. [1988a], 'The Transient Nature of "New" Protectionism', Seminar Paper No. 425 (Stockholm, Institute for International Economic Studies, 1988).

Hamilton, C.B., [1988b], Melo, J. de and Winters, L.A. 'Voluntary Export Restraints: A Case Study Focusing on Effects in Exporting Countries' Seminar Paper No. 464 (Stockholm, Institute for International Economic Studies, 1988).

Hamilton, C.B. [1990a], 'The New Silk Road to Europe', Seminar Paper No. 468 (Stockholm, Institute for International Economic Studies, 1990).

Hamilton, C.B. [1990b], 'European Community External Protection and 1992: Voluntary Export Restraints Applied to Pacific Asia', Seminar Paper No. 478 (Stockholm, Institute for International Economic Studies, 1990).

Hamilton, C.B. [1991], 'European Community External Protection and 1992: Voluntary Export Restraints Applied to Pacific Asia', *European Economic Review*, Vol. 35, 1991, pp. 378-87.

Héritier, A. [1996], 'The Accommodation of Diversity in European Policy-making and its Outcomes: Regulatory Policy as a Patchwork', *Journal of European Public Policy*, 3/2, pp. 149-67, 1996.

Hoeller, P. and Louppe, M.-O. [1994], 'The EC's Internal Market: Implementation, Economic Consequences, Unfinished Business', *Economics Department Working Papers*, No 142 (Paris, OECD, 1994).

Houthakker, H. S. [1965], 'New Evidence on Demand Elasticities', *Econometrica* 33.

Jacquemin, A. and Sapir, A. [1988], 'International Trade and Integration of the European Community: An Econometric Analysis', *European Economic Review*, Vol. 32, 1988, pp. 202-12.

Koekkoek, A., Kuyenhoven, A. and Molle, W. [1990], 'Europe 1992 and the Developing Countries: An Overview', *Journal of Common Market Studies*, Vol. XXIX(2), December 1990, pp. 111-131.

Kruger, L.G. [1992], 'EC-92: Standards and Conformity Assessment', study paper submitted to the Subcommittee on International Economic Policy and Trade and the Subcommittee on Europe and the Middle East of the Committee on Foreign Affairs (US House of Representatives, June 1992).

Langhammer, R. [1990], 'Fuelling a New Engine of Growth or Separating Europe from Non-Europe?', *Journal of Common Market Studies*, Vol. XXIX(2), December 1990, pp. 133-56.

Melo, J. de and Messerlin, P.A. [1988], 'Price, Quality and Welfare Effects of European VERs on Japanese Autos', *European Economic Review*, Vol. 32, 1988, pp. 1527-46.

Melo, J. de and Winters, L.A. [1990], 'Do Exporters Gain From VERs?', *Discussion Paper No. 383* (London, Centre for Economic Policy Research, 1990).

Neven, D.J. and Roller, L. [1991], 'European Integration and Trade Flows', *European Economic Review*, Vol. 35, 1991, pp. 1295-1309.

Nicolas, F. and Repussard, J. [1995], *Common Standards for Enterprises* (Luxembourg, Office for Official Publications of the EC, 1995).

OECD [1985], *Costs and Benefits of Protection* (Paris, OECD, 1985).

Pelkmans, J. [1987], 'The European Community's Trade Policy Towards Developing Countries' in C. Stevens and J. Verloren van Themaat (eds), *Europe and the International Division of Labour* (London, Hodder and Stoughton, 1987).

Pelkmans, J. and Winters, A. [1988], *Europe's Domestic Market* (London, Royal Institute of International Affairs, 1988).

Previdi, E. [1997], 'Regulatory Policy Formation and Enforcement in the Single Market' in H. Wallace and A.R. Young (eds), *Participation and Policy Making in the European Union* (Oxford, Oxford University Press, 1997).

Price Waterhouse [1988], 'The "Cost of non-Europe" in Financial Services', *Research on the 'Cost of non-Europe' – Basic Findings*, Vol. 9 (Luxembourg, Office for Official Publications of the EC, 1988).

Sapir, A. [1989], 'Does 1992 Come Before or After 1990? On Regional Versus Multilateral Integration', *Discussion Paper No. 313* (London, Centre for Economic Policy Research, 1989).

Sapir, A. [1993], 'Sectoral dimension', in P. Buigues *et al.* (eds), 'Market services and European integration: the challenges for the 1990s', *European Economy/Social Europe*, Reports and Studies No 3 (Luxembourg, Office for Official Publications of the EC, 1993).

Sapir, A. [1995], 'Europe's Single Market: The Long March to 1992', *Discussion Paper No. 1245* (London, Centre for Economic Policy Research, 1995).

Sbragia, A. [1993], 'EC Environmental Policy: Atypical Ambitions and Typical Problems?' in A.W. Cafruny and G.G. Rosenthal (eds), *The State of the European Community, Vol. 2: The Maastricht Debates and Beyond* (Boulder, Colorado, Lynne Rienner, 1993).

Schuknecht, L. [1992], *Trade Protection in the European Community* (Chur, Harwood Academic Publishers, 1992).

Silberston, A. [1984], *The Multifibre Arrangement and the UK Economy* (London, HMSO, 1984).

Smith, A. and Venables, A.J. [1988], 'Completing the Internal Market in the European Community: Some Industry Simulations', *European Economic Review*, Vol. 32, 1988, pp. 1501-25.

Smith, A. and Venables, A.J. [1991], 'Counting the Costs of Voluntary Export Restraints in the European Car Market', in E. Helpman and A. Razin, (eds), *International Trade and Trade Policy* (London, MIT Press, 1991).

Tarr, D. and Morkre, M. [1984], *Aggregate Cost to the United States of Tariffs and Quotas on Imports* (Washington DC, Federal Trade Commission, 1984).

Trela, I. and Whalley, J. [1989], 'Unravelling the Threads of the MFA', Seminar Paper No. 448 (Stockholm, Institute for International Economic Studies, 1989).

US Chamber of Commerce [1993], *Europe 1992: A Practical Guide for American Business*, Update No. 4 (Washington DC, US Chamber of Commerce, August 1993).

USITC [1993], *1992: The Effects of Greater Economic Integration Within the European Community on the United States: Fifth Follow-up Report*, Investigation No 332-267 (Washington DC, United States International Trade Commission, April 1993).

USITC [1996], *The President's Trade Policy Agenda and the President's 1995 Annual Report on the Trade Agreements Program* (Washington DC, United States International Trade Commission, March 1996).

USTR [1996], *1996 National Trade Estimate Report on Foreign Trade Barriers* (Washington DC, Office of the United States Trade Representative, Executive Office of the President, 1996).

Velia, M. [1996], 'Trade Policy and Adjustment in the Textile and Clothing Industry: The European Commission and Mauritius' (DPhil thesis, University of Sussex, 1996).

Wallace, H. and Young, A. R. [1996], 'The Single Market: A New Approach to Policy', in H. Wallace and W.Wallace (eds), *Policy-making in the European Union* (Oxford, Oxford University Press, 1996).

Winters, L.A. [1988], 'Completing the Internal Market: Some Notes on Trade Policy', *European Economic Review*, Vol. 32, 1988, pp. 1477-99.

Winters, L. A. [1990], 'Import Surveillance as a Strategic Trade Policy', *Discussion Paper No. 404* (London, Centre for Economic Policy Research, March 1990).

Winters, L.A. [1991], 'Voluntary Export Restraints and the Prices of UK Imports of Footwear', *Weltwirtschaftliches Archiv*, Vol. 38, 1991, pp. 523-43.

Winters, L.A. [1992], 'Integration, Trade Policy and European Footwear Trade', in L.A. Winters (ed.), *Trade Flows and Trade Policy After '1992'* (Cambridge, Cambridge University Press, 1992).

Winters, L.A. and Brenton, P.A. [1991], 'Quantifying the Effects of Non-tariff Barriers: The Case of UK Footwear', *Kyklos,* Vol. 44, 1991, pp. 71-92.

Woolcock, S. [1991], *Market Access Issues in EC-US Relations: Trading Partners or Trading Blows?* (London, Royal Institute of International Affairs, 1991).

WTO [1995], *Trade Policy Review: European Union 1995* (Geneva, World Trade Organization, 1995).